The Cubs Win the Pennant!

6/22/05
Park Ridge, Ill.

Jack —

To my good friend from Maine days. May these pages bring back fond memories of those happy days of our youth — and the players who left their mark in Chicago" ways — P. Nuts, Banks, Caracella, Passeau, Hardy, Broons, Wyse, Nicholson, Pafko, Johnson, Lonnie Merullo, Hommage Prim, Grimm et al.

Days — R."

happy!
Paul

The Cubs Win the Pennant!

Charlie Grimm, the Billy Goat Curse, and the 1945 World Series Run

JOHN SKIPPER

McFarland & Company, Inc., Publishers

Jefferson, North Carolina, and London

LIBRARY OF CONGRESS CATALOGUING-IN-PUBLICATION DATA

Skipper, John C., 1945–
    The Cubs win the pennant! : Charlie Grimm, the billy goat
curse, and the 1945 World Series run / John Skipper.
      p.   cm.
    Includes bibliographical references and index.

    ISBN 0-7864-1816-8 (softcover : 50# alkaline paper) ∞

    1. Chicago Cubs (Baseball team)—History. 2. Grimm,
Charlie. I. Title.
GV875.C6C54 2004
796.357'64'0977311— dc22   2004007081

British Library cataloguing data are available

On the cover (background, Wrigley Field): Cubs manager Charlie
Grimm (courtesy Baseball Hall of Fame Library); Goat (Clipart.com)

Manufactured in the United States of America

McFarland & Company, Inc., Publishers
  Box 611, Jefferson, North Carolina 28640
   www.mcfarlandpub.com

For all the players and all the fans
who for all the years have lifted their heads high
and proclaimed, "Wait till next year!"

Contents

Introduction

On October 14, 2003, the Chicago Cubs were five outs away from going to the World Series. They had a 3–0 lead against Florida in the sixth game of the National League Championship Series. They were ahead, three games to two, and had their best pitcher, Mark Prior, 18–6 during the regular season, sailing along toward a shutout. Then, suddenly — it seemed like no longer than a couple of minutes — Moises Alou narrowly missed catching a foul ball in the first row of the stands down the left-field line when a fan, trying to catch it, reached above Alou's glove and deflected it. Damage, but no real harm yet. Moments later, Alex Gonzalez, a Cubs shortstop who made just 10 errors during the regular season, booted a potential double play ball. Before long the Marlins had tied it and then taken the lead. Then Mike Mordecai, a 35-year-old reserve who drove in eight runs all year, hit a bases-loaded double. The Marlins scored eight runs in the inning to take an 8–3 lead and never looked back. The next night, Florida won the seventh and deciding game, 9–6, and the Cubs were denied a trip to the World Series. Again.

It was the closest they had come since 1989 when they fought gamely in a best three-out-of-five series with the San Francisco Giants. In game four, with the Cubs trailing two games to one, Cubs pitcher Mike Bielecki took a 1–0 lead into the bottom of the eighth inning. The Giants loaded the bases, prompting manager Don Zimmer to bring in his ace reliever, lefthander Mitch Williams, to face Will Clark, the Giants' star first baseman who was having a stellar playoff series. Clark whistled an eye-high fastball into center field for a base hit, driving in the only two runs the Giants needed to send the Cubs home, once again prevented from being in the World Series.

Rick Wrona, a reserve catcher on that team, said something happened the night of the first playoff game at Wrigley Field, as the players were being introduced, that he'll never forget.

"I was standing on the dugout steps, waiting to run out on the field when my name was announced. Ron Santo, the old Cubs third baseman (and now a Cubs radio broadcaster), came up to me and said, 'Just think of all the men who played so many games on this field and never got a chance to do what you're doing tonight. When you go out there tonight, you're representing all of them.' I tell that story a lot," said Wrona.

"Just think of all the men who played so many games on this field...."
"This field"—Wrigley Field—plays a big part in Cubs history because of its beauty, its durability over the years, and its history: the site of Babe Ruth's "called shot" in the 1932 World Series (the "did he or didn't he" discussion continues more than 70 years later); Gabby Hartnett's "homer in the gloamin'" on September 28, 1938; Ernie Banks' "let's play two" spirit; Cubs pennants in 1929, 1932, 1935, 1938, and 1945 and their near misses in 1969, 1984 and 1989; their one-game playoff victory over the Giants in 1998; and all the stars who have graced the premises, including Jurges, Cavarretta, Hack, Sauer, Sandberg, Sosa and so many, many more. Wrigley Field was the scene of Ernie Banks' 500th home run off Pat Jarvis of the Atlanta Braves on May 12, 1970, and Pete Rose's 4,191st hit, tying him with Ty Cobb for most hits in baseball history, on September 8, 1985.

"The Friendly Confines," as Banks calls the park, was built in 1914 and was known as Weeghman Park in honor of owner Charles Weeghman, whose ballclub, the Whales, was in the fledgling Federal League that lasted two years. When poor finances forced the league to shut down after the 1915 season, Weeghman purchased the Cubs from the famed Taft political family of Cincinnati. When William Wrigley bought controlling interest in the ballclub, the name of the park was changed to Cubs Park in 1920 and to Wrigley Field in 1926.

When Philip K. Wrigley took over ownership of the ballclub in 1932 after the death of his father, he instilled a philosophy about the ballpark that remains today. Wrigley believed that there weren't many things you could guarantee the paying customer. You couldn't guarantee a Cubs win or that someone would hit a home run or pitch a shutout. One thing you could guarantee, according to Wrigley, is that visitors could see a ballpark that was a showcase, a sight to be remembered. The famed Wrigley Field bleachers and hand-operated scoreboard were built in 1937, the same year Bill Veeck, Jr., planted the now familiar green ivy on the outfield walls. The ballclub has had its ups and downs over the years, but the ballpark remains a fabulous tourist attraction. "Players have good years and bad years. The stadium is always the star," said one writer.

As Santo and Wrona, players of two different eras, stood side by side on the dugout steps on that crisp October evening in 1989, it wasn't difficult for any Cubs fan to remember some of the famous exploits on that field from the men who had come and gone.

Five years earlier, in 1984, the Cubs won their division title as Rick Sutcliffe, a big right-handed pitcher and mid-season acquisition from the Cleveland Indians, went 16–1 for the Cubs to lead the way. Chicago disposed of the San Diego Padres easily in the first two playoff games at Wrigley Field and headed for San Diego needing just one more win to get into the World Series. While the two teams headed west for the remainder of the series, Don Johnson, a second baseman on the Cubs last championship team of 1945, got in his car in California, accompanied by his wife, and headed for Chicago for the World Series. But the Padres won the next three games and the Cubs' hopes were dashed again. As for Johnson's trip to Chicago, "We turned around in Albuquerque," he said.

"Just think of all the men who played so many games on this field..."
In 1969, the Cubs, under the direction of Leo Durocher, had an All-Star infield of Santo at third, Don Kessinger at short, Glenn Beckert at second and Ernie Banks at first — with Billy Williams in the outfield and Ferguson Jenkins anchoring the pitching staff. They won an 11-inning thriller on opening day on a home run by Willie Smith and remained in first place for 155 days. On August 13, they sported a 73–43 record and were 8½ games ahead of the second-place New York Mets. But the Cubs stumbled at the same time as the Mets got hot. By August 27, Chicago had lost 7 out of 8 and led New York by only two games. On September 10, the Mets took over first place and never looked back. Chicago was thwarted again.

"Just think of all the men who played so many games on this field..."
There was Ken Holtzman, a left-handed pitcher (and a member of that '69 team), who threw two no-hitters in a Cubs uniform including one in 1969. And there was "Sad Sam" Jones who in May of 1955 became the first black man to throw a no-hitter as the Cubs beat Pittsburgh with Jones walking the first three men in the ninth inning — and striking out the next three.

There was Don Cardwell, traded to the Cubs from the Phillies in May 1960, who threw a no-hitter in his Cubs debut — and nine years later was a member of the '69 Mets team that overtook the Cubs. There was Ken Hubbs, the promising Cubs second baseman of the early 1960s who was killed in a plane crash in 1962, and Frank Ernaga, whose first four hits for the Cubs in 1957 were two homers, a triple, and a double — and a year later was out of baseball.

There were Dick Drott and Moe Drabowsky and Glen Hobbie, three right-handed pitchers in the late 1950s who the Cubs envisioned as being the trio that would turn the club's fortunes around. It didn't happen. There was Ernie Broglio, who had won 21 and 18 games in two seasons with the Cardinals, a man the Cubs thought so highly of that they traded their young outfield prospect, Lou Brock, to get him. Broglio got a sore arm. Brock got into the Hall of Fame.

There was Harry Chiti, a Cubs catcher in the early 1950s, the youngest player in the major leagues two years in a row. There was Hank Sauer, the tobacco-chewing outfielder who won the Most Valuable Player award in 1952, and Bob Rush, a pitcher who, like Sauer and Chiti, had the misfortune of playing for some terrible Cubs teams in the 1950s and who spoke for two generations of ballplayers when he said, "We were optimistic every spring. Everyone starts out the same."

"Just think of all the men who played so many games on this field…"
Cubs futility is part of baseball lore now, for the historian, the researcher, or the fan has to go back almost 60 years, to 1945, to find a Chicago Cubs team that made it to the World Series. It is a classic year not only in Cubs history but in baseball history for it is remembered as the last "war year" for major league baseball, the last year when ballclubs sent their best athletes off to the armed services and then tried to field the best teams with whoever was left. Sometimes the play was erratic. Sometimes it was comical. But it served the purpose that President Franklin D. Roosevelt hoped it would when he asked four years earlier for the games to continue — America needed the diversion, the entertainment, he said.

And so it was that on September 29, 1945, Paul Erickson, a blond-haired, fireballing pitcher for the Chicago Cubs, threw a curve ball to Tommy O'Brien of the Pittsburgh Pirates with two outs in the bottom of the ninth inning. O'Brien's knees buckled just a bit, like any hitter's knees do when he is expecting the high hard one and gets the rainbow curve instead. He had reason to be surprised. It was young Erickson's first curve ball of the inning. Some claim it was his first curve ball of the year. Before it settled into catcher Mickey Livingston's mitt, it crossed home plate at roughly waist-high level. Strike three, three outs, game over. Cubs win 4–3 and with it they won the National League championship. There wasn't another moment like it for the rest of the century.

Their journey to the National League pennant in 1945 is recounted in the following pages, a marvelous story told in part by some of those who participated in it, men who provide a "living history" with their recollections. As this book project unfolded, a strange thing happened, one of those quirky numbers things that seem to happen so often in baseball. The author's goal was to contact every living member of the 1945 team so that he could weave together their recollections along with all the statistical data available and tie all the research together into a clear, concise and complete historical record of the season. As it turned out, the number of players who were able to contribute turned out to be nine, one of baseball's magic numbers, and they provide the starting lineup for this work. Their thoughts and recollections are buttressed by hundreds of hours of research to verify dates and places and to provide the raw data that document what they had to say. The facts, figures and statistics are the footnotes to history. The men who played the games put faces on the footnotes.

There is Hank Borowy, the lean Yankee pitcher who, like Sutcliffe 39 years later, was a mid-season Cubs acquisition. Now a man in his mid-80s, he had no problem remembering how he wanted to start the seventh game of the World Series after having pitched five innings in game five and four innings in game six. In reflecting on it almost 60 years later, he compared the feeling he had on that October day in 1945 to the feeling of sexual desire that takes over a man in the heat of passion.

And in contrast, there was Hank Wyse, a 22-game winner who was the ace of the staff until Borowy was acquired and who was passed over by manager Charlie Grimm to pitch that seventh game. If Borowy was the man who got the date to the prom, Wyse felt like he was the jilted suitor who was forced to stay home from the dance.

Claude Passeau, interviewed at the age of 90, recalled the third World Series game in which he pitched the greatest game in Series history up to that point — a one-hitter — and said it was the first one-hitter of his career in which his team actually won the game. An injury to Passeau in the sixth game was the start of the unraveling of his team's chances to win the series.

Second baseman Don Johnson, the man who turned around at Albuquerque in 1984, recalled, at the age of 85, several key games in the 1945 season and admonished the author to be sure to get his batting average right. It was .302. Shortstop Lenny Merullo said he still bears the marks from getting spiked in the 12th inning of the sixth game of the World Series. Backup catcher Dewey Williams thinks the outcome of the World Series would have been different if the manager and coaches had listened to him about who should have pitched the seventh game. First baseman Phil Cavarretta, well past 80, spoke with the same gruffness and directness that made him a tough competitor and someone who didn't particularly care if he was liked. Outfielder Andy Pafko, who was to play on championship teams with the Cubs, Brooklyn Dodgers and Milwaukee Braves, talked with great pride about how he drove in the winning run in the pennant-clinching game and how lucky he was to be a 24-year-old kid in the World Series with the Cubs.

And then there was Erickson, the man who threw the pitch that thrust the Cubs into the World Series and who, more than a half-century later, was polite and wished the author well and offered some thoughts on the 1945 season but admitted that at his age, he couldn't remember much. He died a few months later.

These were the men who took the field for this book, my starting nine. I am indebted to each of them, for without them, the book would be hollow, a silent echo chamber. It is published in memory of Johnson, Wyse Williams, Passeau and Erickson, all of whom helped make it possible but died before the book was completed.

"Just think of all the men who played so many games on this field..."
The author wishes to thank Roger Johnson, son of Don Johnson, and Claude Passeau, Jr., son of Claude Passeau, for not only their help but, more importantly, their willingness to help and the family of Andy Pafko, whom the author contacted after finding a "Pafko Family Tree" on the Internet. Through their help, the author located and interviewed the kind man identified on the family tree as "Grandpa Andy."

Thanks also to my colleague and friend, Bob Link, for his editing advice and encouragement; to Arian Schuessler, whose knowledge and skill in photography and photo editing was a huge help; to Michael Grandon, who hears most of my manuscripts before he ever reads them and is kind enough to put up with me; to Andrew Alexander and Ernest Kallay, library directors, and staff members at the Mason City Public Library for their kind assistance; to the National Baseball Hall of Fame,

Front row, from left: Stan Hack, Don Johnson, Harry Lowrey, Phil Cavarretta, Andy Pafko, Charlie Grimm (manager), Bill Nicholson, Paul Gillespie, Lenny Merullo, Hank Borowy. Second row, from left: Claude Passeau, Mickey Livingston, Paul Derringer, Len Rice, Dewey Williams, Ray Prim, Bob Chipman, Hy Vandenberg, Frank Secory, Heinz Becker, Red Smith (coach). Third row, from left: Andy Lotshaw (trainer), Hank Wyse, Lon Warneke, Ray Starr, Paul Erickson, Ed Hanyzewski, Roy Johnson (coach), Walt Signer, Ed Sauer, Roy Hughes, Billy Schuster, Milt Stock (coach). Seated in front: Jim Chalikis, batboy.

The Sporting News, the Society for American Baseball Research and the Chicago Cubs organization for their help.

My greatest gratitude goes, as always, to the captain of my team, Sandi Skipper.

John C. Skipper
Mason City, Iowa
May 2004

I

The Return of Charlie Grimm

"I honestly feel that it would be best for the country to keep baseball going."
— *President Franklin D. Roosevelt*

It was a baseball season like few others, a season in which the over-the-hill gang got a second chance, when some physically impaired individuals got a once-in-a-lifetime chance, when there was no All-Star game because of travel restrictions and, in the view of many, there weren't any bona fide All Stars anyway. It was the last "war year" and it was the last time in the 20th century that the Chicago Cubs won the National League pennant.

In 1945, many of the best athletes in the country, or at least those who were the most physically fit, were fighting overseas, leaving positions open at home for erstwhile ballplayers throughout the United States. Some were teenagers still in high school; some were men approaching middle age. All were trying to fill the gap and preserve the national pastime until the frontline ballplayers got home.

In 1945, Americans could mail a first-class letter with a three-cent stamp and buy a gallon of gasoline for a quarter. They could buy a three-bedroom brick home for $15,000 and buy a week's groceries for less than $20. The nation's population was 139 million and most adults were working — the unemployment rate was 1.9 percent. The minimum wage had recently been raised to 40 cents an hour. Life expectancy in the United States had risen to 65.9 years.

Americans flocked to movie theaters to see *Going My Way*, starring Barry Fitzgerald and Bing Crosby, and *The Lost Weekend*, *National Vel-*

vet and *A Tree Grows in Brooklyn*. They read John Steinbeck's *Cannery Row* and listened to a young Italian singer from New Jersey named Frank Sinatra sing "Put Your Dreams Away." Tall, leggy Bess Myerson, a brunette from New York, was chosen as Miss America.

People were reading *Time, Newsweek, Look,* and *Life* magazines to keep up with the news as well as *Reader's Digest,* the *Saturday Evening Post* and *Photoplay* for more leisurely reading. *Radio Mirror* magazine made a slight name change that foretold the future in broadcasting. "Television" was added to the title. Also, *Ebony* magazine, published by and primarily for African-Americans, made its debut.

Americans turned on their radios to hear H.V. Kaltenborn report the news and hear war correspondents such as Edward R. Murrow provide news accounts from battlefronts. They laughed at the radio antics of Edgar Bergan and Charlie McCarthy, Fibber McGee and Molly, and the most popular radio performer of the era, Jack Benny.

NBC was the oldest and most popular radio network but CBS made gains in April with the debut of "Arthur Godfrey Time," starring a red-haired, freckle-faced, ukulele-playing host who later was one of television's early stars. On June 14, a third major network was born when the former "NBC Blue" network, which had been under separate ownership from NBC for two years, formally took its new name, the American Broadcasting Company — ABC.

Sir Alexander Fleming and two associates from Great Britain won the Nobel Prize for medicine for their discovery of penicillin and John Hersey won the Pulitzer Prize for fiction with his book *A Bell for Adano*.

In Grand Rapids, Michigan, city officials tried something new with their water supply; they fluoridated it, the first city in the country to do so.

Events in two other areas of the country, 30 days apart from one another, signaled that the world was becoming an increasingly dangerous place because of man's inhumanity to man. On July 16, in Alamagardo, New Mexico, American scientists successfully tested a new weapon by detonating an atomic bomb. Exactly one month earlier, on June 16, world leaders launched a noble experiment with the formation of a global organization called the United Nations. An unrelated incident gave Americans a fright on July 28. A U.S. B-25 bomber, well away from any combat, flew off course and crashed into the Empire State Building between the 78th and 79th floors, killing 13 people.

In St. Louis, a young, curly-haired broadcaster named Harry Caray began a broadcasting career doing radio play-by-play of St. Louis Cardinal baseball games. A half-century later, his trademark home run call of "it may be, it could be, it is" was part of the American sports lexicon.

America was a lot of things in 1945, but more than anything else, it was a nation at war. The United States, like the rest of the world, had been making adjustments for years to do its part on the home front to support the thousands of service men and women abroad in World War II. They bought war bonds. They grew "victory gardens." They worked in defense factories. They read the newspapers daily and listened to their radios to monitor the grim news of the war casualties. On April 12, 1945, their commander in chief, President Franklin D. Roosevelt, died of a cerebral hemorrhage in Warm Springs, Georgia. On April 30, German dictator Adolph Hitler, whose madman tactics had consumed so much of Roosevelt's time and thoughts in his last years, committed suicide as his empire was crumbling around him. On May 8, Germany formally surrendered. On August 6, U.S. forces dropped an atomic bomb on the city of Hiroshima, Japan, and three days later, exploded another atomic bomb, this one on the city of Nagasaki, Japan. On August 18, Ernie Pyle, the greatest of war correspondents, was killed in a non-combat traffic accident overseas. On September 2, Japan surrendered, bringing the war to an official end. Three months later, on December 9, General George S. Patton, the feisty, fiery Army troop commander who had survived many military battles, was killed in a peacetime jeep accident.

Nearly 16 million Americans served in the armed forces during World War II with a heavy toll — 408,000 killed and 670,000 wounded. Women were serving and were starting to get some recognition. The March 12 issue of *Time* magazine had a cover story on Captain Mildred McAfee of the U.S. Naval Reserves.

The U.S. government helped those who returned with the passage of the GI Bill, which paid for college tuition and books and provided $65 a month for any service man or woman seeking higher education or paid $20 a week for 52 weeks for others. Returning GIs could get a home loan at 4.25% interest with no money down and house payments of about $50 a month.

Sports in the United States carried on, providing a diversion from the woes of everyday life for millions of fans. One notable exception was the Wimbledon tennis matches, which were canceled because Great Britain, the home of Wimbledon, was too engrossed in the war. Oklahoma A&M won the NCAA college basketball championship by defeating New York University, 49–45. Army was the nation's top college football team, finishing with a record of 9–0–0. The Toronto Maple Leafs won hockey's Stanley Cup by defeating the Detroit Red Wings, 4 games to 3. Hoop Jr. won the Kentucky Derby.

Baseball, long regarded as America's national pastime, made many concessions to the war effort. Its biggest contribution was in the number of ballplayers who left the playing fields for the battlefields. Some sacrificed what would have been the most productive years of their careers to serve their country. There were other concessions too. Chicago Cubs owner Philip K. Wrigley intended to install lights at Wrigley Field in Chicago but donated the steel to the war effort instead. Later, Wrigley was instrumental in developing a women's professional baseball league that created a new niche in the sports/entertainment world made famous 50 years later by the movie *A League of Their Own*. The Racine Belles, Muskegon Lassies, Fort Wayne Daisies and Grand Rapids Chicks played "hardball" on the field but had chaperones off the field and had strict instructions to be "ladylike" in their dress and actions.

After the Japanese bombed Pearl Harbor on December 7, 1941, thrusting America into World War II, baseball commissioner Kenesaw Mountain Landis and the two league presidents, Will Harridge of the American League and Ford Frick of the National League, were all of one mind. Baseball would make whatever sacrifices were necessary for the war effort, including suspension of play altogether if that was deemed necessary.

On January 14, 1942, Judge Landis, a staunch Republican and unabashed anti–New Dealer, wrote a letter on behalf of baseball and in the spirit of patriotism to the man in the White House whom he detested politically. In it, he informed the president:

"Baseball is about to adopt schedules, sign players, make vast commitments, go to training camps. What do you want it to do? If you believe we ought to close down for the duration of the war, we are ready to do so immediately. If you feel we should continue, we would be delighted to do so. We await your order."

Baseball got its answer in a letter from President Roosevelt to Landis dated January 15, 1942:

My dear Judge:
Thank you for yours of January fourteenth. As you will, of course, realize the final decision about the baseball season must rest with you and the Baseball Club owners—so what I am going to say is solely a personal and not an official point of view.
I honestly feel that it would be best for the country to keep baseball going. There will be fewer people unemployed and everybody will work longer hours and harder than ever before.

And that means that they ought to have a chance for recreation and for taking their minds off their work even more than before.

Baseball provides a recreation which does not last over two hours or two hours and a half and which can be got for very little cost. And, incidentally, I hope that night games can be extended because it gives an opportunity to the day shift to see a game occasionally.

As to the players themselves, I know you agree with me that individual players who are active military or naval age should go, without question, into the services. Even if the actual quality of the teams is lowered by the greater use of older players, this will not dampen the popularity of the sport. Of course, if any individual has some particular aptitude in a trade or profession, he ought to serve the government. That, however, is a matter I know you can handle with complete justice.

Here is another way of looking at it — if 300 teams use 5,000 or 6,000 players, these players are a definite recreational asset to at least 20,000,000 of their fellow citizens— and that in my judgment is thoroughly worthwhile.

> With every best wish,
> Very sincerely yours,
> Franklin D. Roosevelt

Thus, baseball proceeded, buoyed by what came to be known as the "green light" letter from Roosevelt. For the next four years, quality of play was diminished considerably as older ballplayers, who might have been considered "washed up" under normal circumstances, got new life as they replaced younger athletes who had gone off to war. As ESPN.com's Rob Neyer described it 60 years later, "Baseball endured, thanks to rosters stocked with baby-faced rookies, grizzled old minor leaguers and 4-F ballplayers...."

Germany invaded Poland on September 1, 1939. The war in Europe had begun. The U.S. government started making preparations for its own possible future involvement by instituting a military draft, the first ever during peacetime, in the fall of 1940. The law required men between the ages of 21 and 35 to register for the draft.

The first major league player to be drafted was Phillies pitcher Hugh "Losing Pitcher" Mulcahy, so nicknamed because he lost 76 games in the previous four years for awful Philadelphia teams. Mulcahy reported to Camp Edwards, Massachusetts, on March 8, 1941. When Pirate pitcher Oad Swigart and Senator hurler Lou Thuman got drafted, it raised nary an eyebrow, the same as when Dodger outfielder Joe Gallagher answered the call. But when Detroit slugger Hank Greenberg was drafted on May 7, it changed the dynamics of the American League pennant race. Greenberg hit .340 and had 41 home runs and 150 runs batted in for a 1940

Tiger team that won the American League championship. Without him, the Tigers plunged to fourth in 1941.

After the Japanese bombed Pearl Harbor on December 7, two days before baseball's winter meetings were to begin in Chicago, hundreds of ballplayers were drafted or volunteered to join the armed forces. *The New York Times* reported in January of 1945 that of 5,800 men playing professional baseball in 1941, all but 400 were in the military or had been in the military. Many who left in 1941 and 1942 did not return until the war was over. Some returned to the game but never regained their old form. Some could not compete effectively for their old jobs against younger athletes who had replaced them. There were some who seemed to pick up where they left off, including Greenberg, Bob Feller, Ted Williams and Stan Musial.

Team travel in major league baseball was adjusted to minimize needless long trips in order to preserve gasoline and oil. In 1945, the All-Star game, scheduled for Fenway Park in Boston, was cancelled. The "All-Star" talent pool was thin and the game would have required too much travel by players from various parts of the country to get to Boston.

Another concession to the war was spring training sites. Baseball executives asked the 16 major league teams to hold their spring training sessions north of the Mason-Dixon line and east of the Mississippi River, once again to minimize travel. The Brooklyn Dodgers trained at Bear Mountain, New York. The Boston Braves held camp in Connecticut while the Red Sox worked out at Tufts College in Boston. The St. Louis Browns, Detroit Tigers, Cincinnati Reds, Cleveland Indians, Pittsburgh Pirates, Chicago White Sox and Chicago Cubs all trained in Indiana, while the St Louis Cardinals were in Cairo, Illinois.

With so many ballplayers in the service, teams had to dig deep into their systems to fill their squads and some, out of compassion, made room for returning ballplayers whose injuries would ordinarily have kept them from playing. Pete Gray, an outfielder for the Browns, was an example of someone filling a roster spot created by vacancies caused by the war. An outfielder, Gray managed to bat and field despite having only one arm. He lost his right arm in a truck accident when he was a boy. He learned to hit lefthanded. In the field, he would catch a ball with the glove on his left hand, then put the ball under his arm, drop the glove, grab the ball and throw it back in to the infield. Gray hit .218 in 77 games and had six doubles and two triples among his 51 hits. He did not play after 1945.

Bert Shepard was an example of an owner's compassion. Shepard was a P-38 fighter pilot whose plane was shot down while he was flying his 34th mission over Germany. He woke up in a hospital in Ludwigwist, Germany, with his right leg amputated. Shepard came back to the States and was signed by the Washington Senators, mostly as a goodwill gesture by Senators owner Clark Griffith, and got into one game. With Boston clubbing Washington 14–2, Shepard got the chance to give the rest of the bullpen a rest. He pitched 5⅓ innings and allowed only one run on three hits. Like Gray, Shepard did not play after 1945.

A survey done prior to the 1945 season showed that 509 players who were considered "regulars" on their ballclubs were in the armed services. The minor leagues lost 3,576 players to the war, dwindling their numbers down to 1,188. Many teams used players who were well into their 40s, in some cases bringing them out of retirement. Men who had not played for several years found themselves back on the ballfields, doing their patriotic duty of keeping the national pastime alive.

At the start of the 1945 season, the Brooklyn Dodgers had four players on their roster over the age of 40. Catcher Clyde Sukeforth, 43, who got into 18 games, hadn't played since 1934. Another catcher, Ray Hayworth, 41, got into a couple of games as a pinch hitter. Outfielder Floyd "Babe" Herman, 42, who appeared in 37 games, hadn't swung a bat in the big leagues in eight years. Even manager Leo Durocher, who turned 40 in July, was on the roster and got one hit in five at-bats as a pinch hitter. In all, 11 of the 16 major league teams had rostered players who were 40 or older. The senior member of this senior class was Cincinnati Reds pitcher Horace Lisenbee, who turned 47 on September 23 and was 1–3 in 31 appearances. At the opposite end of the age spectrum was Brooklyn's Tommy Brown, a 16-year-old second baseman, who, as Baseball Hall of Fame Historian Jerome Holtzman points out, was almost young enough to be Lisenbee's grandson. He was not, however, the youngest major leaguer. That distinction is still held by Joe Nuxhall, a pitcher who appeared in one game for the Reds in 1944 at the age of 15.

American League teams were also hustling to find anyone at any age who could fill gaps in their rosters. On September 4, 1945, the New York Yankees, losing 10–0 to the Detroit Tigers, brought in Paul Schreiber to relieve. Schreiber, 42, was New York's batting practice pitcher and hadn't thrown in a major league game since 1923. He gave up no hits in 3⅔ innings. He didn't fare as well in one other appearance when he gave up four hits in ⅔ of an inning.

Perhaps the strangest baseball development of all in the 1945 baseball season, certainly in comparison to everything that has happened since then, occurred on September 29 in Pittsburgh. The Chicago Cubs, under the direction of affable manager Charlie "Jolly Cholly" Grimm, won the National League pennant.

The story of the Cubs' climb to success begins about 16 months earlier, on May 1, 1944. Chicago, a winner on opening day, had now lost nine in a row and was buried in last place in the National League.

Owner Phil Wrigley's hunch in hiring Jimmy Wilson as manager three years earlier had not paid off. Wilson had been a curious pick to begin with to succeed manager Gabby Hartnett in 1941. Wilson managed the lowly Philadelphia Phillies for five seasons, 1934–1938, in which the ballclub finished seventh three times and eighth twice and in its best season, 1935, finished 25 games below .500. He and the Phillies parted ways with two games left in the 1938 season and Philadelphia sporting a record of 45–103. Wilson's career winning percentage of .401 as a manager is the lowest of any manager at the helm for 1,000 games or more.

When Philadelphia let him go, it appeared his managing days were mercifully over. He had been around the game for a long time, long enough to have connections. And he had always been regarded as a good baseball man saddled with bad teams. Wilson hooked on as a coach with Cincinnati and was coaching for the Reds on August 1, 1940, when tragedy struck the ballclub. Willard Hershberger, a 30-year-old catcher who suffered from periodic depression, had what he thought was a bad game against Boston. He went back to his hotel and killed himself by slitting his wrists. Wilson, an old catcher, went back on the active roster at the age of 40 to share catching duties with the veteran Ernie Lombardi. The Reds won the pennant but Lombardi came up lame at the end of the year. Wilson was pressed into service in the World Series. He responded by getting six hits in 17 at-bats and was a sparkplug, albeit an aged one, for the world champion Reds. Wrigley admired Wilson's spunk, ignored his previous failures as a manager, and hired him to replace Gabby Hartnett, the Cubs' star catcher who helped lead them to a pennant in 1938 but under whose guidance the club had slipped to fourth in 1939 and fifth in 1940. Wilson took over a ballclub that had two established stars, third baseman Stan Hack and first baseman Phil Cavarretta, a promising power-hitting outfielder in Bill Nicholson, and a pitching staff anchored by veteran Claude Passeau. Two young pitchers with great potential, Hank Wyse and Hi Bithorn, were a year away from the big leagues.

Unfortunately for the Cubs, in Wilson's first three years, the club never won as many games as it had in any year in Hartnett's tenure.

Worse, the veteran Hack announced his retirement at the end of the 1943 season, preferring to go home to his ranch rather than to play another season for Wilson.

The ballclub was at low ebb and far from the proud days that began when Chicago became a charter member of the National League in 1876. In that year, Chicago took its place in baseball history alongside St. Louis, Hartford, Louisville, Boston, New York, and Philadelphia. And they finished in first place. Al Spalding, pitcher and manager, won 47 games and lost 13. Spalding helped form the National League and later started a sporting goods company that still bears his name. The rest of the pitching staff, a guy named

Gabby Hartnett was a great Cub catcher who took over as manager for Charlie Grimm in 1938 and guided the club to the National League championship.

McVey, won five and lost one. Adrian "Cap" Anson was the starting third baseman who would later become a star first baseman. In 1879, he also became manager of the White Stockings, as they were known back then, and led them to championships in 1880, 1881, 1882, 1885 and 1886. More than a century has passed, and no Cubs manager has equaled Anson's feat of five championships. Frank Chance won four. Charlie Grimm won three.

Anson remained at the helm through the 1897 season but the Cubs hit a championship drought after 1886 and would not finish on top for another 20 years. At the time, it seemed like a long dry spell. Recent history has shown it to be, by comparison, mercifully short.

Tom Burns managed the ballclub in 1898 and 1899. At the turn of the century, Tom Loftus, who had previous managing experience with Cincinnati and Cleveland, took the helm for a couple of years but departed after a sixth-place finish in 1901. The following year, Frank Selee took over. Selee, a bald-headed man with a flowing mustache, wore a business suit and bow tie in the dugout. He looked more like the town banker than the leader of a ballclub, but he was one of the premier managers of the 19th century, managing Boston from 1890 through 1901 and winning championships in 1891, 1892, 1893, 1897 and 1898.

When Selee came to the Cubs, he made several defensive changes over the next few years, moving catcher Frank Chance to first base, third baseman Joe Tinker to short and shortstop Johnny Evers to second. He developed two great starting pitchers in Mordecai "Three Finger" Brown and Ed Reulbach. The Cubs finished fifth in 1902 but won 15 more games under Selee than they had under Loftus the previous year. By 1904, the Cubs were solid contenders. They finished second, winning 93 games, 40 more than the year before Selee took over.

But Selee became ill with tuberculosis and was forced to resign. In four years, he would be dead at the age of 49. He picked first baseman Chance to succeed him and the Cubs flourished with the team Selee developed. Chicago finished third in 1905 but then won National League championships in 1906, 1907, 1908 and 1910. They finished second to Fred Clarke's Pittsburgh Pirates in 1909 and second to John McGraw's New York Giants in 1911. After a third place finish in 1912, Chance resigned.

Second baseman Evers was picked to replace Chance. In hiring Evers, the Cubs started two patterns they would repeat at the end of the century. They hired five managers in five years and also hired former players who were fan favorites with no proven managerial talent.

Evers took over in 1913 and was gone after a third-place finish at 88–65. Hank O'Day, former pitcher and future umpire, lasted a year, 1914 — a year best remembered not for the Cubs, who finished fourth, but for the "Miracle Braves," who won the National League pennant and then disposed of Connie Mack's Philadelphia A's in the World Series. In 1915, former catcher Roger Bresnahan managed the Cubs to a 73–80 fourth-place finish. Then came Tinker, the old shortstop, whose team finished fifth with a 67–86 mark in 1916. By the following year, the Cubs found a man they stuck with, Fred Mitchell, who lasted four years and brought home a championship in 1918.

It was at about this time that the Cubs were going through some front-office changes that would change the focus and direction of the team.

William Wrigley, who made his fortune in the chewing gum business, got involved with the Cubs as a civic gesture as well as an investment, because control of the ballclub had been gained by stockholder

Charles Taft of Cincinnati in 1915 upon the death of Chicagoan Charles Murphy, who had controlling interest.

After the 1915 season, the Federal League, which had raided players from the American and National Leagues, folded. Charles A. Weeghman, who had owned the Federal League's Chicago Whales, and businessman William Walker made a pitch to buy the Cubs. They approached another tycoon, J. Ogden Armour, and asked him to put up $500,000. Armour declined but said he was in for $50,000 if nine other investors could be found for the same amount. Armour called Wrigley, who agreed to buy in. In fact, Wrigley contributed $100,000.

This group took over the ballclub on January 20, 1916, with Weeghman being the leader and Wrigley a member of the board of directors. Within a year, Weeghman found himself in serious financial trouble and borrowed money from Wrigley, using Chicago Cubs stock as collateral. When Weeghman could not repay the loan, Wrigley became the largest single stockholder in the ballclub, although he did not have controlling interest.

In December of 1918, the board named Mitchell, the Cubs manager, as the president of the ballclub and businessman William L. Veeck as vice president. (Veeck's son, Bill Veeck, Jr., later worked for the Cubs and planted the vines that still adorn the outfield walls in Wrigley Field. He also became famous as a baseball executive in his own right, owning the Cleveland Indians, St. Louis Browns and Chicago White Sox.) The National League prohibited a team's field manager from also being president of the ballclub, so Mitchell stayed on as field manager and Veeck became president of the Cubs.

By the end of the 1921 season, Wrigley and another stockholder, A.D. Lasker, found themselves in frequent disagreements about how the team was being run, on and off the field. In the end, Wrigley bought out Lasker and became principal owner.

Wrigley was an interested owner but left most of the details of the day-to-day running of the ballclub to Veeck. Wrigley used the fortune he had made in the chewing gum business in some unusual ways that benefited the team. In 1922, he bought an island—Catalina Island, off the coast of southern California—and had 350 bungalows and a hotel constructed on it. He then arranged for daily boat rides to and from the island and advertised it as a great holiday get-away place for Hollywood stars and anyone else who could afford it. He also established it as the spring training mecca for the Cubs.

Meanwhile, the Cubs meandered in the National League standings, not scaring anyone with their record. Wrigley became anxious to have a winner and to procure the players that would help bring the club to the top. In this vein, after the Cubs finished fifth in 1924, Veeck and Bill Killefer, who was now field manager, pulled off a deal with the Pittsburgh Pirates that landed veteran shortstop Rabbit Maranville and a first baseman named Charlie Grimm.

Killefer stepped aside as manager in favor of Joe McCarthy, a brilliant baseball strategist and evaluator of talent. Under McCarthy's direction, the Cubs won the pennant in 1929 and McCarthy's reputation soared. He bolted the Cubs to manage the New York Yankees, where his teams and their successes are legendary. McCarthy managed the Yankees for 16 years, won eight pennants, and had seven World Series championships. He remains the all-time leader in winning percentage for both the regular season and for World Series games. Meanwhile, in 1931, the Cubs turned to temperamental second baseman Rogers Hornsby, one of the game's greatest hitters, to be their manager.

Early in 1932, a pivotal year in Cub history, William Wrigley died. His son, Philip, inherited the chewing gum empire, Catalina Island with all its trimmings and the Chicago Cubs. In mid-season, the ballclub was in turmoil. Hornsby had alienated many players with his caustic comments and insults. He was a disciplinarian and a perfectionist and had little patience for ballplayers who did not have the desire, commitment and talent that he possessed. He was a bad match for the Cubs, who needed someone with just the opposite personality to take hold of the club.

William Veeck's choice was the banjo-playing first baseman, Grimm. The new manager instilled an attitude in his players to have fun, move the runners around the bases, play good defense and don't walk too many opponents. Under Grimm, the Cubs won 37 of 57 remaining games and won the National League pennant. Chicago won again in 1935 and was headed toward the top in 1938, but Grimm didn't think the ballclub was playing up its potential — and he blamed himself. After talking it over with Wrigley and Veeck, Jolly Cholly decided it would be best if he stepped aside. Veteran catcher Gabby Hartnett took over and guided the Cubs to their third championship in seven years. But they dropped to fourth place in 1939 and to fifth in 1940. That prompted Wrigley's decision to bring on Wilson.

He had two sixth-place finishes with the Cubs in 1941 and 1942 and had moved them up to fifth in 1943, his best year statistically as a manager with a 74–79 record. On opening day, April 18, 1944, Hank Wyse won a 3–0 pitching dual with Cincinnati's Bucky Walters at Crosley Field. The following day, young Ed Hanyzewski lost a 2–1 heartbreaker to Elmer Riddle of the Reds. On April 20, the Cubs' Bill Fleming pitched well enough to win but didn't as Cincinnati prevailed for the second straight day, 2–1. The final margin might have been higher had not Mike Kosman, a pinch runner for the Reds, been thrown out at the plate in what turned out to be his only appearance ever in a major league game.

The Cubs home opener was April 21, the first of a three-game series with the defending National League champion Cardinals. St. Louis handed the Cubs their third straight loss, 4–0. Two days later, the Cardinals won a doubleheader, 11–3 and 5–4. The Cubs had now lost five in a row, including all three home games. A stop at Pittsburgh on April 26 resulted in a 6–1 loss to the Pirates and their young fireballing righthander Preacher Roe, who later on would have some great seasons with the Brooklyn Dodgers. The Cardinals then swept the Cubs in St. Louis so that on April 30, Chicago had a 1–9 record and showed no signs of turning it around. Wilson was dismissed as manager and coach Roy Johnson took over for one game, which the Cubs lost 10–4 to Cincinnati for their 10th straight loss.

Wrigley needed someone who could transform a lethargic, discontented group of athletes and mold them into a winning ballclub. The call went out again to Charlie Grimm. "Jolly Cholly" was the son of a house painter who wanted his boy to carry on the family business. But Grimm chose baseball instead and became one of the game's most colorful characters and consistent first basemen, both at bat and in the field. The St. Louis Cardinals took a brief look at him in 1918 but he established himself as a member of the Pittsburgh Pirates, where he played six years before being traded to the Chicago Cubs. He played 12 years for the Cubs, the last five as player-manager, before giving up his first-base duties to a 17-year-old kid fresh out of high school—Phil Cavarretta, whom Grimm managed on three Cubs pennant-winning teams. By the time Grimm's playing career was over, he had 2,299 hits with 394 doubles, 108 triples and 79 home runs and a lifetime batting average of .290. He was named the best defensive first baseman in the National League nine times.

As was noted, his first stint as Cubs manager came on August 2, 1932, when the Cubs fired the humorless Hornsby and Chicago went on to capture the National League pennant—the first time in baseball history that a mid-season replacement manager won a championship. The Cubs lost the World Series to the New York Yankees but were back on top in 1935, helped immensely by a mid-season 21-game winning streak. They lost to the Detroit Tigers in the World Series. In 1938, after Grimm resigned on July 20, the Cubs rallied to win the pennant under Hartnett, who became the second manager in baseball history to win a pennant as a mid-season replacement, Grimm being the first.

Grimm went to the Cubs radio broadcast booth for three years, teaming first with Pat Flanagan on WBBM in 1938 and then with former player and manager Lew Fonseca on WJJD in 1939 and 1940. Grimm and Flanagan broadcast the Cubs-Pirates game on Sept, 28, 1938, when Hartnett hit a home run into the darkness—the famed homer in the gloamin'—that helped seal the pennant for the Cubs. The radio job gave Grimm the opportunity to tell his stories and have a little fun with the fans. It was the custom for a team's public address announcer to tell the crowd that day's paid attendance in about the seventh inning. The attendance figure was given to the broadcasters before the official announcement. Knowing the exact figure, Grimm and Fonseca would offer guesses on the radio as to the attendance, always coming very close to the figure they already knew. Then they would marvel at how good they were at guessing the attendance. One day, Fonseca "guessed" the exact figure, amazing the unsuspecting audience. From that point on, the men said they weren't going to guess the size of the crowd any more—because it was no longer a challenge.

Cub manager Charlie Grimm, "Jolly Cholly," won a pennant when he took over as Cub manager in 1932, won again in 1935, started the year as Cubs manager when they won again in 1938 and guided them to the 1945 championship. "Every time we call on Charlie, we win," said Cub owner Philip Wrigley. (Photograph courtesy of Baseball Hall of Fame Library)

In 1941, when Hartnett was removed as Cubs manager and replaced by Wilson, new Cubs general manager Jim Gallagher hired Grimm as one of Wilson's coaches.

Shortly thereafter, Bill Veeck Jr. purchased the Milwaukee Brewers minor league club and needed someone not only to lead the team but also to help put customers in the seats. With the Cubs' blessing, Grimm took on the responsibility. The Brewers won the American Association championship in 1943 — another title for Grimm. By 1944, he was the toast of Milwaukee. His Brewer ballclub was winning and Charlie was entertaining the fans with his antics on the field and his stories off the field. Meanwhile, the Cubs were reeling. They had lost 10 in a row after winning on opening day and seemed destined for a long, lonely stay in the second division. The ballclub wanted to bring Grimm back to Chicago but Grimm was reluctant to leave Milwaukee unless a successor to him could be found who could keep the ballclub winning and the fans entertained. The Brewers hired Casey Stengel and Grimm returned to the Cubs.

Grimm took over on May 5 and the Cubs proceeded to lose their first three games under his direction, bringing the losing streak to 13. On May 11, just before Cubs starter Ed Hanyzewski took the mound at Wrigley Field, Grimm showed him and the rest of the team what life was going to be like under his direction. He gave Hanyzewski a four-leaf clover, which he wore under his cap. The Cubs beat the Phillies 4–3 to snap the losing streak. It was also the ballclub's first win of the year in the friendly confines of Wrigley Field.

Giving Hanyzewski the four-leaf clover was typical of Grimm's approach to managing a team. "I had fun playing baseball. I tried to make it fun for my players," he said in his 1968 autobiography *Baseball, I Love You: Jolly Cholly's Story.* "I was Jolly Cholly and I always thought a pat on the back, an encouraging word or a wisecrack paid off more than a beautifully executed piece of strategy."

The record shows Grimm was no slouch on strategy. Over the years, his teams executed the fundamentals well — they often were among the league leaders in most bunts, fewest walks and fewest errors. In 1945, his team led the National League in hitting, pitching and fielding. And Don Johnson, his number two hitter in the lineup, finished first in the National League in sacrifice bunts with 22. Peanuts Lowrey and Andy Pafko, his number three and five hitters, finished tied for second with 21 sacrifice bunts each.

He tried to maintain a balance of playing to win while having fun doing it. Once, while coaching third base as managers often did in those days, Grimm watched Cardinal shortstop Marty Marion make two consecutive spectacular plays to retire Cubs batters. After the second one,

Grimm keeled over in the coaching box as if he had fainted. The crowd loved it.

On another occasion, when a Cubs pitcher hit a home run, Grimm told players on the bench to each grab a bat. As the pitcher crossed home plate and headed for the dugout, he was greeted by teammates who had formed two rows with the bats held up and extended to form an arch for him to run through to get to the dugout.

Still another time, when the Cubs were losing badly in a game and one batter after another was being retired, manager Grimm leaned over the front of the dugout, scooped out some dirt with his hand and buried the lineup card.

"He loved baseball and everybody loved him," said Lenny Merullo, who played for Grimm for eight years and was a member of the 1945 World Series squad. "Charlie would never have been a computer kind of guy. He liked to play hunches. And boy, could he tell the stories."

As the Cubs tried to rebuild in 1944 and 1945, Grimm unleashed a story that became one of his favorites. With so many good ballplayers in the armed services, ballclubs filled out their rosters with men who were categorized as "4-F" by the military, meaning they were deemed ineligible to serve, usually because of some sort of disability. Grimm said a young man approached him one day and told he wanted to play for the Cubs, that he could help them. The man explained that he was 4-F — so he could be in uniform as soon as Grimm wanted him.

The man said, "I can hit like Ruth, run like Cobb and field like DiMaggio."

"If you think you can do all that, you must be nuts," said Grimm.

"That," said the man, "is why I'm 4-F."

Another Grimm story: He said a scout approached him excitedly and told him about a pitcher he found who threw a perfect game, struck out every batter, and only two batters hit foul balls off him. "Send me the guys who hit the foul balls. We need hitters," said Grimm, or so the story goes.

He could not mastermind a fairy-tale finish in 1944. After Hany-zewski beat the Phillies on May 11, the Cubs lost three more in a row to bring their record to 2–16. But Grimm got 16 wins from Wyse and 15 from the veteran Passeau, and Nicholson had his greatest year, hitting 33 home runs, driving in 122 runs and scoring 116, leading the league in all three categories. When the Cubs beat Pittsburgh 7–2 on August 5 at Forbes Field, it was their 11th straight win and they climbed to within one game of .500 at 46–47. It was as close as they would get. The Cubs were 74–69 under Grimm and finished in fourth place.

Nicholson was the team's established star. He finished second to Marty Marion of the Cardinals in Most Valuable Player voting. On July 23, he hit four consecutive home runs, two in each game of a double-header against the Giants. When he came to bat with a chance to hit his fifth straight homer, Giant manager Mel Ott ordered him intentionally walked — even though the bases were loaded. "He was killing us," Ott explained after the game.

Grimm counted on rightfielder Nicholson to be a key component on the 1945 ballclub if the Cubs were to have any chance of overtaking the three-time defending National League champion Cardinals. In centerfielder Andy Pafko, the Cubs had a hard-hitting outfielder who had the best arm in the National League since KiKi Cuyler (according to KiKi Cuyler, among others). In left field, there was Harry "Peanuts" Lowrey, a speedster who was a great contact hitter and who had just been released from the service. In Nicholson, Pafko and Lowrey, the Cubs had the potential of having the best outfield in the National League.

Phil Cavarretta had MVP potential at first base, if Grimm could get him to control his temper. Cavarretta was the team captain and a firebrand who hated to lose a game or a fight. On the other side of the diamond, third base had been a question mark when Hack, the usually happy-go-lucky guy who made everyone else on the ballclub feel better about themselves, quit when he tired of playing under Wilson. Grimm called him and counseled him, cajoled him and convinced him to come back. Hack and Cavarretta gave the Cubs All Stars at first and third.

Things were shaping up for 1945. But Grimm, owner Wrigley and general manager Gallagher knew that to have a chance to overtake the Giants and Dodgers and challenge the Cardinals, they were going to have to find a way to bolster their pitching staff, which was long on desire but also long on age and short on durability.

II

Pitching Staff:
The Old and the Wyse

"If you do this, I'll take care of you for the rest of your life."
— *Philip Wrigley*

Baseball is filled with examples of pitching staffs dominated by two great starters that were good enough to lead ballclubs to championships. In the 1930s, the Dean brothers, Paul and Dizzy, led the St. Louis Cardinal staff. In 1948, the Boston Braves had "Spahn and Sain and pray for rain," referring to their aces, Warren Spahn and Johnny Sain. In the 1950s, the Milwaukee Braves won two consecutive championships with Spahn and Lew Burdette leading the way. The Dodgers of the 1960s had Sandy Koufax and Don Drysdale.

In 1945, the Cubs had two capable starters in Hank Wyse and Claude Passeau, both of whom were capable of winning 20 games. Passeau had already done it once and Wyse seemed ready to hit the 20-win mark. Beyond these two hurlers, though, the Cubs' pitching staff was, for the most part, an aging group of athletes, and there wasn't much depth.

Wyse was coming off a 16–15 year with the below .500 1944 Cub team and much was expected of him in 1945. As early as March 24, Grimm predicted he would win 20 games. A righthander, he never overpowered anybody with his speed, but he moved the ball around, keeping hitters off balance, and had a great sinkerball. And he could pitch a lot of innings. "He was rubber-armed," said teammate Len Merullo.

At 27, he was the youngest in the Cubs starting rotation. A spinal injury had kept him out of the military. After the 1944 season, Wyse got a job in a war plant in Miami, Ohio, and, in a freak accident, fell off a welding platform, injuring his back. Because of the injury, he was forced to wear a corset for much of the 1945 season. But he fulfilled Grimm's March prediction, winning 22 games and losing 10 and leading the pitching staff in innings pitched with 278⅔.

Wyse, a native of Oklahoma, was a handsome kid who was frequently kidded by teammates because of his youthful good looks and skin so smooth that he had little facial hair to shave. He broke into professional baseball in 1940 on the same Cubs farm team at Tulsa that had Dizzy Dean, who was trying to make his way back to the major leagues.

Wyse stayed with Tulsa until 1942 when the Cubs brought him up. He got into four games and had a 2–1 record. In 1943, he was 9–7 in 38 games, setting the stage for the next two seasons when he won a combined total of 38 games.

In a 1998 interview, Wyse verified the concerns of Cub management about the lack of depth on the pitching staff. He said Wrigley and Grimm met the pitchers at mid-season and told them they thought the club had a chance to win it all. They said they were hoping to find another pitcher to solidify the staff and take some of the pressure off Wyse. According to Wyse, Grimm told the starting pitchers that until the club could come up with another pitcher, the starters might have to go on two or three days rest.

Wyse said he told the bosses he wasn't sure he could do that. "Mr. Wrigley said, 'if you do this, I'll take care of you for the rest of your life'," said Wyse.

So Wyse went to the mound often and was spectacular in July, starting nine games in 28 days, carrying out what Wrigley and Grimm wanted him to do. Wyse won eight of his nine starts and the Cubs went 26–6 for the month to take over first place and never relinquish it.

On July 1, Wyse beat the New York Giants 4–3 in the second game of a doubleheader at the Polo Grounds. It was the first win in what would be an 11-game winning streak that elevated the Cubs from fourth place to first place, a position they held for the rest of the year.

On July 8, Wyse, again pitching the second game of a doubleheader, beat the Philadelphia Phillies 9–2 at Shibe Park. The win was the Cubs 10th in a row and put them on top of the National League where they remained for the rest of the season.

Four days later, on July 12, the Cubs beat the Boston Braves, 6–1, at Wrigley Field as Wyse stopped Tommy Holmes' hitting streak at 37. It remained the modern National League record until Pete Rose hit safely in 44 straight in 1978.

On Sunday, July 29, Wyse and Hank Borowy, making his first start with the Cubs, beat the Cincinnati Reds 4–1 and 3–2 in a doubleheader at Wrigley Field in the first showing of the 1–2 pitching punch that would lead the Cubs the rest of the way. Wyse's incredible July:

July 1— beat New York 4–3   July 19 — beat Brooklyn 3–1
July 5 — beat Boston 3–2   July 22 — lost to Philadelphia 11–6
July 8 — beat Philadelphia 9–2   July 26 — beat Cincinnati 2–1
July 12 — beat Boston 6–1   July 29 — beat Cincinnati 4–1
July 15 — beat New York 7–2

As for Wrigley's promise to take care of Wyse for the rest of his life, "I'm still waiting," Wyse said with a laugh in the 1998 interview, 21 years after Wrigley's death.

Passeau, at 36, nine years older than Wyse, had arm problems that almost caused him to retire early in the season. He was a seasoned, right-handed veteran pitcher who believed the plate belonged to him — and he didn't hesitate to throw "message" pitches to batters who cramped his style.

HANK WYSE

Hank Wyse fulfilled his manager's prediction when he won 22 games, despite suffering back problems that caused him to wear a corset most of the season.

Hank Sauer, who later played for the Cubs, recalled a time when he was a rookie with Cincinnati and faced Passeau and homered off him. "As I'm rounding second base, he yells at me, 'You bush son of a bitch, you're going down next time.' And sure enough. The next time up, down I go. And the next time after that, too. One time after he knocked me down, he looked at me on the ground and said, 'Try hittin' that way.' That was Claude Passeau."

The pride of Millsaps College in Jackson, Mississippi, Passeau jumped from Class-A ball to the major leagues in 1935 and played sparingly with the Pittsburgh Pirates. Then he established

Claude Passeau had bone chips in his elbow that nearly caused him to retire twice. He won 17 games in 1945 and threw a one-hitter in the World Series. His injury in the sixth game of the series was the turning point.

himself by winning 51 games in four years with a Philadelphia Phillies team that wasn't very good before being traded to the Cubs in 1939. He won 20 games with the Cubs in 1940, 14 in 1941, 19 in 1942 and 15 each in 1943 and 1944 to earn the reputation of being a consistent winner.

He also had the reputation of throwing a spitter and, while Passeau was not beyond using whatever edge he could to baffle opposing batters, the drop on his pitches was also caused by his unusual grip of the baseball. He was plagued with finger injuries throughout his career and he was given to gripping the ball more loosely than most pitchers as he tried to avoid blisters.

Passeau started the 1945 season in great pain from calcification of bone chips in his right elbow. Scheduled to be the opening day starting pitcher, Passeau sat out and eventually went home to Mississippi where he contemplated calling it quits. He was getting old (for a ballplayer), he was hurting, and he was doing pretty well financially because of some investments he had made in the tungston oil business. In fact, Passeau had thought about quitting the year before but stayed with the Cubs and compiled a 15–9 record and an earned run average of 2.89. He decided to come back to the Cubs in 1945, also, after staying home in Mississippi for a couple of weeks nursing his sore arm.

When he returned, he threw a shutout in his first start, beating Cincinnati 4–0 on April 25. Grimm was reluctant to put him in the regular rotation right away, wanting time for his arm to heal completely. In his next start on May 13, Passeau lost a 3–2 decision to the Boston Braves. He then reeled off nine straight victories before losing again to the Braves, this time 3–1 on July 12. That loss, in the second game of a doubleheader, ended a Cubs 11-game winning streak. For Passeau, the loss preceding his nine-game streak and the loss that ended it both came at the hands of Boston starter Nate Andrews, who won only five other games all year. By year's end Passeau was 17–9 with a 2.46 earned run average.

The Passeau winning streak:

May 23 — 5–3 win over Philadelphia	June 24 — 6–3 win over St. Louis
June 3 — 3–1 win over Boston	June 28 — 11–8 win over Brooklyn
June 10 — 7–4 win over Cincinnati	July 3 — 24–2 win over Boston
June 15 — 8–1 win over Cincinnati	July 7 — 3–0 win over Philadelphia
June 20 — 5–3 win over Pittsburgh	

"You know," he said, many years after his retirement, "it's a funny thing in baseball. There are certain teams you can beat. Others give you trouble. It seems like I could beat Chicago (when he played for the Phillies), St. Louis, Pittsburgh and Cincinnati and break even with the rest."

Passeau made the National League All-Star team four times and is remembered as being the pitcher who served up the three-run homer to

Ted Williams with two out in the ninth inning of the 1941 All-Star game as the American League came from behind to win 7–5. Passeau, ever the competitor, talked about the Williams homer 50 years later and pointed out that an error prior to the home run kept the inning alive and that all three runs were unearned.

Passeau helped himself with his defense throughout his career. He went from September 21, 1941 to May 20, 1946 without making an error, fielding the ball cleanly 273 times during that time period.

The rest of the Cubs staff was suspect. The veterans' best days were behind them and the youngsters were untested under pennant-race pressure. At the start of the 1945 season, a lot was expected of 38-year-old veteran Paul Derringer, who had more than 200 wins in his career but who had not had a winning season since 1941. Derringer, a righthander, had a career filled with ups and downs, partly because he played on some good teams and some bad ones. He pitched for Rochester in the International League in 1929 and 1930 and won 40 games, earning him a shot at the big leagues. He was 18–8 in 1931, his rookie year with the St. Louis Cardinals. Two years later, he was 0–2 with the Cardinals when they traded him to Cincinnati for Leo Durocher. While Durocher became part of the Cardinals famed "Gashouse Gang," Derringer struggled to a 7–25 record with the Redbirds and a 7–27 record for the season.

Two years after that, he won 22 games for the Reds, the first of four seasons when he won 20 or more games. He was the starting and winning pitcher for the Reds in the first night game in Cincinnati in 1935. In 1940, he threw two one-hitters, was the winning pitcher in the All-Star game and helped the Reds to their second successive National League championship. His battery mate late in the year and in the World Series was Jimmy Wilson, his future manager at Chicago before Grimm arrived.

All of that was well behind him when Derringer was sold to the Cubs in 1943. He had two mediocre years, 10–14 in 1943 and 7–13 in 1944, and clearly showed that he was nearing the end of the road. Grimm intended on using Derringer as the third or fourth man in the rotation. But Wyse arrived at spring training nursing the sore back and Passeau had such a sore elbow that he went home. When Derringer looked good in beating the White Sox in an exhibition game the weekend before the season started, Grimm named him as the Cubs starting pitcher on opening day. And he beat the Cardinals 3–2 at Wrigley Field, one of only six times all year that the Cubs beat the Cardinals. "Ooom Paul," as Grimm called him, went on to have his finest season since 1940, winning 16 and losing 11.

Derringer finished his career with 223 career wins, including 32 shutouts and 10 wins in which the final score was 1–0. He appeared in the World Series four different years with three different teams. He never pitched in the major leagues after the 1945 season.

Rounding out the starting rotation was Ray Prim, a veteran left-hander who spent most of his career in the minor leagues. But like so many other ballplayers of his day, Prim got his big chance in the big leagues during the war years and made the most of it.

He was nicknamed "Pop" by some of his teammates because of his silver-graying hair and "Cutie" by others because of the screw ball he could throw that could handcuff opposing batters. Prim had been around a long time. He started in the Cotton States League in 1928 and pitched off and on for the Washington Senators in 1933 and 1934, appearing in 10 games, two as a starter and eight in relief, and losing his only two decisions. He moved to the Philadelphia Phillies in 1935 and compiled a 3–4 record in 29 games, six as a starter. He did not make a major league appearance again for eight years. In between, he was a star with the Cubs' Los Angeles farm club in the Pacific Coast League. Prim had three 20-win seasons in a seven-year stretch, prompting the Cubs to bring him up to the big club in 1943. He appeared in 29 games for the Cubs and had a 4–3 record with one complete game in five starts. But the next year, he was back with Los Angeles where he posted a 22–10 record and an earned-run average of 1.70.

So the Cubs brought him back for one more try in 1945, using him as their number four starter and in relief. This time, Prim responded with a great season, but not right away. Through the end of June, he was much like he had been in his previous stints in the big leagues, unimpressive, with only two wins.

But the Cubs got hot in July and Prim was a big part of their success. From July 6 through July 22, he won five games as both a starter and reliever and in one stretch had 27 consecutive scoreless innings, including two consecutive shutouts. He blanked Boston 2–0 on July 13 and came back five days later to stifle the Dodgers, 5–0. The scoreless streak was broken on July 22 when Philadelphia's Vince DiMaggio homered off him, but the Cubs and Prim still won the game, 8–5. By the end of the season, Prim had compiled a 13–8 record with a 2.40 earned-run average, best ERA in the National League. He also led the league in fewest walks per innings, 1.25, and in fewest hits per nine innings, 7.73. In total, opponents averaged less than one base runner per inning off him.

Prim's July winning streak:

July 6 — winner in relief in 11–3 win over Philadelphia
July 8 — winner in relief in 12–6 win over Philadelphia
July 13 — starter and winner in 3–0 win over Boston
July 18 — starter and winner in 5–0 win over Brooklyn
July 22 — starter and winner in 8–5 win over Philadelphia

Prim was originally a righthander but burned his right hand as a youth and permanently damaged tendons. So he switched and became a lefthander and was able to make a career out of it.

Bob Chipman was a 26-year-old relief pitcher and spot starter who the Cubs got in a 1944 trade with the Brooklyn Dodgers for infielder Eddie Stanky. Chipman, a lefthander, did not throw hard but had excellent control. While he was never a star in the big leagues, he is one of the few Cubs pitchers on the 1945 championship team who hung on for several more seasons in the big leagues.

He broke in with Brooklyn in 1941, and while he was too late in arriving to play in the World Series, he did make an appearance in the Dodgers 100th victory that year. Leo Durocher used him sparingly in three years but he pitched pretty well. He worked eight innings without allowing an earned run between 1941 and 1943. So "Mr. Chips," as he was called, was sent to the Cubs for Stanky after posting a 3–1 record with the Dodgers at the start of the 1944 season. He was 9–9 with the fourth place Cubs, giving him his best season record of 12–10.

In 1945, he made 25 appearances for the Cubs and had a 4–5 record. More important, he started 10 times and had three complete games, including one shutout, a 3–0 victory over Pittsburgh on April 22. While it was early in the season, it was an important victory because the Cubs needed a lift, with Passeau out with an elbow injury and Wyse still nursing a sore back. On May 30, Chipman won the second game of a doubleheader as the Cubs beat the Giants 11–2 after losing the opener 8–6. The games were played before the largest Wrigley Field crowd in seven years— 42,565. Chipman beat Bill Voiselle. It was the Giant hurler's second straight loss after winning his first eight. After the Cubs purchased Hank Borowy from the Yankees on July 27, Chipman made only two more starts as manager Charlie Grimm went with a set rotation of Borowy, Wyse, Passeau and Prim.

On September 29, Chipman came into the game in relief of Borowy and recorded the second out of the ninth inning. When Paul Erickson came on to strike out the next batter, the Cubs had won the National League championship. Chipman started the next day in the final game of the season and defeated the Pirates 5–3, the Cubs 98th win of the season.

At 39, Hy Vandenberg was the oldest pitcher on the Cubs roster and, at 6 feet 4 inches and 220 pounds, was also the biggest. He had an indistinguished big league career prior to coming to the Cubs. As a 29-year-old rookie for the Boston Red Sox in 1935, Vandenberg appeared in three games, gave up 12 runs on 15 hits in 5⅓ innings, and returned to the minor leagues sporting a 20.25 earned run average with the Red Sox, who never gave him a chance to redeem himself. He spent a year in the minors and then came up with the New York Giants in 1937. In his only appearance, he threw a complete game but gave up seven runs on 10 hits in suffering his first major league loss. He appeared in six games with the Giants in 1938, in two more in 1939, and got his first big league win with New York in 1940 when he also lost a game for the Giants.

Vandenberg, who was 35 years old going into the 1941 season, spent three years in the military and then was picked up by the Cubs and Grimm, starving for pitching, in 1944. He responded with a 7–4 record in 35 games, including nine starts. At the start of the 1945 season, with Passeau out with an injury and Wyse hurting with a sore back, Vandenberg, the old man of the pitching staff, found himself in the role of a spot starter and mainstay in the bullpen. He had his best year in the big leagues, with a 7–3 record that included seven starts, most of them before Borowy joined the team from the New York Yankees on July 27.

On June 15, in his first start of the year, Vandenberg surprised everybody, including Grimm, when he threw a masterpiece. The only expectation was for him to throw enough innings to give the rest of the staff a breather. Instead, Vandenberg narrowly missed a no-hitter when he beat Cincinnati 3–0 in the second game of a double header at Crosley Field. Al Libke hit a double off him in the first inning for the Reds' only hit of the game. Vandenberg lost his next start 6–4 to the Cardinals and Harry Brecheen at Wrigley Field but came right back to beat the Dodgers 3–1 at Ebbets Field on June 29. On July 4, Vandenberg beat the Braves 4–1 at Wrigley Field, the Cubs' fourth win in what would be an 11-game winning streak.

He appeared in three games in relief in the World Series, pitching six innings and allowing no runs on one hit. Grimm considered starting him in the seventh game but went with Borowy instead. Borowy, who had won two previous games, got shelled as the Cubs lost 9–3. Vandenberg, so close to achieving a pitcher's dream of starting the seventh game of a World Series, never appeared in another major league game.

Paul Erickson was a big blond righthander who first came up with the Cubs in 1941. He was the stereotype fireballer — someone who could throw as hard and as fast as anyone in baseball. There were no radar guns in Erickson's day to record the speed of his pitches, but those who saw him pitch and who had to hit against him claim he was in the 90-to-95 mile-an-hour range. But his relief appearances were often an adventure, an exercise in suspense, because he walked almost as many batters as he struck out. In his eight-year major league career, Erickson struck out 432 and walked 425 in 814⅓ innings pitched, an average of better than one walk every two innings or close to five walks per game.

He was also a bit of an eccentric. He began his professional career in Ponca City, Oklahoma, in 1937, where he overpowered batters with his fastball. In 1939, pitching for St. Joseph in the Western League, he led the league in strike outs with 198. When Erickson showed up at Wrigley Field for a camp for young hopefuls in 1941, Bob Lewis, the Cubs traveling secretary, greeted the young man and showed him where he needed to go to dress and prepare for his tryout, as Lewis did with all of the youngsters when they arrived. When everyone was accounted for, Lewis left the ballpark and went across the street to a bar to grab a quick sandwich and a beer. When he sat down, he saw a familiar face across the way. Erickson was there, also having a sandwich and a beer. Lewis informed him politely but sternly that he should be at the ballpark.

Erickson said he knew where he should be. But he said he was so excited about the tryout that he had forgotten to eat lunch. And in order to try out, he had to have his strength. So lunch was vital. As he told Lewis in the bar that day, "This is serious." He finished his lunch, went across the street, and made the team.

On May 18, 1945, Grimm gave Erickson his first start of the season as the Cubs were mired in a slump. They had lost five games in a row and found themselves in fourth place, 8½ games behind the league-leading Giants. The day before, New York scored six runs in the eighth inning to beat the Cubs 8–5. It was the Giants 12th win in 13 games and increased their season record to 20–5 while the Cubs were stagnant at 10–12.

So Erickson got the starting assignment the next day at Brooklyn but was wild, and when he did find the plate with the ball, the Dodgers hit it. Brooklyn won 15–12 in a game in which Brooklyn's Luis Olmo homered and tripled, each with the bases loaded, a feat that has not been repeated. To add to Olmo's odd day, he also had a double in the game, achieving three-fourths of "the cycle." Only the single eluded him.

Erickson didn't start again until May 26 but beat Philadelphia 2–1 in a pitching duel with former Cub Bill Lee. For the season, he started nine games, relieved in 19 and finished with a 7–4 record, his finest year in the big leagues.

He became known as "Lil Abner," a popular heroic comic strip character of the day because of one particular relief appearance that occurred September 29, 1945, when Erickson came into a ballgame at Pittsburgh in the ninth inning. The season was winding down to its final days and the Cubs needed one win to clinch the National League championship. Hank Borowy, the ace of the staff, took a 4–3 lead into the ninth inning but was tiring. After he gave up an out and a hit, manager Charlie Grimm summoned Bob Chipman who was able to get the second out, but the tying run advanced to third base. Grimm called on Erickson to finish the job. Erickson struck out Pirate pinch hitter Tommy O'Brien on three pitches to clinch the pennant.

An old warrior who had helped the Cubs win two pennants in the past attempted to give them a boost in 1945 as well. Lon Warneke was a star pitcher for the Cubs on their 1932 and 1935 championship teams. Warneke, who put together years of 22–6, 22–10 and 20–13 in 1932, 1934 and 1935, had some great days with the Cubs. He won two games in the '35 series with an earned run average of under 1.00. A year earlier, he nearly threw consecutive no-hitters. On April 17, 1934, Warneke was the opening day pitcher for the Cubs and took a no-hitter into the ninth inning before surrendering a single to the Reds' Adam Comorosky as Chicago won 6–0. Then on April 22, Warneke tossed another one-hitter, this one against the Cardinals and Dizzy Dean. No other pitcher in baseball history has opened the season with consecutive one-hitters. (Bob Feller of Cleveland threw the only opening day no hitter in 1941). Warneke was traded to the Cardinals in 1937 and stayed with them until 1942, when the Cubs bought him back for $75,000. While at St. Louis, Warneke finally got his no-hitter, blanking Cincinnati 2–0.

Warneke, who was a National League All Star in 1933, 1934, 1936, 1939 and 1941, was called into the military and saw limited service in 1942 and 1943 and retired at the end of the 1943 season. When the Cubs opened in 1945 with Passeau and Wyse struggling to get healthy, Grimm, who had managed him in his early days with the Cubs, talked Warneke into coming out of retirement. But Warneke was ineffective for the most part. The desire was there but the zip on the fastball wasn't. He appeared in nine games and had an 0–1 record before retiring for good.

Hiram "Hi" Bithorn was a hard-throwing righthander who was the first Puerto Rican to play in the major leagues. He was 9–14 in his rookie season, 1942, but came back with an 18–12 season in 1943. He led the National League in shutouts with seven and had a 2.60 earned-run average. The Cubs, who had been struggling for several years, pegged Bithorn as a pitcher who, teamed with veterans Claude Passeau and Hank Wyse, could help bring the club back into pennant contention. But Bithorn went into the Coast Guard after the 1943 season and missed the entire 1944 and 1945 seasons. Two years later, he was out of the big leagues.

Bithorn is remembered in Chicago Cubs history for an illustrious moment that occurred on July 15, 1942. He was pitching in relief of Passeau in a game against Brooklyn that had been filled with rough play and incidents of players jawing with one another. At one point, Bithorn went into his wind-up and then whirled and fired the ball in the direction of Brooklyn manager Leo Durocher in the Dodger dugout. Durocher was not injured, Bithorn was ejected, and the Cubs lost the game 10–5.

Eddie Hanyzewski was the Cubs pitcher who, in 1944, was the losing pitcher at the start of the Cubs 13-game losing streak that prompted the hiring of manager Charlie Grimm, and he was the winning pitcher in the game that ended the streak.

Hanyzewski broke in with the Cubs in 1942 and had a 1–1 record in six appearances. He had his best year in 1943, making 16 starts and appearing in relief in 17 games. He posted an 8–7 record. The big righthander had arm problems the next year. He was in only 14 games and slumped to 2–5. Grimm expected him to compete for a spot in the starting rotation in 1945, but arm problems continued to plague him. Hanyszewski appeared in two games early in the season without a decision.

Ray Starr was another old-timer who was briefly on the Cubs pitching staff in 1945. The 39-year-old hurler had the nickname of "Iron Man" because in the minor leagues, he started both games of doubleheaders more than 40 times. His first shot in the majors came in 1932 with St. Louis, where he got into a few games. The same was true in 1933, when he split time with the New York Giants and Boston Braves. He then lingered in the minor leagues for several years before Cincinnati brought him up, at the age of 35, in 1941. Starr won three games and followed that with seasons of 15–13 in 1942 and 11–10 in 1943. His next stop was Pittsburgh before coming to the Cubs in 1945. He got into nine games with the Cubs, but was largely ineffective. One exception was on July 6 when Starr got his only start of the season and beat Philadelphia 11–3 in the first game of a doubleheader, one of five doubleheaders the Cubs played in a two-week span. He gave the regular starters a break and got his only win of the year. He pitched in eight games in relief and did not fare well. Altogether, he worked 13⅓ innings and allowed 17 hits and 7 walks. It was his last season in the major leagues.

Several other pitchers appeared in a few games in 1945. Jorge Comellas, a Cuban, was in seven games and had an 0–2 record. It was his only year in the major leagues. George Hennessey was a righthander who had brief stays with the St. Louis Browns in 1937 and Philadelphia Phillies in 1942 and an even briefer stay with the Cubs in 1945. He got into two games, allowed 3 runs on 7 hits in 3⅔ innings and never played in the major leagues again. Hennessey's 1942 totals with the Philadelphia Phillies remain a statistical marvel. He worked 17 innings, gave up 11 hits and 10 walks while striking out only two, yet emerged with a 2.65 earned-run average.

Walt Signer got into four games with the Cubs in 1943 and into six during the 1945 season in which he pitched seven innings, allowed three runs on 11 hits, walked five, struck out none and did not play after that in the major leagues. Mack Stewart was another pitcher who came up with the Cubs in 1944 and had a brief stint with them in 1945. He appeared in 16 games, 15 in relief, and surrendered 48 hits and 18 walks in 40⅔ innings, his last innings in the major leagues.

The Cubs were without the services of righthander Bill Fleming, who had been with the club for four years and who posted a 9–10 record in 1944. After seeing limited service in his first three seasons, Fleming appeared in 39 games in 1944, threw nine complete games and seemed on the verge of reaching his full potential. But he went in the Army after the 1944 season and missed all of 1945, a familiar baseball story in the war years.

Fleming was likely to have won in double figures in 1945. His departure, along with Bithorn's absence, Prim, Vandenberg and Derringer's age and the ailments of Wyse and Passeau all pointed to another long season for the Cubs. When Grimm assessed his situation in spring training 1945, he put the typical "Jolly Cholly" spin on his hopes for the upcoming season — optimistic but realistic. "We'll finish higher than fourth," he told the press.

Even with that modest prediction, given the circumstances, he might have been accused of going out on a limb.

III

The Starting Lineup

"Hack has more friends than Durocher has enemies."
— Attributed to many

Pat Pieper, the Cubs field announcer, had the same message for
Wrigley Field patrons at the start of every game. Pieper, who started his
career with the Cubs in 1914 by yelling into a megaphone, now sat against
the box seat wall behind home plate, wearing his well-worn, sweat-
stained straw hat and enunciating each syllable as he spoke into a microphone with a raspy voice that was a familiar sound at Wrigley Field. "If
sandpaper could talk," said one wag, "it would sound like Pat Pieper."

"Attention. Attention please. Have your pencils and your score-
cards ready, and I will give you the correct lineups for today's ballgame."

He would then provide the batting orders for each team, starting
with the visitors. After announcing the lineup for the opponent, Pieper
would pause and say, "... And for the Cubs ..." and then would pause
again so as not to be drowned out by the roar of the crowd. Next, he
would tell who was batting in what order for Chicago, and it didn't vary
much during the spring and summer of 1945: Stan Hack, third base;
Don Johnson, second base; Peanuts Lowrey, left field; Phil Cavarretta,
first base; Andy Pafko, centerfield; Bill Nicholson, rightfield; Mickey
Livingston, catcher; Len Merullo, shortstop; and whoever the starting
pitcher was that day.

Barring injuries, the only variations were at shortstop where Roy
Hughes shared duties with Merullo and at catcher where Paul Gillespie
and Dewey Williams gave Livingston a breather.

At age 24, Pafko was the youngest Cub. He was a big, strong, farm
kid from Wisconsin who had one of the strongest, most accurate throwing arms in the National League — the best in a Cub outfield since KiKi

39

Cuyler in the 1920s, said manager Charlie Grimm. Pafko said he developed strong forearms and hands from doing chores on the family farm with his five brothers. Those chores included milking 16 cows a day. Sometimes, he said, the Pafko brothers would get up an hour early so there would be another hour of daylight at the end of the day and they could play ball.

Pafko started in organized ball with Eau Claire in his home state in 1940. By 1943, he had progressed to Los Angeles in the Pacific Coast League where he was the league's Most Valuable Player. He also got his first shot at the big leagues.

On September 24, 1943, Pafko made his debut with the Cubs. "I was called up to the Cubs with three other guys and I had never been in Chicago in my life," said Pafko. "It was a rainy, misty morning and we got to the ballpark and just looked around and said, 'Boy oh boy, so this is Wrigley Field.'

"And I walked in the clubhouse and there was Stan Hack, the first major league player I ever met. What a nice guy. He had that big smile of his and he said, 'Welcome to the Big Leagues.' I'll never forget it."

The record book bears out Pafko's recollection of a rainy, misty day. The weather was so bad that there were only 314 fans in the stands— the lowest paid attendance in Wrigley Field history as Pafko went two-for-three, a double and single, and drove in four runs as the Cubs beat the Phillies 7–4 in a game played in a downpour and called at the end of five innings.

Almost two years later, on May 30, 1945, Pafko and the Cubs played in front of 42,565, the largest Wrigley Field crowd since the pennant year of 1938, as the Cubs and Giants split a doubleheader. In the first game, the Giants' Mel Ott surpassed Honus Wagner for the National League record in total bases as the Giants won 8–6. Pafko hit a three-run homer in the second game as Chicago won 11–2.

Pafko remembers the 1945 season as a tough fight to hold off the St. Louis Cardinals from winning their third straight pennant. "We had to battle the Cardinals all year and they were tough," he said. "They came at you with pitchers like Howie Pollet, Harry 'The Cat' Brecheen and Max Lanier. What a thrill for a kid like me, two years in the big leagues to make it to the World Series. And the night we won the pennant, I drove in the winning run with a sacrifice fly." Pafko's run-scoring fly to right provided the margin of victory as the Cubs beat Pittsburgh 4–3 in the first game of a doubleheader to clinch the National League championship. Then they won the second game 5–0, marking the 20th time the Cubs swept a doubleheader in 1945.

Andy Pafko, at age 24, was the youngest Cub. He was one of the club's best hitters and had a great arm in the outfield. He threw out two Detroit base runners trying to go from first to third on base hits in the World Series. Pafko had tremendous forearm development that he said he got milking cows while growing up on a Wisconsin farm. (Photograph courtesy of Baseball Hall of Fame Library).

Pafko said the Cubs won because of the balance of talent — good pitching, good hitting, good defense and an interesting balance of personalities.

"Phil Cavarretta at first base. What a hustler. What determination. It would be accurate to describe Cavvy as a serious individual. Always had his nose in the game. Don Johnson at second. Now there was a journeyman ballplayer, spent a lot of time in the minor leagues, but when he got his shot, made the most of it. A gentleman, too. Lenny Merullo was our shortstop. He was a funny guy, always doing things to keep us loose. Had a bad year in '45 but was a real team player. And Smiling Stanley Hack at third. Steady. What a steady ballplayer. We had Peanuts Lowrey in left field. He was fast and he was a tough little out. I was in center and Bill Nicholson played right field. Another guy who didn't have a good year, but boy, what a power hitter. They used to call him 'Swish' and I know how it happened. You hear a lot of reasons for it, like he struck out a lot. But I think it started in Brooklyn. Fans saw him taking practice swings in the on-deck circle and it made a swishing sound. They started calling him Swish and it stuck. Our starting catcher, Clyde McCullough, was in the military so we had Mickey Livingston and Dewey Williams and they did all right.

"Boy, did we have the pitching. Claude Passeau, Hank Wyse, Paul Derringer — and Hank Borowy — we got him from the Yankees and wouldn't have won it without him. And then we had Ray Prim. He didn't have overpowering stuff but he was experienced.

"I played for Charlie Grimm twice — at Chicago and later with Milwaukee. He was my favorite manager. Charlie liked to keep things loose. He was a cut-up. Back in those days the managers also coached, usually at third base. You never knew what he was going to do. We'd lose a game and he'd come in and say, 'OK boys, let's get 'em tomorrow.' Everybody enjoyed playing for him."

In 1943, when Pafko came up so the Cubs could look at him in September, he hit .379 with 22 hits in 58 at-bats. In 1944, his first full year, he hit .269 with six homers and 62 runs batted in. In 1945, with Hack, Johnson and Lowrey all hitting in front of him and all having good years, Pafko hit .298 with 12 home runs and 110 runs batted in.

Hack, the Cubs third baseman for the better part of two decades, had been the top lead-off hitter in the major leagues in the 1930s, scoring 100 or more runs seven times. He sprayed the ball to all fields and was a great bunter. He was named to the National League All-Star team four times and played in the World Series four times with the Cubs. He was also a smooth-fielding infielder, leading the National League in putouts five times and in assists and fielding percentage twice. Hack was part of a great Cubs infield in the 1930s that had Billy Jurges at shortstop, Billy Herman at second base and Grimm and then Cavarretta at first. But his lasting legacy for those who knew him, played with him or against him, or simply saw him play was his friendly nature. One opposing player said, "Hack has more friends than (Leo) Durocher has enemies."

In 1935, the Cubs tried a promotion based on Hack's popularity that backfired. Just as they do today, ballclubs back then marketed items featuring images of their most popular players. This was long before bob-

Stan Hack retired in 1944 but came back at the urging of new manager Charlie Grimm. He was the lead-off hitter for the 1945 championship team. (Photograph courtesy of Roger Johnson.)

blehead dolls came into existence. The Cubs had a much simpler idea. They passed out hand-sized mirrors to paying customers with Smiling Stan's picture on the back. When the game started, so many fans in the bleachers used the mirrors to try to reflect the sun into opposing batters' eyes that umpires stopped the game and ordered all the mirrors confiscated.

Hack began his professional career with Sacramento, where he hit .352 in 1931 and so impressed Cubs brass that Bill Veeck, Sr., traveled to the west coast to sign him personally. He played with the Cubs in parts of 1932 and 1933 and became the regular third baseman in 1934. He was hard working on the field and fun loving off the field, which made him a good match with manager Charlie Grimm. He played for Grimm's pennant winners in 1932 and 1935 and with the 1938 championship team that Grimm managed until Gabby Hartnett took over in mid-season.

Hack appeared only as a pinch runner in the 1932 World Series against the Yankees and hit .227 in 1935 against the Tigers. But he hit .471 with eight hits— seven singles and a double in four games against the Yankees in 1938 and had 11 hits and a .367 average in the seven-game series against Detroit in 1945 for a lifetime World Series average of .348.

In the 1935 series, the Cubs were up three games to two and were engaged in a 3–3 tie in the ninth inning of the sixth game. Hack led off the ninth with a triple and was stranded as the next three batters went down harmlessly. Detroit scored in the bottom of the ninth to win the game and then went on to win the seventh game. A Chicago newspaper later published a cartoon depicting Hack, standing on third base with an anchor chained to his leg, depicting the Cubs' futility in bringing him home. Hack, showing his characteristic sense of humor, was back in Detroit three years later for the All-Star game in 1941. Before the game, he went out on the field, looked at third base, and told an onlooker, "I just wanted to see if I was still standing there, waiting for someone to drive me home."

Hack did not get along well with Wilson, Grimm's predecessor who took over for Hartnett. At the end of the 1943 season, Smilin' Stan said he'd had enough and announced his retirement. When Wilson was fired in May 1944, Grimm replaced him and called Hack, talking him out of retirement.

Lenny Merullo remembers that in spring training in 1945, rookie Pete Elko, who had signed as an outfielder but also played third base, had a great spring and pushed Hack to keep his third base job. Hack responded by hitting .323 for the pennant-winning Cubs and played the first 41 games of the season without making an error. Elko, who played in 16 games for the Cubs in 1943 and 1944, went into the military in 1945 and never played in another major league game.

On August 30, Hack became the 82nd player in major league history to achieve 2,000 hits. But a bigger hit came on October 8 when his 12th inning double drove in the winning run in the sixth game of the World Series.

Second baseman Don Johnson was a career minor league ballplayer who got his chance to play in the big leagues at the age of 31 when Lou Stringer was drafted into the Army in 1943. Johnson played in a few games and returned the following year as a 32-year-old rookie, hit .278, and made the All-Star team. He made the All-Star team again in the 1945 pennant-winning year when he hit .302.

Johnson was the son of Ernie Johnson, an American League infielder in the 1920s. Ernie Johnson, a shortstop, played on the New York Yankee pennant winner in 1923, but he didn't play much. The Yankees' regular shortstop in those days was Everettt Scott, who set the record for most consecutive games played — 1,307 — between 1916 and 1925, a record later broken first by Lou Gehrig in 1939. Cal Ripken, Jr., topped Gehrig in 1997.

Don Johnson said he had three mentors who influenced his career: his father; Hollis Thurston, a former major league pitcher whom he met when both were playing for San Francisco in the Pacific Coast League; and Yankee second baseman Joe Gordon.

Johnson went to Oregon State College but quit in 1932 when he signed to play for the Seattle minor league ballclub in the Pacific Coast League, managed by his father. It was a special relationship but it didn't last long. Ernie Johnson was relieved of his duties in June of 1932. Don played with Seattle two more years and then was released. The next year he played for Reading, Pennsylvania, in the New York–Pennsylvania League but was released two weeks into the season. He said it was at this point that he would have quit baseball had it not been for his father's encouragement. He played for the San Francisco Missions in 1936 and 1937, where he met Thurston. The two sat side by side in the dugout, where Thurston explained the intracies of the game, said Johnson. Then in 1939, Johnson played on a Tulsa ballclub with Dizzy Dean, who was trying to work his way back to the major leagues.

Dean had been a star pitcher with the St. Louis Cardinals until he was hit in the foot by a line drive hit by Cleveland's Earl Averill in 1937 All-Star game. In trying to come back from the injury, Dean altered his delivery and was never as effective as he had been before he got hurt. The Cardinals shipped him to the Cubs and Dean helped Chicago win the 1938 pennant. But by 1939, he was at Tulsa, trying to regain his old form.

Johnson said Dean's actions matched his reputation. He often had as many as three phones hooked up in his hotel room because of money matters he was tending to, which included betting on the horses. But he said Dean was generous. In those days, minor league players got $1.20 a day meal money and Dean, who was wealthy from his days in the big leagues, often boarded the team bus after everyone else had gotten on board and passed out sandwiches and soft drinks he had purchased for the team.

In 1943, Johnson played for Charlie Grimm's Milwaukee Brewers team, and that turned out to be his big break. He came up to the Cubs

Don Johnson was a career minor league player who didn't make it to the major leagues until he was 32 years old. He hit .302 for the pennant-winning Cubs. (Photograph courtesy of Roger Johnson)

later that year after Stringer got drafted. In 1944, Cubs manager Jimmy Wilson was fired and was replaced by Grimm, who had always liked Johnson at Milwaukee.

Johnson, who did not serve in the military because he had a wife and three young children, met Joe Gordon at an exhibition game in

Tulsa. He said the New York Yankees always played an exhibition game with Tulsa in the years before World War II. Johnson got up enough nerve to take Gordon aside before the Yankee-Tulsa game in the spring of 1941 and asked him what tips he could provide for a second baseman pivoting on a double play.

He recounted his talk with Gordon in a *Sporting News* interview in 1944. "I had been trying all the different methods," he said. "Some insisted that you should straddle the bag. Others said the only way to do it was to touch the bag and then step back and still others said you had to hit the bag with a certain foot and then take so many steps. The net result was that I wasn't good at any of them.

"When I asked Gordon about it that spring, he told me very bluntly and simply: There is no set way of making a double play. Forget all about this foot and so many steps and all that rot. There's only one way to make a double play — get to the bag in a hurry and get rid of that ball as fast as possible.

"That was all I needed. From that point on, I became a good double-play man. And I'm certain that whatever skill I developed in that department is the reason for my being up here," said Johnson.

He always thought he could have made it to the big leagues sooner had he not played every infield position in the minors as he tried to hang on with one club or another. Tulsa manager Roy Johnson told him in 1941 that he was going to be the regular second baseman. Then he had the conversation with Gordon that he said elevated his career.

While Gordon's advice helped him become a better defensive second baseman, 40 years later, Johnson marveled at the ability of one of his successors — Ryne Sandberg. "I couldn't hold that guy's glove," he said in a 1997 interview.

His best day at the plate in the majors was also the Cubs all-time best day at the plate. On July 3, 1945, Johnson got five hits and scored five runs in a 24–2 win over Boston. The Cubs got 28 hits in that game, which is still the team record.

One of his most valuable contributions is almost lost in the statistics. Johnson led the National League in sacrifice bunts in 1945 with 22. Hitting second in the lineup, behind Hack and ahead of Cavarretta, Nicholson and Pafko, his bunting helped set the table for some big innings.

The road to the big leagues was a winding one for Peanuts Lowrey. He was signed by the Los Angeles Angels of the Pacific Coast League for $1 after impressing scouts at a tryout — or at least impressing them enough to spend a dollar on him. From there he was sent to Moline, Illinois, in the Three-I League and then spent some time at Ponca City, St. Joseph and Tulsa before making it back to the Angels in 1940. He went to Milwaukee in 1942, when Charlie Grimm was managing. The Cubs brought him up at the end of the season but he did not impress. He hit only .190 in 27 games and drove in only four runs. In 1943, given the chance to play every day, Lowrey hit .292 and would have earned a starting spot in the Cubs outfield, but the military called him for duty. He did not return until 1945. By that time, Grimm, his manager with Milwaukee, was back with the Cubs and Lowrey was back in the outfield. He played in 143 games and hit .282. Batting third in the lineup, behind Stan Hack and Don Johnson, Lowrey drove in 88 runs but also helped keep rallies alive with his bunting. He had 21 sacrifice bunts during the season, tying him with Pafko for second in the National League. Only teammate Johnson, hitting ahead of him in the lineup, had more, leading the league with 22.

Lowrey's nickname of "Peanuts" was a lifelong one, said to have been given to him by his grandfather because as an infant, he was "as small as a peanut." Lowrey was born in Culver City, California, in the heart of movieland and as a child landed some bit parts in silent movies. As an adult, he had a speaking role in one movie, *The Winning Season*, in which Ronald Reagan played Grover Cleveland Alexander. Lowrey once described his role this way: "I was the player who plunked Reagan with a ball between the eyes as he was heading for second."

When the Cubs made their move in the 1945 pennant race, Lowrey's hitting played an important part. In the club's 11-game winning streak in July, which propelled them from fifth to first place, a spot they didn't relinquish, Lowrey hit .373. The winning streak started with a July 1 win against the Giants when Lowrey drove in the winning run with an eighth-inning single.

Clean-up hitter and team captain Phil Cavarretta had been a Cub since his graduation from Lane Tech High School in Chicago in 1934. He played hard and didn't worry about being liked. Even teammates were wary of him. "We used to have a hell of a time with him," said shortstop Lenny Merullo. "He was a very tough competitor and was always ready to fight."

Second baseman Johnson said he often kept his distance in the locker room. "I was lucky," said Johnson. "My locker was two or three down from his. Phil was a competitor who didn't hesitate to chew you out if he didn't think you were getting the job done," said Johnson.

Merullo recalled a time Cavarretta instigated a fight with Brooklyn over a play that had occurred the day before — a play Cavarretta wasn't even involved in. It happened when Dodger second baseman Eddie Stanky, an ex-Cub, tagged Merullo in the face with the ball as Merullo slid into second, trying to break up a double play. Merullo and Stanky got into a pushing and shoving match that emptied both benches. When umpires broke up the scuffling, Merullo was ejected from the game.

Cavarretta, who was Merullo's roommate, was incensed. He told Merullo that Dodger shortstop Pee

Harry "Peanuts" Lowrey was the Cubs' left-fielder. He didn't hit for power but he got several game-winning hits during the Cubs' stretch drive in September. (Photograph courtesy of Baseball Hall of Fame Library)

Wee Reese had taken a swing at him and Merullo shouldn't let him get away with it. So the next day, before the game, at Cavarretta's urging, Merullo approached Reese to talk to him about the previous day's fight. Dodger outfielder Dixie Walker overheard the conversation and took a swing at Merullo. Another fight broke out, and this time it took Brooklyn police to break it up. But captain Cavarretta, through his roommate Merullo, had served notice that misdeeds against the Cubs would not go unnoticed or without retaliation.

Merullo said Cavarretta often used his elbows to make his way through crowds of fans who wanted autographs or just to get a look at him as he arrived at the ballpark or when he left after a game. Merullo and Nicholson broke him of the habit, pleading with him to understand that the fans were just well wishers.

Cavarretta broke in with the Cubs as a teenager after spectacular years pitching and hitting for Lane Tech High School, leading the school, located not far from Wrigley Field, to the Illinois state baseball championship two years in a row. He then led his American Legion team to

Phil Cavarretta was a hard-hitting, tough-talking first baseman who won the batting title and was the National League's most valuable player in 1945. He was such
a tough competitor that team mates had to break him of the habit of elbowing his
way through crowds of fans outside the ballpark. (Photograph courtesy of Baseball Hall of Fame Library.)

a national championship. He was given a tryout by the Cubs and, batting against star righthander Lon Warneke, Cavarretta hit the first pitch into the right-field bleachers.

After signing with the Cubs, he hit .316 with Peoria, hitting for the cycle in his first game, on May 15, 1934. The Central League folded early in 1934 and the Cubs sent him to Reading in the New York–Pennsylvania League where he hit .308. Chicago brought him up at the end of the 1934 season and he was the starting first baseman and captain for the next 20 years, playing in the World Series in 1935, 1938 and 1945.

He was a left-handed hitter who could hit for power. But more often, he sprayed the ball all over the park for 22 years, compiling a lifetime batting average of .293. A hearing problem kept him out of military service. His career was filled with big hits. On September 25, 1935, 19-year-old Cavarretta homered against the Cardinals for the only run of the game as the Cubs won their 19th straight en route to the National League championship. On July 30, 1943, Cavarretta and Nicholson hit back-to-back home runs against the Dodgers at Ebbets Field off Johnny Allen. Cavarretta's blast hit the right-field foul pole and was retrieved and kept in the game. Nicholson hit the next pitch for a home run, providing the oddity of the same ball being hit out of the park on consecutive pitches.

In 1944, Cavarretta tied Stan Musial of the Cardinals for most hits with 197. But his best year was the next year, the pennant year. On May 11, 1945, Cavarretta got four hits as the Cubs beat the Phillies 7–1. He had another four-hit game on August 5, as the Cubs, now in first place, defeated Cincinnati 12–5.

He won the 1945 batting title with a .355 average and was chosen the league's most valuable player. Though the Cubs lost the World Series to Detroit, Cavarretta was the leading hitter on both teams with a .426 percentage with 11 hits in 26 at-bats.

His legacy had three components: hitting, hustling and his competitive mean streak.

Future teammate Eddie Miksis summed it up. "Phil was a no nonsense guy. Hard-headed and win at any cost. That was Phil."

Nicholson was a popular power hitter with the Cubs who had his best year in the major leagues in 1944 — and one of his worst in 1945. "He was a big, handsome son-of-a-gun. He always had a big chew of tobacco in his mouth," said Merullo. "Sometimes, he'd go get a drink of water with that chew in his mouth and he'd start talking and you could hardly understand him."

Between the 1944 and 1945 baseball seasons, Nicholson worked at a defense plant in Maryland and missed 1945 spring training because of questions by the military as to whether he should be allowed to play. While he waited for answers, Nicholson worked out with the Philadelphia Phillies. On April 14, three days before opening day, he got the go-ahead to join the Cubs. But he had missed spring training and he never regained the form he displayed in previous years that made him one of the most formidable hitters in the National League.

In 1944, Nicholson led the league with 32 home runs. He had 122 RBIs and scored 116 runs and lost to Marty Marion of the Cardinals by one vote for Most Valuable Player honors. He was one of the most feared hitters in the league, so much so that on July 23, 1944, New York Giant manager Mel Ott ordered his pitcher, Andy "Swede" Hansen to walk him with the bases loaded. It was the second game of a doubleheader in which Nicholson had homered three times in the first game and had homered once already in the second game. There wasn't much strategy to it. "He was killing us," said Ott after the game, which the Giants won 12–10.

Nicholson earned an appointment to the U.S. Naval Academy but could not pass the physical because he was color-blind. Instead, he went to Washington College in Chestertown, Maryland, where he played football, basketball and baseball. As a fullback on the football team, he led his school to its only undefeated season in 1934. He was a guard on the college basketball team but is best remembered as a slugging outfielder in baseball. He was so impressive that the Philadelphia A's signed him right out of college. He batted 12 times for the A's without a hit and was sent to the minors. While playing for Chattanooga in the Southern League, his manager, former Cubs star KiKi Cuyler, taught him how to open his stance, be patient in the batter's box, and quit lunging at pitches. Cuyler also told the Cubs about him. He came up to the Cubs in 1939 and immediately became one of the fan favorites. His color-blindness kept him out of World War II. He averaged 28 home runs a year for the Cubs between 1940 and 1944 before hitting only 13 for the pennant winner in 1945, but he contributed 88 runs batted in, third on the team behind Phil Cavarretta and Andy Pafko.

Nicholson led the National League in home runs and runs batted in both the 1943 and 1944 seasons. Prior to that, Babe Ruth and Jimmy Foxx were the only other two players to be that productive in two consecutive seasons.

Thompson "Mickey" Livingston proved early on in his career that he could take a lick. In 1939, while playing for Springfield in the Southern League, Livingston chased after a foul ball and, having tossed his mask aside, rammed his head into the dugout roof while wearing only his baseball cap. From that point on, he suffered from recurring headaches that prompted an early exit from the Army because he was unable to wear a helmet without excruciating pain.

He was playing for the Philadelphia Phillies when the Cubs, seeking to fill the void left by Clyde McCullough going into the military, got him in a trade for pitcher Bill Lee. He homered his first time up as a Cub in Wrigley Field.

Livingston signed with the St. Louis Cardi-

Bill Nicholson, the National League home run champion in 1943 and 1944, had a season-long slump in 1945 but remained a fan favorite. He was almost always seen on the field with a large chaw of tobacco in his cheek. (Photograph courtesy of Baseball Hall of Fame Library)

nals in 1935 but after being assigned to five different clubs in a six-week span, he asked for his release. The Cardinals granted it. He stayed out a year and then came back to pro ball in 1937, got into two games with the Washington Senators in 1938 and got three hits in four at-bats, including two doubles. But that wasn't enough to save his job as Livingston was shipped back to the minor leagues where he suffered the head injury the following year.

He came up with the Phillies in 1941 and stayed in the majors for 10 years. He caught in more than 100 games in only one of those years, 1943, in time split between Philadelphia and Chicago. Though he was considered the Cubs' starting catcher on the 1945 championship team,

Mickey Livingston took over catching duties when Clyde McCullough was called to the military. A head injury kept him out of the service.

he appeared in less than half of their games, 71, sharing duties with Dewey Williams and Paul Gillespie.

Merullo was the Cubs regular shortstop for four years but lost his starting job late in 1945 because he was in a season-long slump. Like team mate Bill Nicholson, Merullo was struggling in a year when most of the other regulars were having good years.

"It broke my heart but I understood," said Merullo years later. "I hadn't been playing very well. I was in kind of a funk and Charlie (Grimm) went with Roy Hughes who was a veteran, a good ballplayer and a better hitter than I was." Hughes, who was also the starting short-stop in the World Series, hit .261 in 69 games. Merullo finished the season with a .239 average in 121 games.

As evidenced by his understanding about being benched, Merullo had a lot of respect for manager Grimm. "He was just outstanding. He was great with the players, he could handle the press and he was a crowd pleaser. You can't beat that," he said.

Merullo grew up in the Boston area and developed a love for the Cubs because of some good fortune he had in high school. He used to frequent Braves Field, where Boston's National League team played, and developed some acquaintanceships with Cubs personnel when they came to town. One day, the Cubs equipment manager gave him a uniform and told him to dress and work out with the ballclub. He did this several times while still a teenager in high school and received tips on hitting and fielding from Cubs players and coaches.

Merullo played for Villanova College, where he had been recruited by Harry Stuhldreher, the quarterback in the famed Notre Dame "Four Horsemen" backfield. Stulhdreher was the Villanova football coach and had seen Merullo play high school baseball. He tipped off the Villanova baseball coaches who went to see Merullo play and convinced him to come to Villanova.

After college, Merullo signed with the Cubs. He went to spring training at Catalina Island in 1939 where he was touted as being the next Billy Jurges, referring to the outstanding Cubs shortstop of the 1930s. Merullo tried so hard to live up to the advance billing that he hurt his throwing arm and played in only six games, with Moline in the 3-I League in 1939. But he was healthy and played in 162 games for Tulsa in 1940 where the fun-loving Merullo was no match for former major league standout Dizzy Dean, a zany character on and off the field who was trying to regain his pitching prowess with a stint at Tulsa. Dean called Merullo one of the best defensive shortstops he had ever seen.

Ironically, Merullo is probably best known in the big leagues for a day of defensive gaffes. He made four errors in the second inning of the second game of a doubleheader on September 13, 1942 in Boston. Three of the four errors occurred on the same play, a dubious major league record. Merullo let a ground ball get through him, then fumbled the relay from leftfielder Bill Nicholson, then threw wildly to the plate. His son, Len Jr., was born earlier on the same day and has been known since the date of his birth as "Boots."

Merullo, looking back on his career years later, said he realizes he is best remembered for his four-error day and the fight with Pee Wee Reese and Dixie Walker at Ebbets Field that resulted in his expulsion two games in a row — the second one before the game even started.

Lenny Merullo once made four errors in a game. He was the Cub starting short-stop in 1945 until he was benched late in the season with a hitting slump. "It broke my heart," he said.

"Those are records that will probably never be broken," he says with a laugh.

One of the reasons the Cubs won the pennant in 1945 is because of the ballclub's remarkable record against the Cincinnati Reds, winning 21 of 22 games. The game they lost was a 4–3 decision on August 4, and Merullo says he was partly to blame. Recalling the game almost 60 years later, he said, "I foolishly tried to stretch a double into a triple and was thrown out. That probably cost us the ballgame."

The Cubs starters helped the pitching staff by playing outstanding defense most of the time. Only Merullo at shortstop could be described as less than sure-handed. He made 36 errors in 121 games. Cavarretta played in 132 games and committed only nine errors, an improvement over 1944 when he was charged with 13 miscues. Johnson was vastly improved at second. In his rookie 1944 season, he made a whopping 47 errors, keeping many rallies alive for opposing teams. In 1945, he cut that total to 19 in 138 games. Hack was his usual steady self at third base, playing in 150 games and committing 14 errors, five less than his total in 1944 when he appeared in only 93 games.

Chicago's outfield saved a lot of runs with fine defensive play. Pafko in center made only two errors in 140 games for a .995 fielding percentage. Lowrey in left had four errors in 138 games for a fielding percentage of .987. In right field, Nicholson, who had a tough year at the plate, kept the Cubs in a lot of games with his defense. He made three errors in 151 games and had a .990 fielding percentage. In addition, Nicholson had 12 assists and four of those were double plays in which he threw out base runners trying to advance after a catch. Lowrey had 17 assists and Pafko had 11.

Cubs pitchers fielded their positions well. Claude Passeau went through the entire season without making an error.

The Cubs bench in 1945 included several old-timers who tried to fill in and help wherever they could and one line-driver hitter who had the biggest bunions in baseball.

Heinz Becker was described as the kind of ballplayer who could wake up at 3 a.m., get out of bed and start hitting line drives. In 1945, he was a 30-year-old veteran of many years in the minor leagues who faced two obstacles in becoming a regular on the Cubs. He was a first baseman — and nobody was going to displace MVP Phil Cavarretta at that position. Also, Becker had terrible foot problems. One of his feet was so deformed that players said his ankle touched the ground when he walked and he suffered from bunions that often made him hobble.

But he also had three things in his favor. He was the ballclub's only switch hitter, he could hit, and manager Charlie Grimm liked him. Grimm had him on his Milwaukee ballclub where Becker hit .342 in 1942 and lost the batting title by two points to Eddie Stanky. The 1944 Brewers are regarded as one of the best teams ever in the minor leagues. They were managed by Grimm until he was called back to the Cubs in May. Thereafter, Casey Stengel was the manager. The Brewers won 102 games, lost only 51 and compiled a team batting average of .307. Their leading hitter was Becker, who hit .346 with 10 home runs and 115 runs batted in.

Becker had an unusual upbringing. He was born in Germany during World War I and became the only German-born major league ballplayer during World War II. He lived in Germany until he was seven years old and later spent some of his growing-up years in Venezuela and then in Dallas, Texas, as his father switched careers from being a brewer to being a cattle rancher. Grimm and Cubs teammates enjoyed the way Becker talked because they said his accent was part German, part Texan.

He got into organized baseball in 1938 and signed with the Cubs in 1942. His bad feet created some adventurous—and dangerous—fielding situations. Merullo recalled an incident in batting practice when Becker was at first base and a ball was hit to short. Merullo threw the ball to Becker, who stretched for it but otherwise did not move. The ball hit him in the forehead and he went down in a heap. "We thought he was dead," said Merullo.

Becker got his first chance with the Cubs in 1943 when Wilson was still the manager. Appearing in 24 games, he could only manage 10 hits in 69 at-bats for a .145 batting average. Worse yet, he only drove in two runs. So he was dispatched back to Milwaukee. Then came the fabulous 1944 with the Brewers under the direction of Grimm and Stengel that led to his second chance with the Cubs. When he got back to the major league club in 1945, this time with Grimm as manager, he came through. Becker hit .286 and had a .421 slugging percentage. And he got some clutch hits. On August 13, playing in place of the injured Cavarretta, Becker had a single, double and triple in a 4–1 win over the Philadelphia Phillies.

After the season, he had surgery on his feet, but his days on the Cubs were numbered. Chicago had the veteran Cavarretta and a promising young first baseman, Eddie Waitkus, who was about to emerge on the big league scene. By 1947, Becker was playing for Cleveland.

Clyde McCullough was a tough, cocky catcher who was one of the last catchers in the big leagues to work without a chest protector. He bristled at all the attention Walker Cooper got as a catcher for the St. Louis Cardinals. Cooper was the perennial All Star for a team that won three consecutive pennants from 1942 through 1944. McCullough thought he was as good as Cooper and didn't hesitate to say so.

Merullo said, "McCullough was just the opposite of Mickey Livingston, who was quiet and went about his business. McCullough had natural ability and a great arm. He always said he was going to be the greatest. Each year McCullough would say he was going to kick Walker Cooper's ass and each year, Cooper would walk away with all of the honors."

McCullough broke in with the Cubs in 1940. He had his greatest game on July 26, 1942, when he hit three consecutive home runs—but his homers accounted for all of the runs in a 4–3 loss to the Phillies. Those were three of the five homers McCullough hit all year. Less than a month later, on August 24, 1942, McCullough had the unusual distinction for a catcher of taking part in a triple play against the Cincinnati Reds—a routine double-play ball with runners on first and third in which the third out was made at the plate when the runner on third tried to score.

McCullough was in the Navy for all of the 1944 and 1945 seasons but was allowed by Commissioner Happy

Dewey Williams was a back-up catcher who was used primarily for his defensive skills and his handling of pitchers.

Chandler to participate in the World Series. He was the first player in baseball history to have appeared in a World Series without having played during the regular season. He got up once as a pinch-hitter in the seventh game and struck out.

Dewey Williams was the backup catcher for Livingston during the 1945 season and prided himself on his handling of pitchers. He began his professional career as an outfielder with Macon in the Southern League in 1937 where Milt Stock, later to be a Cubs coach, was the manager. When he was with the Atlanta Crackers in 1940, he played every position except shortstop and pitcher. He settled in to be a catcher when former major league catcher Paul Richards, the manager at Atlanta, took him under his wing. Williams was batting .313 with Toronto in 1944 when the Cubs brought him to the major leagues.

Williams said it was his hitting, not his catching, that held him back. He took great pride in his ability behind the plate. "Anytime we got ahead by a run or two from the sixth inning on, I'd put my stuff on. I knew I'd be coming in," he said. "The other catchers couldn't field or throw as good as I could but they could hit a little better."

Richards was a major league catcher for eight years in the 1920s and '30s and came back and caught for Detroit during the war years. In between, he managed the Atlanta Crackers where he and Williams connected. Williams said he would sometimes come back to the dugout and see Richards, the manager, putting on some catching gear, as if he anticipated Williams coming out of the game soon. "You learn real quick that way," said Williams.

He played in 79 games with the Cubs in 1944 and, backing up Livingston, appeared in 59 games in the championship season, hitting .280 in 100 plate appearances. Ironically, it was Richards, his old mentor, who got the key hit, a bases-loaded double, in the seventh game of the World Series, to help sink the Cubs.

Paul Gillespie, another reserve catcher, appeared in 75 games for the 1945 Cubs, 45 as catcher, one as an outfielder, and 29 as a pinch hitter. He broke into professional baseball as a catcher at Brownsville, Texas, in 1938. In 1939, he played for Lake Charles, Louisiana, as an outfielder but then went back to catching in 1940 when he played in Elmira, New York. His next stop was Salina, Kansas, in 1941 where he hit a single, double and triple in his first game. The well-traveled Gillespie also played for Knoxville and Oklahoma City in 1941 and was with three teams in 1942 as well — Oklahoma City, Tulsa and the Chicago Cubs.

He played for Chicago in five games but then entered the Coast Guard. He returned to the Cubs at the end of the 1944 season, long enough to get into nine games. In 1945, he did well in a reserve role, hitting .288 in 75 games. He had his best game in the major leagues on August 15, when he hit two homers and a single and drove in six runs as the Cubs beat the Dodgers 20–6. In 1946, McCullough was back in his starting role, with Livingston and Williams backing him up. Gillespie was the odd man out. He never played in the majors after 1945. The Cubs public relations office in 1945 made it known that Gillespie was the first Cubs player ever to have a crew-cut hair style.

Roy Hughes was a veteran major league infielder who served as a utility man for the Cubs until Merullo fell into a batting slump in late 1945. Hughes replaced him at shortstop and was the starting shortstop in the World Series. His big league career started with the Cleveland Indians in 1935. As the Indians regular second baseman in 1936, Hughes hit .295 and appeared in 152 games. He stayed with the Indians through 1938 and then went to the St. Louis Browns. He shared time with the Browns and Philadelphia Phillies in 1939 and played the entire 1949 season with Philadelphia.

Then it was back to the minor leagues for a few years. In 1943, he played for the Los Angeles Angels and was considered one of the best hitters in the Pacific Coast League. The Cubs brought him up in 1944 when Hack retired. After Grimm talked Hack out of retirement, Hughes became a utility man again. He played 66 games at third base and 52 at shortstop in 1944. In the Cubs championship year, Hughes had the statistics to prove he was a utility man. He was in 36 games as a shortstop, 21 at second base, nine at third base and two at first base.

One of his most memorable days in the major leagues had nothing to do with hitting or fielding. While a member of the Cleveland Indians, Hughes was arrested in the dugout for failing to make alimony payments to his ex-wife.

Infielder Seymour "Cy" Block seemed like a "can't miss" prospect when the Cubs acquired him from the Dodger organization. In 1941, he led the Sally League in hitting with a .357 batting average and had 112 RBIs. He and Stan Musial of the Cardinals were touted by *The Sporting News* as being the top rookies in the National League. Block went to spring training with the Cubs at Catalina Island in February 1942 but was sent down to Tulsa in the Texas League before the season started. He was called up at the end of the season and hit .364 in 12 games. In six minor league seasons, he hit .325, .315, .313, .357, .276 and .364. He seemed destined for a brilliant major league career but instead went in the Coast Guard for three years. He was discharged in September 1945 in time to get on the Cubs' roster and to be eligible for the World Series. He got into one game as a pinch runner.

Before he went in the service, Cubs' manager Wilson had him playing second base in spring training, a backup to Lou Stringer. When he got out of the service, Grimm was the manager and Don Johnson was an All Star at second base. He appeared in only six more major league games. Block got out of baseball and went into the insurance business, where he became a millionaire.

Billy Schuster was a utility infielder known more for his maverick personality than for his baseball accomplishments. He liked the nightlife and was known as "Broadway Bill" when he played for Los Angeles in the Pacific Coast League. Schuster got his first taste of the major leagues with the Pittsburgh Pirates in 1937, when he got into three games. The

Pirates brought him up for two games in 1939 and then released him. He played in the coast league for four years before coming up with the Cubs in 1943, appearing in 13 games at the end of the season. He played two more seasons and hit .191 in limited duty for the '45 Cubs.

In the 12th inning of the sixth game of the World Series, a game the Cubs had to win to stay alive, Schuster got in as a pinch runner and scored the winning run on a double by Hack, pushing the series into a seventh game.

Schuster is remembered in Cubs folklore for pulling the hidden ball trick on the great slugger Jimmy Foxx, who was well past his prime but was hanging on as a war-time replacement with the Philadelphia Phillies. Foxx doubled in a game against the Cubs and was taking his lead off second base when he noticed that Schuster, who had concealed the ball in his glove, was now approaching the legendary ballplayer. Foxx is reported to have seen the ball, looked up at Schuster and said, "If you tag me with that thing, I'll kill you." Schuster tagged him, then dropped the ball on the ground and ran for the dugout, according to the oft-told story.

Johnny Moore was 43 years old and had been out of major league baseball for eight years when the Cubs picked him up as a war-year warrior. He started his career with the Cubs in 1928 but didn't play regularly until 1932, when the Cubs traded slugging outfielder Hack Wilson to the New York Giants. Moore didn't hit with power but he did hit .305 as the Cubs won the National League pennant. He slipped to .263 in 1933 and the Cubs dealt him to Cincinnati. Playing for both the Reds and the Philadelphia Phillies, Moore hit .334 in 1934, the first of four successive seasons when he hit over .300. After the 1937 season, he went to the Pacific Coast League where he played until the Cubs brought him up in 1945. He pinch hit six times and got one hit. Moore retired with a lifetime batting average of .307.

Len Rice was a third-string catcher on the Cubs roster. Rice had always been a hard-luck player. He lost a kidney as a result of a high school football injury and incurred several career-threatening injuries playing baseball in the Nebraska State League, so many in fact that the St. Louis Cardinals, who had signed him, let him go. He played for Grand Island, Lincoln, Ogden, Tucson, Columbia, Syracuse, Cincinnati, Syracuse again and then for the Cincinnati Reds before coming over to the Cubs. He hit .232 in 45 games for the Cubs.

Lloyd Christopher was an outfielder who began the 1945 season with the Boston Braves and appeared in one game for the Cubs as a defensive replacement. He did not bat.

Johnny Ostrowski was a third baseman-outfielder who broke in with the Cubs in 1943 but did not get much playing time on a team that had Stan Hack at third base and Peanuts Lowrey, Andy Pafko and Bill Nicholson in the outfield. Ostrowski got into four games in 1945 and made the most of them, hitting .300 with three hits in 10 at-bats.

Like Ostrowski, Reggie Otero had the misfortune of playing behind a Cubs legend. Otero, a Cuban-born first baseman, saw action in only 14 games, playing behind Cavarretta and Becker. Otero batted 23 times and had nine hits and five runs batted in. He never played in the major leagues again — so his lifetime batting average is .391.

Frank Secory was an outfielder who played in the major leagues for six years but did not crack the starting lineup much because the Cubs outfield was pretty well set with Lowrey in left, Pafko in center and Nicholson in right. Secory got into one big league game as a member of the Detroit Tigers in 1940 and got into two games with the Cincinnati Reds in 1942. The Cubs gave him a longer look in 1944 and he responded by hitting .321 with 18 hits in 56 at-bats, including four home runs. But in 1945, with Lowrey back from the service, Nicholson coming off the best year of his career and Pafko blossoming into one of the top outfielders in the league, Secory didn't get much playing time and hit only .191 in 35 games.

Secory played for the Milwaukee Brewers, where he got the attention of Grimm who later brought him up to the Cubs. At Milwaukee, Secory had the nickname of "Atlas" because of his strength. He once hit a ball off the tower lights in the outfield.

He came off the bench in the World Series to get the biggest hit of his career. In the 12th inning of the sixth game, Secory pinch hit for the injured Merullo and singled, starting a rally that resulted in Schuster, running for Secory, scampering home with the winning run.

In 1946, in a reserve role with the Cubs, Secory hit three home runs. Two of them were in extra innings. He is the last player in major league history to have more home runs in extra innings than in regulation play during a season. The only other players to accomplish this are Jack Coombs of the 1911 Philadelphia A's and Birdie Tebbetts of the 1937 Detroit Tigers, each of whom hit two home runs for the season — and both were in extra innings — and Ross Youngs of the 1923 New York Giants who, like Secory, hit three homers for the season and two were in extra innings.

Ed Sauer was a reserve outfielder who, like Secory, didn't get much playing time because of the play of starting outfielders Pafko, Lowrey and Nicholson. Sauer, who won the Most Valuable Player award in the Southern Association in 1943, came up with the Cubs at the end of that season. He played in a total of 37 games in 1943 and 1944. In the championship season, he hit .258 in 49 games and was hitless in two pinch-hitting at-bats in the World Series. Sauer's brother, Hank, was a star with the Cubs from 1949 to 1955.

Three Cubs players who had been regulars before the war had the misfortune of missing the pennant-winning season and the World Series.

Lou Stringer was the Cubs regular second baseman in 1941 and 1942 after Billy Herman was traded to Brooklyn. He played in 145 games in 1941 and hit .246. In 1942, he played in 121 games and hit .236. He spent the next three years in the military. When he returned, his old manager, Wilson, was long gone, having been replaced by Grimm, and Don Johnson had established himself as the Cubs second baseman. "I was just a mediocre ballplayer," Stringer said years later, "and Charlie Grimm was crazy about Don Johnson."

Dom Dallessandro, an outfielder, broke in with the Boston Red Sox in 1937 but became a regular in the Cubs outfield in 1940. He hit .268, .272, and .261 in his first three years with the Cubs, then slumped to .222. In 1944, with Grimm as manager, "Dim Dom," as Grimm called him, had his best year in the majors, hitting .304. But he was called into the military in 1945 and when he returned, the Cubs had an experienced outfield in Lowrey, who had replaced Dallessandro in left field, Pafko and Nicholson.

Bobby Sturgeon was the starting shortstop in 1941 and hit .245 in 121 games. He went into the service during the 1942 season and did not return to the Cubs until 1946, missing 3½ seasons when he was in his early 20s and just developing as a ballplayer. He also missed what would be his only opportunity to play in the World Series.

IV

The Season Begins

"One good relief pitcher could make a lot of difference."
— *Charlie Grimm*

All major league clubs faced depleted personnel because of the war. The Cubs fared better than most other teams because they only lost one regular, McCullough, their catcher, in 1945. Three others in the starting lineup — Pafko, Lowrey and Livingston — had served and had been discharged, as had reserve catcher Gillespie.

Grimm was succinct in describing his team. "We were fortunate in that many of our regulars were not acceptable for military service," he told the press. It was a more diplomatic way than saying many of his players were old or "4-F."

The St. Louis Cardinals were not as fortunate. The Cardinals, winners of three consecutive championships, were favorites to win a fourth in 1945 but were beset, even before the season started, with some incidents and circumstances that, in the end, they could not overcome. On February 15, before spring training had started, Major Billy Brooks Southworth, son of Cardinal manager Billy Southworth, was killed when a plane he was flying crashed in New York. The young Southworth had been the first professional ballplayer to enlist, joining the Army Air Corps in December of 1940. Southworth had flown 25 bombing missions over Germany and had returned from all of them unharmed. It was an unthinkable tragedy that a veteran pilot of his stature would die in a military plane crash unrelated to the war and in his own country. He was on a routine flight from Long Island, New York, to Florida when he ran into difficulty and attempted an emergency landing at LaGuardia Airport. But Southworth overshot the runway and his plane plunged into Flushing Bay. Manager Southworth, stunned by the loss of his son, was still grieving at home when the Cardinals began spring training in Cairo, Illinois in March.

The Cardinals lost their top hitter, Musial, their starting catcher, Walker Cooper, and one of their starting pitchers, Max Lanier, to the military. Musial had hit .347 and driven in 94 runs for the 1944 championship team. Cooper had hit .317 with 72 RBIs. But his value to the Cardinals was much more than just his hitting. In 1944, Cooper was the starting Cardinal catcher in 88 games. The Cardinals won 63 and lost 25, a winning percentage of .716. It was this intangible — Cooper's contributions to a championship team by just his presence behind the plate, an accomplishment not associated with gaudy statistics — that made him so valuable and envied by catchers like McCullough.

Lanier also represented a big loss. He had won 17 games, lost 12 and had a 2.65 earned-run average. The Cardinals did not appear to have any pitcher on the horizon who would equal Lanier's win total from 1944. Also gone to the military were outfielder Danny Litwhiler, pitcher Fred Schmidt and infielder George Fallon.

Trouble continued to haunt the Cardinals. Walker Cooper's brother, Mort, a pitcher who was 22–7 in 1944, was upset with Cardinal owner Sam Breadon because he thought Breadon lied to him and his brother about a salary freeze. They had not gotten pay raises. When Mort learned that the 1944 MVP, shortstop Marty Marion, had gotten a salary increase, he blew up. Breadon tried to appease the pitcher and agreed to renegotiate with him. But when Cooper, still infuriated with his boss, failed to show for a scheduled start in a road game at Cincinnati, Breadon traded him to Boston for pitcher Red Barrett.

Despite all of these off-the-field problems, the on-the-field Cardinals beat the Cubs in 16 of their 22 head-to-head contests and finished in second place, just three games behind Chicago.

The Giants, bolstered by the hitting of their manager and future Hall of Famer, Mel Ott, and aging catcher Ernie Lombardi, 37, who had one more good year left in him, got off to a fast start but faded by mid-season and finished fifth. Brooklyn had a feisty manager, Leo Durocher, and a feisty second baseman, Eddie Stanky, who had been a Cub the previous year. Stanky led the league in walks and in participation as a fielder in double plays, in assists and in errors. The Dodgers finished third.

The Cincinnati Reds, the best National League team in 1939 and 1940, also struggled to put a decent wartime team on the field. They went to spring training in Bloomington, Indiana, depending on three old-timers to aid a depleted pitching staff — Hod Lisenbee, 46, who had not pitched in nine years, when he was 1–7 with the Philadelphia A's in 1936; Walter "Boom Boom" Beck, 40, whose record over the past five years was a cumulative 2–10 and whose nickname came from what opposing batters did to his pitches; and Guy Bush, 43, once a stellar pitcher with the Cubs, but who hadn't pitched in the majors since 1938 when he was 0–1 in six games with the Cardinals.

The Philadelphia Phillies, who had finished last in six of the past seven years, were destined to make it seven out of eight. By June 30, when they had won only 17 games, manager Freddie Fitzsimmons was fired and replaced with Ben Chapman, who guided the club to 29 more wins. Chapman, an outfielder by trade, was so desperate for pitching that he put himself on the mound 13 times and compiled a 3–3 record. He was one of 19 Phillie pitchers who combined to lose 108 games.

Another indication of how major league ballclubs had filled their rosters with would-be ballplayers: By 1950, only 30 players who appeared in at least one major league game in 1945 were still in the major leagues—5.7 percent of the 529 who played in the last war year.

Meanwhile, at the start of spring training 1945 for the Cubs, no one could have envisioned where the journey would end. Where it started was strange enough, at a resort in French Lick, Indiana, about 2,000 miles east of where the ballclub usually trained on Catalina Island off the coast of southern California. The Cubs had trained at Catalina since 1922, when William Wrigley, Jr., owner of the ballclub and father of current owner Philip Wrigley, bought the island and made it a playground for millionaires. Wrigley had 350 bungalows constructed and arranged for two steamers to make periodic two-hour treks back and forth from the mainland to the island. He sold package deals that included transportation, housing, meals and sight-seeing. He built a mansion at the top of a hill overlooking all of the tourist trappings. And he brought the Cubs to the island for spring training every year. It was not unusual for movie stars, vacationing on Catalina, to work out with the Cubs.

But beginning in 1942, acting on orders of the commissioner to train closer to home to save fuel costs, the Cubs chose French Lick, a resort town of about 2,000 citizens, about 88 miles south of Indianapolis. It was the home of two lavish hotels, the West Baden and the French Lick Springs, just a couple of miles from one another. Each hotel offered their guests a plush complex complete with mineral water springs and an atrium in which guests could watch birds fly above them as they sat and chatted with friends over drinks. There were accommodations for biking, running, baseball, golf and other outdoor activities. Inside, in addition to the atrium and fancy guest rooms, there were elegant ballrooms. The hotels played host to many important guests over the years, including major league baseball teams, former New York governor and presidential candidate Al Smith, and gangster Al Capone.

Perhaps the most unique feature of the French Lick lifestyle — the thing that attracted wealthy guests from all over the country — was the mineral water, promoted and marketed as "Pluto Water." This precious commodity was said to be a liquid that was a primary step in attaining good health because of its capability of "cleaning out" the systems of those who partook in it. "If Nature Can't, Pluto Water Can" was its advertising motto. Stripped of all the marketing hyperbole, Pluto Water was a laxative.

Hotel guests were invited to have their Pluto Water at the start of the day. After they had a glass of it, they were given canes and invited to take a walk in a nearby woods to enjoy the out-of-doors fresh air and delightful scenery. Outhouses were situated throughout the woods for the convenience of those who had consumed the Pluto Water. It was easy to tell when an outhouse was in use: a cane would be hanging on the door handle. It was considered rude to return to the hotel from the walk in the woods without your cane.

History does not record how many Chicago Cubs, if any, participated in this routine. Merullo remembers seeing many wealthy, elderly patrons avail themselves of the special water but he chose to pass up the chance and does not recall seeing any teammates take part. So it is not possible to determine if Pluto Water played any part at all in developing the National League championship team in 1945. In 1947, Pluto Water was banned by the Federal government, which deemed it injurious to a person's health.

The Cubs made two personnel moves before the season started, one involved an eccentric outfielder who had been a minor league phenom who never lived up to expectations in the big leagues; the other involved a future Hall of Famer who had reached the end of an illustrious career.

On February 21, the Cubs sold outfielder Lou Novikoff, "The Mad Russian," to their Los Angeles farm club. Novikoff was one of the greatest minor league hitters of all time but the only way he matched his reputation in the big leagues was through some of his zany antics. A four-time minor league batting champion, Novikoff won the Pacific Coast League Triple Crown in 1940 with a .343 batting average, 41 home runs and 171 RBIs while playing for the Los Angeles Angels. But his defense was often nonexistent. His approach to handling fly balls was once described as "waiting for the ball to drop and then smothering it with his hands." Worse yet, Novikoff had what turned out to be an incurable fear of vines, not a good thing for an outfielder who would have to play half of his major league games in Wrigley Field.

With the Cubs, Novikoff would allow balls to go over his head and hit the wall rather than go back into the vines to try to make the catch. Grimm, wanting to salvage Novikoff because of his potential as a hitter, tried to cure him of his fears in the field. Grimm said he thought maybe Novikoff was afraid the vines were poison ivy. So one day before a game, he went to the outfield with Novikoff, tore some of the

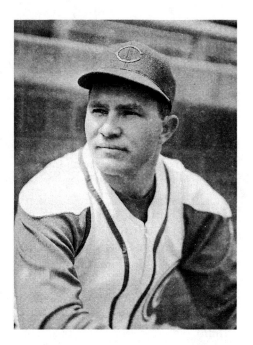

Lou Novikoff was one of the greatest hitters in minor league history but never reached his potential in the major leagues. When the Cubs sent him to the minors prior to the 1945 season, a bitter Novikoff said he had been "sold down the river."

green vines off the wall and rubbed them all over his face and arms, hoping to prove they were harmless. But nothing worked and Novikoff was consistently a liability in the outfield. In Los Angeles, he once fell while chasing a fly ball and said he tripped on the foul line, which he claimed was crooked. In another game, he was a runner on second and tried to steal third — but the bases were loaded. "I couldn't resist. I had such a good jump," he said.

Management had a Lou Novikoff Day in Los Angeles for him in 1941. Novikoff hit two home runs and two singles and threw a man out at the plate. That was more or less a typical day for Novikoff in the Pacific Coast League. He topped off the ceremonies honoring him by taking the microphone and singing "My Wild Irish Rose."

But he didn't play well in the major leagues. After his Triple Crown Year with Los Angeles in 1940, Gallagher brought him to the Cubs where he played parts of four seasons and only once appeared in more than 100

games. That was in 1942 when he played in 128 games and hit .300 but
with just 7 home runs and 64 RBIs.

Gallagher got tired of waiting for Novikoff to develop. He had three
good young outfielders in Lowrey, Nicholson and Pafko—and Secory
showed signs of being an adequate backup. So the Cubs asked waivers
on Novikoff—"the biggest dud in major league history," according to
one sports writer. Eventually, Chicago took him off waivers and sent him
down to Los Angeles where he had been a fence buster. The Cubs figured
he could make more money for them down there than in the big leagues.
Novikoff's reaction: "I've been sold down the river."

On March 5, Jimmie Foxx, one of baseball's all-time home run leaders, signed with Philadelphia after having endured a miserable year at
the plate with the Cubs in 1944. Foxx, who played 17 years in the American League and who was all-time second in home runs with 534 when
he retired, played seven games for the Cubs at the end of the 1942 season and hit .205. He retired in 1943 but came back the next year as a
pinch hitter and role player. At Philadelphia, he got up 20 times with
just one hit and was 0-for-11 as a pinch hitter. He hit seven home runs
in limited duty. It was during this time that he was victimized by Schuster's hidden ball trick. Not long after that, he retired for good.

On March 10, the first 11 Cubs players arrived for spring training.
Grimm welcomed the pitchers and catchers who were the first to report
and before long, he was feeding Chicago sports writers the pabulum of
pre-season pleasantries. "You can say that the Cubs won't settle for fourth
this year. The way we're shaping up will make us plenty formidable when
the bell rings. I'm 100 percent optimistic about our chances," he told the
press.

While the Cubs players enjoyed the luxuries of the French Lick
resort, they had to battle the weather. Heavy rains flooded the ballfields
and forced the club to work out on the fairways of nearby golf courses
on several days and work out in the ballroom on other days. It was a
bizarre start to what would be a bizarre season.

Wrigley, Gallagher and Grimm, while not as hard hit as most other
clubs by seasoned players going off to war, still had to field a team made
up of men who fit one of three categories: they were either too old for
the armed services, had served and been honorably discharged and now
were trying to get back into their pre-war playing shape, or had been
rejected by the military for medical reasons.

The Cubs had 12 players on their spring training roster over the age
of 32. Their pitching staff would be dependent on full seasons from Van-

denberg, 39, Derringer and Prim, both 38, and Passeau 36. Starting third baseman Hack was 35, second baseman Johnson was 32, shortstop Hughes was 34 and catcher Livingston was 30. The outfield was relatively young with veteran Nicholson at age 30, Lowrey at 26 and Andy Pafko at 24.

The younger Cubs had an assortment of abnormalities that kept them out of the armed services and did not give them the appearance of a pennant contender. Livingston suffered from chronic headaches, the result of banging his head on a dugout roof chasing a foul ball several years before. Cavarretta had a hearing deficiency. Nicholson was color-blind and had diabetes that was getting progressively worse but was not diagnosed until years later. Wyse had back problems that were made more severe when he fell off a scaffold while working as a welder after the 1944 season. Passeau was past military age but was among the walking wounded at spring training with painful bone chips around the elbow of his pitching arm.

In fact, the chance for the Cubs to get off to a quick start in 1945 was dealt a huge blow on April 3, two weeks before opening day, when Grimm announced that Passeau would be lost to the team for several weeks because of the bone chips. He went home to Mississippi to nurse his sore arm and contemplate whether it would be worth it to return to the team when his arm healed. Derringer, another veteran, earned the opening day start because of his performance in a 15–2 drubbing of the White Sox in one game of the crosstown three-series prior to the start of the regular season.

On April 17, five days after President Roosevelt died at Warm Springs, Georgia, and a day after U.S. troops reached Nuremberg, Germany, as the war raged overseas, the Cubs opened the season by defeating St. Louis 3–2 behind Derringer. Elsewhere on opening day, Cincinnati beat Pittsburgh 7–6 in 11 innings in a game that featured a fifth-inning grand-slam home run by Reds centerfielder Dain Clay. The homer was a symbol of oddities fans came to expect in 1945 — for it was Clay's only home run of the year, though he came to bat 645 times.

On April 19, the Cardinals disposed of the Cubs 8–2 to even both of their records at 1–1. Meanwhile Ott's Giants completed a three-game sweep of the Boston Braves and were the only undefeated team in the National League after just three games. The next day, Pittsburgh's Rip Sewell beat the Cubs 5–4 to get his 100th career win. On April 21, the Cubs came back to beat the Bucs in a doubleheader at Forbes Field with Derringer picking up his second win and Chipman winning for the first time. The Cubs won six in a row between April 21 and April 28 and found themselves in first place, if only for a day, on April 28. In one of the wins, on April 25, Passeau made his first start of the year and beat Bucky Walters and the Reds 4–0 at Crosley Field. For Passeau to be back so soon, and to have thrown a shutout in his first start, was a great morale boost for Chicago.

In their fifth straight win, on April 27, Derringer beat the Pirates' Sewell 7–3. Sewell allowed just four hits in four innings but his teammates committed four errors. The Cubs' defense was also shaky. All three of the Pirate runs were unearned because of a dropped fly ball. It was Derringer's third straight win to start the season, a hugely pleasant surprise for Grimm and the Cubs.

The Associated Press reported, "Paul Derringer, a seasoned traveler up and down baseball's glory road, was heading for the top again Saturday, and if there aren't too many detours, he might well pitch his Chicago Cubs teammates to a National League pennant."

The next day, Wyse took a no-hitter into the eighth inning before Billy Salkeld singled for the Pirates' only hit of the afternoon as the Cubs won 6–0. The Pirates came back the next day to end Chicago's winning streak at six by sweeping a doubleheader at Wrigley Field by scores of 6–2 and 5–4. The Cubs came out of April with a 7–4 record, a half game behind the New York Giants.

Baseball owners elected a new commissioner in April. U.S. Senator Albert "Happy" Chandler of Kentucky was picked to succeed the late Judge Kenesaw Mountain Landis, who had served as the sport's first and only commissioner from 1920 until his death in 1944. Chandler was approved by 11 of the 16 owners on the first vote, but since a three-fourths majority was required, another vote was necessary. His selection was unanimous on the second ballot.

"The important thing now is to keep the game on its present high plane," said Chandler. "It's an honest game and has to be kept that way. After the war, there is another matter. The young kids coming along have got to have a chance to get into the game. Baseball is going to have an important place in the post-war sports program."

At the same April 24 meeting in which Chandler was elected commissioner, owners also agreed to have interleague exhibition games played on July 9–10. They would be in lieu of the annual All-Star game that was scrapped because of all the travel that would have been involved at a time when gas was being rationed. Interleague games would involve teams of the same city — Cubs versus White Sox, Giants versus Yankees,

Browns versus Cardinals, Phillies versus A's— plus teams in close proximity to one another: Cincinnati versus Cleveland, Brooklyn versus Washington and Detroit versus Pittsburgh.

There was talk of canceling the World Series unless two teams from the same city won their respective league championships, which would limit the field to the Cubs and White Sox in Chicago, the A's and Phillies in Philadelphia (an outlandish thought), the Browns and Cardinals in St. Louis who had played in the 1944 series, and the Yankees, Giants and Dodgers in New York.

May 1, 1945	*W–L*	*Pct.*	*GB*
New York	8–4	.666	__
Chicago	7–4	.636	0.5
St. Louis	5–4	.555	1.5
Boston	6–5	.545	1.5
Brooklyn	5–5	.500	2.0
Cincinnati	5–6	.454	2.5
Pittsburgh	4–7	.363	3.5
Philadelphia	3–8	.272	4.5

On May 1, United Press International sized up the first few weeks of the major league season and concluded: "If pitching in the early games tells the story, the Detroit Tigers and Chicago Cubs are headed for an October World Series date." The report cited the early season success of Detroit's Hal Newhouser, Dizzy Trout and Al Benton. It noted that the Cubs, though having just a modest 7–4 record, had six complete games. In four of them, opponents had five hits or less. Three Chicago hurlers— Passeau, Chipman and Wyse— already had shutouts.

In May, the Cubs were not much better than a .500 team, much as they had been in April, showing little sign that they would be a pennant contender. On May 9, the lowly Philadelphia Phillies, who had won just three games all year, hung Derringer with his first loss after four straight wins. Ex-Cub Bill Lee got the victory in a 5–3 decision. Between May 13 and May 18, Chicago lost six in a row, and some of them were really ugly losses. On May 14, Dewey Williams hit a game-tying home run in the ninth inning off Bill Voiselle of the Giants, making a rare relief appearance, but the Giants pushed a run across in the 10th inning to win the game 6–5. The next day, New York won again, 5–4, as Derringer lost his second straight. Napoleon Reyes of the Giants had two singles, two walks, a string of six straight hits over two games, and 16 hits in his last 26 at-bats for a .615 average. On May 16, Voiselle won his seventh straight game without a loss, defeating the Cubs 6–0. Wyse had one bad inning for the Cubs, giving up homers to Mel Ott, Phil Weintraub and Ernie Lombardi in the sixth.

One of the low points of the young season occurred the next day, May 17, when the Giants completed a four-game sweep with an 8–5 victory. The loss dropped the Cubs to two games below .500 at 10–12. Worse, it was a game they let get away. The Giants scored six runs in the eighth inning to wipe out a 5–2 Cub lead and pin the loss on Passeau. The Giants improved their season record to 20–5. The Cubs were buried in fourth place, 8½ games out of first. It got worse. After being swept by the Giants at the Polo Grounds, Chicago traveled to Brooklyn where the Dodgers lit up Erickson and several other Cubs pitchers in a 15–12 slugfest. The Dodgers' Luis Olmo had a double, triple and home run in the game. The triple and homer each came with the bases loaded, a feat for one game that has never been duplicated in the major leagues.

While the Cubs were having trouble putting anything together on the field, they got a break off the field on May 21 when the Selective Service agreed to "indefinitely defer" from the military all men 30 years and over. United Press International surveyed major league baseball rosters and determined the ruling would affect 160 ballplayers—with the Chicago Cubs being the biggest beneficiary. Three Cub starters would not have to worry about the draft — Nicholson, who turned 30 in December of 1944, Johnson who was 34 and Hack who was 36. "Seventy-five percent of remaining major leaguers are 4-F or have been honorably discharged," UPI reported.

The Cubs followed the losing streak by winning three in a row, including a doubleheader win over the Dodgers with Derringer finally winning his fifth game on his third try and Wyse winning his fourth. When Passeau beat the Phillies 5–3 at Wrigley Field on May 23, he started a personal nine-game winning streak in which he re-established his reputation as a dominant National League pitcher and a potent part of the one-two punch with Wyse. The May 23 win also brought the ballclub back to the .500 level at 13–13. They lost the next day but then won four in a row, including a 5–3 win over Brooklyn at Wrigley Field that was Derringer's sixth win.

By this time in the season, signs of things to come were beginning to show in individual performances by the Cubs. Cavarretta was hitting .360 and was a legitimate contender for the batting title. Hack was playing his usual game, hitting .300 and snaring everything around him at third base. But Nicholson, who the Cubs had counted on to have another stellar year, was struggling and the ballclub as a whole was streaky and becoming buried in the middle of the National League standings.

The fans still came out to see them. The biggest crowd in seven years— 42,565 — turned out for a Memorial Day doubleheader with the Giants. New York won the opener 8–6 with Prim taking the loss in relief of Wyse. In the second game, Pafko hit a three-run homer and Chipman, making a rare start, threw a three-hitter to beat Giant starter Bill Voiselle, who took his second straight loss after winning eight straight.

Ott, the Giants' player-manager, set the National League record for total bases with 4,888 in the first game, a mark that has been surpassed several times since then. But by the end of the month, his Giants were starting to put some distance between themselves and other contenders, winning 18 games and losing only 7, to take a 6½ game lead over the fifth-place Cubs.

The Giants were the hottest team in baseball for most of May. They won eight in a row between May 2 and May 13 and were high atop the National League standings with a 16–4 mark. After beating the Cardinals 4–3 in the first game of a doubleheader at the Polo Grounds, Mort Cooper beat them in the second game to snap the winning streak. The Giants then reeled off five more victories, giving them 13 out of 14 before they lost the second game of a doubleheader against Pittsburgh on May 20. New York was 21–6 at the end of the day. The Cubs, losers of six in a row, beat the Dodgers in a doubleheader to up their record to 12–13. They were in fourth place, eight games behind the Giants. Chicago won seven of its last 10 games in May but remained in fourth place, 6½ games behind the Giants. The Dodgers finished April with two wins and then won their first nine games in May, showing signs of challenging the front-running Giants. They split two games and then lost six in a row and were in third place, 19–16 and 5½ games behind New York at the end of the month.

The season had already seen some great and not-so-great individual performances. In Cincinnati's opening day win highlighted by Dain Clay's grand slam, the winning pitcher was 46-year-old Lisenbee, making his first major league appearance in nine years. On April 20, Boston's Butch Nieman hit a three-run homer to help the Braves beat the Phillies 6–5. In the Braves' next game, on April 22, Nieman hit a two-run homer in the ninth inning to tie a game the Braves eventually won, 3–2, over the Phillies. Then on April 24, Nieman hit a three-run homer in the ninth inning to help Boston beat the Dodgers 8–6 with Nieman driving in five of the runs. He had three home runs and 10 RBIs in the three-game stretch. In the remainder of the season he hit 11 more homers and drove in 33 more runs.

On May 9, Giant centerfielder Johnny Rucker got a base hit off Cincinnati's Arnold Carter, extending his hitting streak to 18 games — every game the Giants had played. The next day, Frank Dasso would shut him down to end the streak. On May 14, Mel Bosser made his major league debut with the Reds and walked 10 batters in seven innings but managed to escape with a 5–4 victory. His only other professional experience had been in Class D.

JUNE 1, 1945	W-L	Pct.	GB
New York	26–11	.615	__
Brooklyn	21–16	.567	5
Pittsburgh	19–16	.542	6
St. Louis	20–17	.540	6
Chicago	18–16	.529	6.5
Cincinnati	15–18	.454	9
Boston	13–20	.393	11
Philadelphia	10–28	.263	16.5

The Cubs won 14 games in June, still showing no signs of being much better than an average team. In fact, when Paul Erickson lost a 6–4 decision to the Cardinals at Sportsman's Park on June 7, the Cubs found themselves at .500 once again with a 19–19 record. On June 8, Chicago beat the Reds 7–3 behind Derringer, who won his seventh game, equaling his 1994 total. The next day, they won a doubleheader from the Reds. In the second game, Mickey Livingston hit a homer that was reported to be the longest one ever hit at Wrigley Field. But the Cubs continued to be streaky and when they lost a doubleheader to Pittsburgh on June 14, the Pirates snuck into first place. On June 15, Chicago played its second straight doubleheader — and third in five days. Hunting for someone to give the starting rotation a break, Grimm called on 39-year-old Vandenberg to make his first start of the year. Vandenberg gave up a pop fly double to Cincinnati's Al Libke in the first inning — the only hit of the game — as the Cubs won 3–0. The win, in the second game of the twin bill — Wyse had won the first game — seemed to give the ball-club a lift. Derringer won his eighth game the next day and Passeau won his fifth in a relief appearance the day after that. When Wyse beat the Pirates 5–4 on June 22, the Cubs had climbed to six games above .500 at 28–22 and were in second place, 3½ games behind Brooklyn, which had climbed over the Giants and Pirates. The Cubs slipped a little in the last week, ending the month at 31–27, but seemed to be poised to make a move up in the standings—if the pitching, which had been better than anyone expected, would hold up as the days and weeks added up.

Meanwhile, Durocher's Dodgers had started to make their move. Coming off the 11-game winning streak in May, the Dodgers put together two winning streaks, each of seven games in June, and went into first place on June 14 when Brooklyn beat New York 5–4, beating the slumping Voiselle. They stayed in first place for all but one day for the rest of the month. The Giants, who peaked with a record of 25–7 on May 26, 6½ games ahead of second-place Brooklyn, lost 13 of their next 16 and never regained the momentum they had in the first month. They had been in first place every day but one since opening day but would never be on top again for the rest of the season. The Dodgers played through some distractions. On June 9, after Brooklyn defeated Philadelphia 8–7 at Ebbets Field, Durocher was arrested for his part in a fight in which he allegedly beat up a fan.

June had been strange for the Cubs, despite signs of potential at the end. After toppling to a 19–19 record on June 7, the Cubs reeled off four straight wins to put them over .500 to stay, but all four wins were against Cincinnati, which was not a test of strength. In fact, the Cubs were on their way to beating the Reds in 21 of 22 games. The roller coaster continued when Chicago lost their next three, all to Pittsburgh, and then won five in a row, three against Cincinnati at Crosley Field and two against Pittsburgh at Wrigley Field. The pattern of clobbering the lowly teams and having trouble with the good ones continued when Chicago lost three in a row to the Cardinals at Wrigley Field with Derringer, Vandenberg and Prim taking the losses.

While the Cubs were weaving from winning streak to losing streak, Brooklyn and St. Louis, powerhouses of the early '40s, overtook the slumping Giants and moved into first and second places, respectively. On July 1, the Cubs were 32–27 and in fourth place. They had lost four out of five to the Cardinals in June, showing little indication they would have any chance of overtaking the defending champions. Through the end of June, the Cubs had occupied first place on two days—opening day when they beat the Cardinals and shared the top spot with three other teams and April 28 when they crept into first place for the day. But for most of the rest of the first three months, they were in fourth, fifth or sixth place. One ray of hope: As July approached, even though Chicago trailed Brooklyn by five games and were fourth in the standings, they only trailed the Dodgers by two in the loss column.

The starting pitching had held up well. Had there been an All-Star game, Passeau, Wyse and Derringer probably all would have been named to the squad. Grimm needed to find a reliable fourth starter, and some bullpen help wouldn't hurt. Early season rainouts had resulted in the scheduling of several extra doubleheaders, some of them back to back. If the Cubs were to make a run at the pennant, pitching would be the key, as it would for all of the other contenders. And Wrigley, Gallagher and Grimm had the same question they had at the start of the season. Could they reasonably expect as much out of their starters in the second half of the season — in the dog days of the August heat, in the pressure of a September pennant race — as they had gotten from them in the first three months? All managers and general managers have the same answer: You can never have enough pitching.

On June 29, the Phillies, who had played 68 games and lost 50 of them, relieved Freddie Fitzsimmons of his duties as manager and replaced him with Ben Chapman. In Chapman's first two games, the Phillies lost to the Cardinals 9–1 and to Cincinnati 13–5.

As the mid-point in the season approached, baseball writers pondered the lack of any dominating, or, for that matter, exciting teams in baseball and speculated on the reasons. United Press International reported: "A fascinating lack of logic in the major league pennant races was threatening to complicate them hopelessly.... Preponderance of rookies, who are very good or very bad by streaks, and of old-timers, who have physical limitations to keep them from playing their best all the time, are cited as reasons for the inconsistency. Other factors are bad traveling conditions, a lot of night games and constant lineup shuffling made necessary by uncertainty of player personnel."

July 1, 1945	W–L	Pct.	GB
Brooklyn	40–25	.615	—
St. Louis	36–27	.571	3
New York	36–30	.545	4.5
Chicago	32–27	.542	5
Pittsburgh	33–31	.515	6.5
Boston	31–31	.500	7.5
Cincinnati	28–31	.474	9
Philadelphia1	8–52	.257	24.5

July didn't start out with signs of anything changing. The Cubs lost to the Giants 7–4 with Van Mungo besting Derringer in the first game of a doubleheader at the Polo Grounds. But Chicago came back to win the second game 4–3 behind Wyse with the help of Pafko's inside-the-park home run. After a day off, Passeau was the winner in a 24–2 laugher over Boston at Braves Field in Boston. Chicago got 28 hits in that game, which is still the team record for most hits in a game.

The following day, July 4, the Cubs won a doubleheader over the Braves, 5–3 and 7–6, with Erickson, the fireballing righthander who was often erratic with his pitches, getting one of the wins and the veteran Vandenberg getting the other. Derringer worked effectively in relief in both games. In the first game, he shut down a Braves rally with the bases loaded in the eighth inning. In the second game, he pitched scoreless relief to preserve a win as both Pafko and Nicholson homered. The Cubs were now 36–28 and in second place, 3½ games behind the Dodgers.

Wyse was the winner on July 5 as the Cubs completed the sweep of the Braves with a 3–2 victory. The Cubs win, coupled with a Dodger loss, moved Chicago to within 2½ games of the lead. Next it was on to Philadelphia where Chicago won another doubleheader, 11–3 in the first game with Ray Prim, another starter, winning in relief and Derringer picking up win number nine in the second game. Passeau completed a sweep of the Phillies with a 3–0 win on July 7. On July 8, the Cubs played their fourth doubleheader in eight days and beat Philadelphia 12–6 and 9–2 behind Erickson and Wyse.

Major league ballclubs then had a three-day "All-Star break" in which there was no All-Star game but instead several same-city match-ups. The Cubs and White Sox played an exhibition game at Comiskey Park on July 10 that the White Sox won 5–4 in 10 innings before 47,144 fans—the largest crowd of the year in Chicago. The break was a mixed blessing for the Cubs. The advantage: It gave their regulars and, most importantly, their beleaguered starting pitching staff some time off. The disadvantage: The Cubs had won 10 in a row and had some momentum building for the first time all season. They wanted the time off but hoped it wouldn't stop that momentum.

The Cubs had been a good hitting ballclub all year. Only Nicholson was way below what was expected of him. Cavarretta was contending for the batting title, Pafko was on a pace to drive in 100 runs and Hack was back to his old, steady ways, both at the plate and defensively. The starting pitching had been great. Wyse was 12–5, Passeau was 10–4, and Derringer was 9–6. But Passeau was 1–3 after a 9–1 start and Derringer was 5–6 after a 4–0 start, exactly the problem Gallagher and Grimm had anticipated might happen as the season wore on. And another problem was developing. As the pressure of the pennant race mounted, Grimm had more confidence in his starters than in his bullpen and had used Derringer and Prim in relief to preserve two recent victories.

After three days off, the regular season resumed and Wyse beat the Braves at Wrigley Field for the club's 11th straight win in the first game of yet another doubleheader. Passeau pitched well in the second game but lost a 3–1 decision to Nate Andrews. The loss not only broke the Cubs' winning streak but ended Passeau's personal nine-game winning streak.

Chicago then won its next five games and six of its next seven. Prim won his fourth straight and with his third shutout, a 2–0 four-hitter over the Braves. Then the Cubs beat the once-mighty Giants in a doubleheader to open up a four-game lead over the Dodgers. On July 16, Lowrey and reserve catcher Paul Gillespie sandwiched singles around an error in the bottom of the ninth inning as the Cubs beat the Giants again, this time 4–3. Ray Starr got his first and only win of the year in relief of Passeau. Starr had been picked up from Pittsburgh on waivers in hopes of bolstering the pitching staff. On July 17, Voiselle outdueled Erickson as the Giants salvaged one game in the four-game series. The next day, Chicago split with Brooklyn as Lon Warneke, hero of a decade past with the Cubs, made his 1945 "debut" and pitched five shutout innings before getting shelled and losing an 8–5 decision. They came back to beat the Dodgers the next day when second baseman Johnson got three hits in a 3–1 victory, Wyse's 13th win of the year and his seventh straight win.

By the end of the month, the Cubs had won 26 and lost only 6. (The sixth loss wasn't officially recorded until September. On July 20, Chicago was losing to Brooklyn when the game was suspended and finished in September. Brooklyn won 12–5. It went in the books as a loss for the Cubs in July). On July 8, in the midst of the 11-game winning streak, the Cubs climbed into first place, a surprising turn-around for essentially the same team that started the previous season at 1–13 and had been a .500 ballclub during most of 1945. Perhaps the most amazing statistic: The Cubs were 10–1 on the road for the month.

Other teams had some milestone events in July. On July 6, Boston's Nieman came through again in the clutch, this time hitting a pinch-hit grand-slam home run in the Braves' 13–5 win over the Pirates. On July 8, Floyd "Babe" Herman, 42, who hadn't swung a bat in the major leagues since 1937, pinch hit for the Dodgers, got a base hit, and tripped over first base. On July 15, the hapless Phillies lost their 10th straight game, a 3–1 decision to Cincinnati, putting them 42 games below .500 at 21–63 and 30 games behind the first-place Cubs. Earlier in the year, the Phillies had endured a six-game losing streak in late April and early May and then a stretch from May 25 through June 13 when they lost 16 out of 17 before losing the 10 in a row in July. The managerial change, Chapman replacing Fitzsimmons on June 29, hadn't helped.

The defending champion Cardinals, trying to win their fourth straight championship, were beginning to come on. Obviously missing the lineup punch of Musial and Slaughter and the pitching of the veteran Lanier, St. Louis was just an average ballclub for the first two months of the season. But they won 16 games in June and 19 in July so that by August 1, they were in second place, 5½ games out of first.

Meanwhile, though the Cubs were starting to gain some steam, Grimm and general manager Jim Gallagher knew the Cubs' perch on top of the National League was a house of cards that would crumble unless they could find some pitching help — someone to take the load off their two aces, Wyse and Passeau, and take some of the pressure off Derringer, Prim and Vandenberg who were pitching way beyond what was expected of them.

Prim and Chipman were capable of providing spot starts but Grimm had concerns about the bullpen. "One good relief pitcher could make a lot of difference in this National League pennant race," Grimm told the press on July 25. "We've been good with what starting pitching we have but if our relief pitching was better, well…."

Gallagher and Grimm told their starting pitchers they would try to get them some help. Wyse said Wrigley told Passeau and him that they might have to pitch with two days rest instead of the usual three and that there would be a bonus for them if they could do it. But the Cubs brass worried that down the stretch, the ballclub's aging arms would wilt. On July 27, Gallagher pulled off the deal of the decade in the major leagues. How he managed to do it is a secret that died with him nearly 60 years later.

V

The "Pitch and Pray Lineup" Wins It All

> "The Cubs were plenty jittery now but there was nothing any
> of them could do but watch and pray."
> — *Sports writer Warren Brown*

Jim Gallagher was a Chicago sports writer who covered both the Cubs and White Sox and who became general manager of the Chicago Cubs prior to the 1941 season. He was offered the job in the winter, while he was covering the Chicago Bears. Before accepting the job, he sought the counsel of a friend, George Halas, owner and coach of the Bears, who told him he would be a fool to turn it down.

Fellow sports writer Warren Brown, in his 1945 book, *The Chicago Cubs*, described Gallagher as "a man who can shout louder than the next man if it suits his purpose. He can outcuss the most profane ballplayer if the situation arises. He can be quiet and reserved and excellent company, cutting loose with nothing more emphatic than an occasional 'Judas priest.' He can shy away from all contacts and talk to or with no one for long periods of time. He can be most communicative or he can make silent Cal Coolidge of happy memory seem like an entire public-address system turned on full blast."

Brown also said, "He has never crossed a friend nor often forgiven an enemy — and he has many in both categories."

Branch Rickey, general manager of the Cardinals, Dodgers and later the Pirates, didn't think much of Gallagher when the Cubs hired him, calling him "a glorified office boy."

When Gallagher accepted the job of general manager, one of his first actions was to hire Grimm as a coach. Three years later, Gallagher fired manager Jimmy Wilson after the Cubs' horrendous start and called on Grimm to put the pieces back together again.

A general manager's legacy is the deals he makes. Ed Barrow is remembered for bringing Babe Ruth to the Yankees from Boston. Frank Lane at Cleveland is remembered for trading American League home run champion Rocky Colavito to Detroit for batting champion Harvey Kuenn. Some deals have sealed championships for ballclubs. In 1956, Brooklyn and Cincinnati were the favorites to win the pennant. On May 15, the Dodgers purchased the contract of pitcher Sal Maglie from Cleveland. Maglie, who had not won a game for the Indians, went 13–5 for Brooklyn and was just what the Dodgers needed to get to the World Series. Three years later, the Chicago White Sox were in a position to win their first pennant in 40 years but they had to hold off a good Cleveland Indian ballclub. The "Go-Go" White Sox were known for their speed and pitching but did not have any sluggers. On August 25, Chicago traded three players to the Pirates for veteran first baseman Ted Kluszewski, who hit 40, 49 and 47 home runs in successive years with Cincinnati in 1953–1955. Kluszewski hit .297 for Chicago with many clutch hits as the White Sox captured the flag. On June 13, 1984, the Cubs acquired pitcher Rick Sutcliffe in a five-player deal with Cleveland. Sutcliffe, who was 4–5 with the Indians when the deal was made, won 16 and lost only 1 for the Cubs as Chicago reached post-season play for the first time since 1945. It was a deal with results like any of those that Gallagher sought.

In 1941, he was involved in a deal with Brooklyn's Larry MacPhail that helped the Dodgers to a championship. Realizing that the Cubs were going nowhere that year with their present aging personnel, Gallagher traded one of the team's most popular players, veteran second baseman Billy Herman to the Brooklyn Dodgers for a young, unknown outfielder named Charley Gilbert.

William Jennings Bryan Herman had been the Cubs second baseman for 10 years, combining with shortstop Billy Jurges, third baseman Stan Hack and first baseman Phil Cavarretta to give Chicago the best infield in the National League. He was destined for the Hall of Fame. Herman hit over .300 six times for the Cubs but had gotten off to a slow start in 1941, with only seven hits in 36 at-bats, a .194 percentage. For Brooklyn, he hit .291 and helped the Dodgers win the National League pennant, giving him four World Series appearances, counting the 1932, 1935 and 1938 championship seasons with the Cubs. Herman played five more seasons and retired with a lifetime batting average of .304.

Gilbert, an outfielder, had played 59 games with Brooklyn in 1940, his first major league season, and had not played in 1941 when he was traded to the Cubs. For Chicago, he hit .279 in 86 at-bats. He played parts of four more seasons and ended his career with the Philadelphia Phillies in 1947 with a career batting average of .229.

By all accounts, the Herman-for-Gilbert deal was a real steal for the Dodgers and their general manager Larry MacPhail and not an auspicious start for Gallagher as general manager for the Cubs. On August 20, 1941, Gallagher and MacPhail hooked up again. This time, MacPhail picked up veteran Cubs pitcher Larry French on waivers. French was 5–14 with the Cubs and had no record with the Dodgers for the remainder of the season but did appear in the World Series for them and won 15 games the following year before retiring.

Gallagher and the Cubs made some nickel-and-dime deals over the next few years, trading second baseman Eddie Stanky to the Dodgers in 1944 for pitcher Bob Chipman and dumping minor league hitting sensation Lou Novikoff after four less-than-sensational partial seasons with the Cubs. But Gallagher had done nothing in his tenure to rise above Rickey's early assessment of him and the Cubs had not risen significantly in the standings until their sudden surge in July of 1945.

The hole in the Cubs roster was the same as it had been in spring training. After Wyse and Passeau, the strength of the starting pitching was suspect, totally dependent on the aging arms of Derringer and Prim and the spot starters like Chipman and Vandenberg.

In St. Louis, Mort Cooper was furious with the Cardinals. The pitching half of the Cooper brothers (Walker, a catcher, was in the service), Mort thought owner Sam Breaden had put a freeze on salaries and then learned that MVP shortstop Marty Marion had gotten a pay raise. Cooper sulked and became so angry that he missed a road trip and a scheduled start.

Gallagher was plugged in to the National League grape vine and knew Cooper would probably be available. So did Boston, and on May 23, the Braves sent pitcher Red Barrett and cash to the Cardinals in exchange for Cooper. Gallagher was forced to look elsewhere for pitching help.

On July 27, Gallagher came home from a fishing trip and found a message that Larry MacPhail, who was now with the Yankees, had called. Gallagher was tired and thought about just going to bed. In the morning, he would decide whether to return the call. Before retiring, he changed his mind and returned the call. MacPhail offered to sell Yan-

Hank Borowy was one of the Yankees' best pitchers when he came over to the Cubs in a controversial waivers deal on July 27. He had an 11–2 record for Chicago, an interesting statistic considering Yankee president Larry MacPhail said Borowy had a tendency of fading in the second half.

kee star pitcher Hank Borowy to the Cubs for the waiver price of $97,000. Gallagher said yes and thus pulled off the best deal of his life.

That's how the deal was made. Why the deal was made, at least from the Yankees' perspective, is still a mystery.

Borowy was clearly the Yankees' best pitcher during the war years. He began his career with New York in 1942 and posted a 15–4 record, good enough to have won the Rookie of the Year award had there been one then. He followed that performance with a 14–9 record in 1943 and was 17–12 in 1944. His earned-run averages in those three years were 2.52, 2.82 and 2.64. He won 11 games in a row in a span covering the end of the 1943 season and the start of the 1944 campaign.

In 1945, he was sailing along with another good year. Borowy was 10–5 and was leading the Yankees in wins when he was sold to the Cubs.

The waivers option is one of the oldest rules in professional baseball with regard to player personnel transactions. It started in 1885 with implementation of a rule allowing other clubs to claim a player once his team had served notice it intended to release him. If more than one team claimed him, the player could choose which team he wanted to play for. In 1903, two years after the American League was formed, the waiver rule was formalized in major league baseball, allowing other teams to claim players who had been "waived" by their original team. In 1907, the American League added a provision through which a team could withdraw a player from the waiver list if he was claimed by another team. This allowed a ballclub to manipulate which team could claim the player. Eventually, the National League adopted the same practice. The result was that typically, major league teams tested the waiver market to see which teams were interested in players, knowing they could pull them off the list if they didn't like what they saw. Teams were allowed to bid on players in reverse order of the standings. In other words, the last-place team in the American League would have first choice on an American League player on waivers and the process would follow all the way through to the first-place team. If the player was not picked, the process began all over again in the National League, again in reverse order of the standings. Since the Cubs were in first place on July 27, every other team in baseball had a shot at landing Borowy before Chicago even had a chance at him. No other club claimed him, obviously thinking his name would be pulled from the list if a claim was made. So nobody made an offer — until the last eligible team, the Cubs, put up $97,000 and the Yankees accepted.

The baseball world was stunned. National baseball writer Cornelius

Ryan unabashedly called it "the biggest deal in baseball since the war began." No one argued the point. Not only had the Yankees given up their best pitcher, they had shipped him to the other league. He would no longer be pitching in cities where American League fans would pay for a ticket to see him. Washington owner Clark Griffith was outraged. He told *Washington Post* sports columnist Shirley Povich that MacPhail "was a failure in Cincinnati and a flop at Brooklyn and the fact remains he sold the Yankees best pitcher at a time the Yankees need pitching. We ought to keep our stars in our own league. That's what makes our league prosper. Without stars, we'll have a cheaper league and the National League will be laughing at us.

"This deal was detrimental and caused great damage to the best interests of our league. I would have paid a lot of money for Borowy if I had ever thought the Yankees were serious about selling him," said Griffith.

It was a strange week for the Yankees. Five days before the deal was made, the Bronx Bombers' veteran manager Joe McCarthy, who was ailing, took a leave of absence from the ballclub to go home and rest. His illness was not disclosed but there were rumors of alcoholism. There were also rumors he had not gotten along with MacPhail, who had joined the Yankees front office at the start of the year. Answering questions about McCarthy's departure, MacPhail told reporters he doubted if McCarthy would be back with the team. He said the manager seemed to be depressed about how the Yankees were doing. "He just doesn't have good players and that is not his fault," said MacPhail. At the time, the Yankees were in third place, just 4½ games behind Detroit and two games behind Washington with almost half a season left. McCarthy had not said publicly that he intended to resign but when he heard about the Borowy deal, he threatened to quit.

MacPhail offered no complicated explanation. "This was a chance to sell a pitcher who never has been a winner in the last month or so of a season," he said. "Borowy appears to have outlived his usefulness. He has only four victories since April."

Borowy, interviewed in 1995, offered this explanation for the Yankees shipping him off to Chicago. "Aw, hell, they claim I threw a pitch that a guy hit so hard, it went out of the ballpark and into some railroad box car. The next thing you know, I was gone."

The home run in question may have occurred on July 15, 12 days before the waiver deal. Borowy, pitching for the Yankees, gave up a pinch-hit, grand-slam home run to Zeb Eaton, a pitcher for the Detroit Tigers, in a game the Yankees won 5–4. Borowy had gotten off to a great start in '45, winning eight of his first 10 decisions. But since June 30, he had lost three of five starts, bringing his record to 10–5.

Many baseball owners suspected that MacPhail and Gallagher had pulled off some type of back-room deal. Griffith asked the commissioner's office to investigate. No wrongdoing was found but actions were taken to tighten rules governing waivers.

Grimm, reflecting on the deal years later, said he thought MacPhail had lost confidence in Borowy, despite his stellar years with the Yankees, and that dealing Borowy to the Cubs was repaying a favor to Gallagher for sending Billy Herman to MacPhail's Brooklyn team in 1941, helping the Dodgers win the pennant.

Sports writer Brown, an old crony of Gallagher's, had a simpler explanation. In 1941, he said, the Cubs needed cash and MacPhail provided it in exchange for Billy Herman. In 1945, it was MacPhail who needed cash, and he got $97,000 for Borowy. It wasn't skullduggery, said Brown. It was simple arithmetic.

Borowy arrived in Chicago on July 29 in time to win the second game of a double header against Cincinnati in front of 43,786 fans at Wrigley Field, the first of 11 wins he would pick up against only two losses the rest of the year.

Borowy, who was 29 when he joined the Cubs, had been a brilliant pitcher at Fordham University where he compiled a record of 24–1. He was signed by Yankee scout Paul Krichell, who had a great eye for talent and 15 years earlier had signed a young hitter at Columbia University named Lou Gehrig. Borowy spent three years with the Newark Bears in the Yankee farm system before joining the major league club and winning 56 and losing 30 in 3½ years with the Yankees. He had a good

Yankee manager Joe McCarthy was ill and not with the team when Yankee president Larry MacPhail sold Hank Borowy to the Cubs.

fastball and curve ball but his bread-and-butter pitch was a change-up that kept hitters off balance, according to Grimm. He said Borowy would often develop a blister from the seam of the ball, which gave him trouble with the Yankees but that Cubs trainers were able to keep under control. He was a tough competitor who quickly became the pitcher Grimm felt he could depend on. And with good reason. He nearly was 13–0 with the Cubs, losing only at Boston 2–1 on August 10 and 1–0 at St. Louis on August 24. After the loss to the Cardinals, Borowy went 8–0 the rest of the way. Though one of his two losses was to St. Louis, he beat the Cardinals three times in his half-season with Chicago — and the Cubs only beat the defending-champion Cardinals three other times the whole year. Borowy's appearances with the Cubs:

July 29 — Beat Cincinnati 3–2
August 10 — Lost to Boston 2–1
August 15 — Beat Brooklyn 20–6
August 19 — Beat New York 8–0
August 24 — Lost to St. Louis 1–0
August 28 — Beat Pittsburgh 8–3
September 2 — Beat St. Louis 4–1

September 6 — Beat New York 6–1
September 11 — Beat Boston 5–4
September 15 — Beat Brooklyn 7–6
September 19 — Beat St. Louis 4–1
September 25 — Beat St. Louis 6–5
September 29 — Beat Pittsburgh 4–3

Nearly 60 years after the deal was made, the story of how Hank Borowy came to the Cubs is a subject of debate. Borowy said he still didn't know for sure why the Yankees let him go. And Gallagher, who died in 2002 at the age of 97, always said he had a lot of stories inside him and that's where they were going to stay.

While the Cubs were having their 26–6 July to move into first place, the Cardinals won 19, lost only 8 and chased Chicago the rest of the way. St. Louis had no trouble beating the league's best teams, including the Cubs, but played about .500 ball against the Braves, the Reds and the Phillies. By contrast, the Cubs killed the bottom of the league but had trouble with the teams chasing them, notably the Cardinals. For each team, this was a trend that helped determine the outcome of the National League pennant race.

August 1, 1945	W–L	Pct.	GB
Chicago	58–33	.637	—
Brooklyn	54–40	.574	5.5
St. Louis	55–41	.572	5.5
Pittsburgh	49–46	.515	11
New York	50–47	.515	11
Cincinnati	42–48	.466	15.5
Boston	43–52	.452	17
Philadelphia	26–70	.270	34.5

Ott did what he could to keep the Giants in the race. On August 1, he hit the 500th home run of his career, putting him all-time third behind Babe Ruth and Jimmy Foxx, and on August 12 he hit Nos. 501 and 502 in a doubleheader win over Cincinnati. In the second game, pinch hitter Joe Bowman of Cincinnati was retired, keeping his hitting record for the year intact at 0-for-42. At season's end, his average had increased to .088.

The Cubs remained hot. On August 2, they beat the Pirates 1–0 as Derringer outdueled Preacher Roe. The only run of the game scored when Lowrey doubled in the sixth, scoring Johnson who had singled. It was one of many clutch hits Lowrey would get during the month. On August 3, the Cubs beat the Reds in a doubleheader, moving their record against Cincinnati to 17–0 for the year. The winning pitchers were Wyse and Borowy — the second time in a week they had accomplished that feat. Cavarretta, battling Holmes of the Braves for the batting title, had four doubles, a homer and a single and drove in eight runs in the two games. At day's end, he was hitting .354, two points behind Holmes. On August 4, the Reds beat the Cubs for the first and only time all year, 4–3. Merullo blamed himself for the loss. He was thrown out trying to stretch a double into a triple, snuffing out a Cubs rally. But Chicago roared back the next day in yet another doubleheader and against Cincinnati again, winning 12–5 and 5–1. Three days later, they played and won their third doubleheader of the week, beating Boston 5–2 and 3–2 in 12 innings. Nicholson broke out of his season-long slump with a single, a double and a home run in the first game with Prim picking up the win on a five-hitter. In the second game, Wyse won his 17th as Pafko doubled in the 12th inning, scoring Merullo, who had singled ahead of him. Cavarretta continued his hitting tear, going 6 for 10 in the twin bill.

While the Cubs were piling up wins, so were the Cardinals, winning seven of eight; they were 4½ games out at the end of play on August 10. On August 11, Passeau narrowly missed pitching a no-hitter. He held Boston hitless for seven innings, then gave up two hits in the eighth as Chicago won 8–0. The next day, the Cubs got a scare when MVP first baseman Cavarretta collided with Phillie baserunner Fred Daniels and separated his shoulder. Cavarretta would be out for about a month. (It was also on August 12 that Hugh "Losing Pitcher" Mulcahy, the first ballplayer drafted in World War II, returned to the big leagues but did not pitch in the Phillies' loss to the Cubs.) On August 13, Heinz Becker, the man with the worst feet in the majors, filled in for Cavarretta and got a single, a double and a triple in the Cubs' 4–1 win over Philadelphia.

On August 14, news arrived that transcended anything happening on American baseball diamonds. The day would be remembered in history as V-J Day, for "Victory over Japan." World War II was over.

The Associated Press reflected on how the war's end would affect major league baseball. "Although there is little doubt now that a (world) series will be played, both the Cubs and Tigers face hurdles in their flag drives. Among the unpredictable factors is the amount of help to be expected from the returning servicemen. Exact details of the Army and Navy plans for releasing veterans have yet to be announced but it is assumed baseball will receive its share of former players."

The next day, Borowy was the beneficiary of a 19-hit Cubs attack as Chicago beat the Dodgers 20–6. Reserve catcher Paul Gillespie hit two home runs, one a grand slam. Becker and Pafko also homered.

While the Cubs were pounding the Dodgers, the Cardinals continued to have trouble with the league's least talented teams. They split a doubleheader with Philadelphia and fell five games behind the Cubs in the standings. The Cardinals had a record of 43–23 against the Cubs, Dodgers, Giants and Pirates but were just 23–22 against the Braves, Reds and Phillies. The Cubs had broken even at 26–26 against the Cardinals, Dodgers and Giants but were 44–11 against the rest of the league. The Cubs and Cardinals had 12 more games to play against each other. The outcome of those games would likely decide the championship. On August 16, when Brooklyn beat the Cubs and Wyse 2–1 and St. Louis beat the Phillies 4–0, the Cardinals found themselves four games out with 42 to play — including the all-important 12 with the Cubs. Winning pitcher for the Cardinals was rookie Ken Burkhart. A decade later, Burkhart and Warneke and Secory of the Cubs would all be National League umpires.

On August 19, the Cubs beat the Giants 8–0 at the Polo Grounds in Borowy's first return to New York. Joe Reichler, who later in his career would create the Baseball Encyclopedia, reported on the victory for the AP and showed his prowess with the use of statistics. Reichler wrote: "Hank Borowy had the personal satisfaction Monday of having proved in New York that the short gaiter tag hung on him was entirely unjustified.

"In blanking the Giants Sunday, Borowy pitched his first National League shutout and his fifth complete game in a Chicago Cubs uniform. The former Yankee ace, whom Larry MacPhail had sold 'because of his inability to go the distance in the second half of the season' thus demonstrated that if he did have that fault, he has overcome it."

Reichler cited Borowy's statistics so far with the Cubs: 5 games, 5 complete games, 45 innings, 13 runs, 2.60 earned run average, 4–1 record, and just one home run allowed.

The Giants came back to beat Chicago in the next two games of the series, with Wyse and Passeau taking the losses. The defeats were particularly tough because the Cubs didn't capitalize on the lift they got from Borowy's homecoming win. A worse ramification is that they had lost two in a row going into a three-game series with the Cardinals at Wrigley Field. In the opener on August 24, Harry Brecheen beat Borowy 1–0 with the only run of the game scoring on a Merullo error. The Cardinals trailed the Cubs by 4½ games. The following day, Prim and Burkhart battled but the Cardinals came out victorious again, this time by a score of 3–1. In the series finale, Red Barrett stopped the Cubs and Derringer, 5–1. The Cardinals trailed by 2½ games and still had nine games left with the Cubs.

The most disturbing part of the series for Grimm was that the Cubs had been held to two runs in the three games. He was particularly distressed with Nicholson's inability to produce, a problem that plagued the Cubs outfielder all year. In the series against St. Louis, he got two hits in 10 at-bats. Grimm made a phone call and enlisted the help of the National League's greatest hitter, Rogers Hornsby, to work with Nicholson. Grimm determined that Nicholson had developed a hitch in his swing that had thrown off his timing. It was Hornsby's job to help him get rid of it.

After a much-needed off-day, the Cubs beat Pittsburgh 6–3 on the strength of a three-run homer by Lowrey, who continued his torrid hitting in August. The win went to Borowy. Meanwhile, lowly Cincinnati toppled the Cardinals so the Cubs' lead increased to 3½ games. The following day Prim and Vandenberg combined on a nine-hit shutout as Chicago beat Pittsburgh 2–0 — and the Reds beat the Cardinals again. The lead was once again 4½ games, but not for long. When Pittsburgh beat Derrringer and the Cubs 6–4 on August 30, Chicago's lead was 3½ games, going into a four-game series with St. Louis at Sportsman's Park. The loss to the Pirates spoiled the occasion of Hack's 2,000th major league hit, all, of course, with the Cubs.

With the big series against the Cardinals coming up, Grimm was concerned about his ballclub's recent lethargic play. It was a time in which a manager could have held clubhouse meetings to clear the air, enforced curfews, and ordered extra batting and fielding practice. Grimm chose to get the players drunk. He took them to his farm outside St. Louis for what he described as "an old-fashioned picnic." Many of the

Rogers Hornsby, one of baseball's greatest hitters, was hired to help Bill Nicholson break out of his slump. (Photograph courtesy of Baseball Hall of Fame.)

players didn't want to go. Some, acting like schoolboys trying to stay out of school, made up excuses. Reserve outfielder Ed Sauer told Grimm this was the only time he could visit his sick grandmother. Traveling secretary Bob Lewis had arranged to rent a school bus that was at the train station when the Cubs arrived. Grimm had called ahead and had a chef prepare chicken with all the trimmings and plenty of desserts. Another

Grimm friend set up a bar outside where the beer flowed freely. Grimm said before the night was over, Sauer approached him and said, "Now's the time to send me to the plate if you need me." Derringer started shouting, "I'm going to start the first game of the World Series." Nicholson tried to give his best imitation of Vaughn Monroe singing, "Reaching for the Moon." Lowrey picked up a broomstick and gave Johnson a golf lesson. When it was time for the players to get on the bus and head for their hotel, Grimm counted his troops and came up one short. He found Derringer asleep in a rose bush.

The Cubs lost three out of four to the Cardinals with Wyse losing a 4–1 decision on a two-hitter by Harry Brecheen in the opener on August 31 to bring St. Louis within 2½ games of the Cubs with a month to play. Sauer got both hits, one of them a home run.

September 1, 1945	W-L	Pct.	GB
Chicago	76–46	.622	—
St. Louis	74–49	.601	2.5
Brooklyn	69–53	.565	7
New York	67–57	.540	10
Pittsburgh	67–62	.519	12.5
Boston	56–68	.451	21
Cincinnati	49–73	.401	27
Philadelphia	37–87	.298	40

On September 1, Passeau pitched well but was the loser in a 3–2 ballgame with George Dockins picking up the win for the Cardinals. Borowy beat Ken Burkhart in a 3–2 duel in the first game of a doubleheader the next day, but Prim came out on the short end of a 4–0 score in the nightcap, with Red Barrett picking up the win. The series had been another chapter of the same story with Chicago playing well but with Borowy the only pitcher to come out a winner against St. Louis. From Grimm's point of view, though, the club had played better than it had for a while, and the good play continued when they got out of St. Louis.

The Cubs took the train from St. Louis to Chicago and took on Cincinnati in a doubleheader the next day. True to form, they knocked off the Reds 7–2 and 7–1. Derringer got the win in the opener, benefiting from Pafko's grand slam. Wyse won the second game. Meanwhile, the Cardinals dropped a pair to Pittsburgh, 6–5 and 6–2. In the space of one day, the Cubs had made up the ground they had lost to St. Louis in the four-game weekend series and were leading the Cardinals by four games again.

The next day, Pittsburgh and Chicago battled to an 8–8 tie that was called at the end of 12 innings because the Pirates had to catch a train. The Cubs caught something too—the flu bug, which kept Becker, still filling in for Cavarretta, and Johnson out of the starting lineup. Rookie Reggie Otero started at first base and veteran Roy Hughes played second but the Cubs still beat the Giants twice, 5–2 with Prim winning his 11th and 10–2 with Passeau picking up win number 15. Pafko continued his hot hitting with a single, double and home run in the two games. The Cardinals beat Boston but still fell a half-game further behind and were 4½ games out of first. On September 6, Borowy won his seventh game as the Cubs won their fifth in a row, beating the Giants 6–1. The loser was Bill Voiselle, who had started the season with eight straight wins but was headed for a 14–14 season record. When the Cardinals split their doubleheader with the Braves, they slipped to five games back. Their pennant hopes seemingly would depend on how they fared in the five remaining games they had with the Cubs.

One of the pleasant surprises for the Cubs in these early September games was the resurgence of Bill Nicholson as a force in the lineup. Nicholson, the league's best power hitter in 1943 and 1944, just couldn't get it going in the year when everything else seemed to be going the Cubs' way. But in his first five games in September, "Swish" had two homers, three singles and eight RBIs.

Jerry Liska, Chicago sports reporter for the Associated Press, summed it up this way: "His mates say Nicholson, when in the deepest throes of a slump, would sit and stare blankly at the clubhouse walls, trying to figure out the whole thing. Well-meant advice only added to his batting woes. So big Nick finally decided it was mind over matter."

"I just gave up on the 99 different stances everyone was trying to teach me," said Nicholson. "I simply decided to go back to my old way of hitting—just standing up there and cutting at the ball. Trying to think of what I was doing wrong here and there left me tightened up so badly across the shoulders that I couldn't swing freely. I'm loose again now and I'm giving that ball a ride for a change."

On September 13, both the Cubs and the Cardinals were idle because of rainouts. Much attention was on the American League race where the surprising Washington Senators, with a starting pitching staff of primarily knuckle-ballers, climbed to within a half-game of the league-leader Tigers—with a five-game series coming up against Detroit. The Tigers won three out of four (with the fifth game rained out) and had a 2½ game lead with nine to play.

When the Cubs beat the Dodgers in a doubleheader on September 16, it was their 18th sweep of the year, a major league record. They would win two more doubleheaders before the season was over. Prim got his 12th win in the opener, a 3–2 victory in which he allowed but four hits. Wyse won his 20th game of the season 4–2 in the nightcap, fulfilling Grimm's pre-season prediction about him. Lowrey got yet another game-winning RBI in the opener and Johnson had four hits.

The next day, when the Cardinals beat the Phillies and the Cubs lost to Brooklyn, it brought St. Louis to within three games of the Cubs on the eve of a three-game series against Chicago at Sportsman's Park.

There wasn't an empty seat in the house for the opener, a thrilling game in which Red Barrett, whom St. Louis had acquired in the Mort Cooper deal with the Braves, won his 22nd game, including a 4–0 record against the Cubs. Chicago jumped on Barrett for two runs in the first inning with Pafko driving in both runs with a double. But the Cubs could do nothing after that. Whitey Kurowski drove in three runs for the Cardinals, accounting for all of their runs in the 3–2 triumph.

The Cubs got a huge lift the next day when Borowy — who else? — stifled the Cardinals' bats in a 4–1 victory that gave the Cubs their three-game lead once again. In the finale, Brecheen bested Prim 2–0, pulling St. Louis to within two games of the lead with eight to play. Chicago's pitchers had held the Cardinals to eight runs in the three games, but the Cubs managed only six runs in what one writer referred to as "Charlie Grimm's pitch and pray lineup."

When the two teams met again on September 25, Chicago clung to a 1½-game lead. St. Louis had six games left. The Cubs had seven. Southworth knew his troops needed to sweep the series. The Cardinals were 15–5 in their 20 games with the Cubs. Wrigley Field was packed to the rafters as Brecheen tangled with Borowy, and the fans got their money's worth in the very first inning as each team scored twice. The Cardinals took a 3–2 lead in the fifth but the Cubs came back with four runs in the seventh to take a 6–3 lead. Pafko's double with the bases loaded sealed the win, although Borowy tried and gave up two runs in the eighth. Grimm, obviously realizing the importance of the win, once again used one of his starters in relief. Prim finished up as the Cubs won 6–5.

It was a heartbreaker for Southworth and the Cardinals, now 2½ out with three to play. "Pafko's hit with the bases loaded. He broke his bat ... he broke his bat," the Cards manager lamented to writers in the locker room. "We never thought we'd lose that one. There's nothing to say. There can't be any comment from a loser," he said dejectedly.

St. Louis came roaring back the next day, roughing up Passeau by a score of 11–6 with Barrett winning his 23rd and completing a 5–0 season against the Cubs. More important, St. Louis was now 1½ games out with four to play.

But the next day, September 27, something happened that symbolized the whole season for both the Cubs and the Cardinals. Chicago completed its mastery of Cincinnati by sweeping a doubleheader at Crosley Field, 3–1 in the first game behind Wyse, who won his 22nd, and 7–4 in the second game with Derringer, who won his 16th. The Cubs finished their season series with Cincinnati with a 21–1 record. Meanwhile, the Cardinals, who had a 16–6 record against the Cubs, lost to Pittsburgh, 5–2. The Cardinals played the Pirates four times in September without a victory. Their inability to handle one of the league's lesser teams killed them again as they fell three games out going into the last weekend of the season.

September 29, 1945, is a momentous day in Cubs history. Chicago went into Pittsburgh right after the Cardinals left and needed one game to clinch the National League pennant. Grimm handed the ball to Borowy, as he had so many times since the Cubs acquired him from the Yankees in July. Borowy pitched well and had a 4–3 lead in the ninth inning when Grimm went to the bullpen to play lefty-righty percentages as Pittsburgh put the tying run on. Chipman, the big lefty, came in and got the second out of the inning as the tying run advanced to third base. Then Jolly Cholly yanked Chipman and called on Erickson to wrap things up.

Erickson, the big blond eccentric who could throw the ball hard but often had trouble finding the plate, made the final out a dramatic one.

Sports writer Warren Brown described what happened as Erickson faced Pirate batter Tommy O'Brien with the championship hanging in the balance:

"It was Paul Erickson, one of the lesser pitching lights, who put the finishing touch to the Pirates ... Borowy went through this decisive game until the last half of the ninth inning, holding a 4–3 lead. When he encountered some trouble, Grimm replaced him with Bob Chipman, a lefthander who served his purpose. Erickson came in to pitch to pinch hitter Tommy O'Brien, while the tying run was on third base.

"Erickson, a very fast righthander, is given to wildness, and poise in the pitching box is something he has not yet acquired. On his first pitch, Erickson's cap started to fall off. He went through with it. If he had paused, he would have committed a balk, permitting a run to score.

The pitch was a blazing strike. That gave Erickson all the confidence he needed. He made up his mind to show O'Brien a pitch that was really fast. He did, too. It was the fastest pitch Erickson had ever thrown, and very nearly the wildest. It went much closer to O'Brien than to the plate, and in his rush to get out of the way, O'Brien's bat flew up and ticked the ball. What should have been a run-scoring wild pitch thus became the second strike."

So Erickson's first two pitches in this clutch situation were very nearly a balk and a wild pitch. Instead, he had an 0-and-2 count on the batter. Brown described what happened next:

"The Cubs were plenty jittery now but there was nothing any of them could do but watch and pray. Erickson was the least disturbed man on the field. He had decided now that he would be a smart pitcher. He would use his curve in this spot and get the game over. No one on the Pirate squad and O'Brien least of all ever expected that Erickson had a curve or that in a spot such as this he would attempt to throw it. It is possible that Erickson's catcher was a little surprised himself. But there was nothing he could do about it. So a curve is what Erickson threw. A very fine curve at that. One which bent briskly and cut through the very heart of the plate for a called third strike that gave the Cubs the pennant."

The least surprised man on the field was Erickson. It wasn't pretty but Lil Abner had come through in the clutch.

The Cubs won 22 games in September and did what champions always do—fight off the charges of the teams trying to overtake them. The season had started with New York and Brooklyn leading the pack. In the end, it was only the Cubs and the Cardinals in the running down the stretch. Brooklyn finished a distant third, 11 games out of first place.

Later on, when Grimm assessed the Cubs' resiliency in the stretch drive, he didn't mention Nicholson coming to life or the clutch hitting of Lowrey and Pafko. He didn't talk of the MVP year of Cavarretta, the prophesized 20-win season for Wyse (22 actually) or the near retirements of Hack and Passeau. Instead, he looked back to the beer party he threw for his team at his farm outside of St. Louis with a month to go in the season. "It was," he said later, "just the tonic the boys needed."

FINAL 1945 NATIONAL LEAGUE STANDINGS

	W-L	Pct.	GB
Chicago	98–56	.636	—
St. Louis	95–59	.616	2.5

	W-L	Pct.	GB
Brooklyn	87–67	.564	11
Pittsburgh	82–72	.532	16
New York	78–74	.513	19
Boston	67–85	.440	30
Cincinnati	61–93	.396	37
Philadelphia	46–108	.298	52

VI

Surprises and Otherwises

"… A manager's job certainly didn't get easier during the war. If anything, wartime performance for managers should get extra credit."

— *Bill James*

Baseball historians look at Borowy's great second-half run as the reason the Cubs won the National League championship, their last championship in the 20th century, much like the trade for pitcher Rick Sutcliffe in 1984 was the catalyst for the division championship when Sutcliffe went 16–1 for the Cubs.

Noted baseball writer Fred Lieb, in his book *The St. Louis Cardinals*, published just after the 1945 season, wrote that Chicago's acquisition of Borowy "unquestionably cost the Cards a fourth straight pennant." Lieb points out that had the Cardinals won it, they would have joined the ranks of the 19th century St. Louis Browns, John McGraw's New York Giants of 1921–1924 and Joe McCarthy's New York Yankees of 1936–1939 as the only teams to have achieved that distinction. (Four years later, Casey Stengel's Yankees began a string of five straight championships, 1949–1953; finished third in 1954; reeled off four more straight championships, 1955–1958; finished third in 1959; then won five more straight championships, 1960–1964.)

The Cardinals, minus Musial, two Coopers and Lanier, still had some pop in the lineup and a formidable pitching staff led by Red Barrett, the man they got in exchange for Mort Cooper. Barrett finished at 21–9 for St. Louis and 23–12 for the year. The Redbirds also had Harry "The Cat" Brecheen, who was 14–4, and Ken Burkhart, later to become a great National League umpire, who was 19–8.

When Borowy beat the Reds 3–2 in his first Cubs start on July 29, it was the ballclub's sixth straight win, finishing off a month when they had winning streaks of 11, 5 and 6 games and, with 26 wins, got more than 26.5 percent of their totals wins in just that one month. It was unreasonable to think they could continue at that kind of pace, and they didn't. They were 18–13 in August and the pesky Cardinals inched closer in the standings.

Borowy arrived in the heat of the pennant race and the heat of a Chicago summer and was the dominant pitcher in the National League for the last two months of the season. Without him, the club would have depended on old-timers Passeau, Derringer, Vandenberg and Prim, at an average age of 38, to back up the steady pitching of Wyse. One indication of Borowy's worth is this: If one were to subtract Borowy's 11–2 mark from the 40–25 record the Cubs had after he joined them, it shows a 29–23 record for the rest of the staff. Perhaps the most telling statistic is this: Borowy made 15 starts that the old-timers would have had to make had he not been there.

Clearly, the Cubs had needed another pitcher to bolster their staff and the acquisition of Borowy gave them the strength they needed down the stretch. But they were a good team even before Borowy came along. The Cubs led the league in hitting (.277 team batting average), pitching (2.98 team earned-run average, 86 complete games) and fielding (.980 fielding percentage with fewest errors committed, 119.) First baseman Cavarretta won the batting title with a .355 average and was voted the league's Most Valuable Player. Young outfielder Andy Pafko was fourth in MVP voting and Borowy and Wyse were fifth and sixth respectively.

The strength of the Cubs starting pitching, particularly in the first half of the season, was a pleasant surprise. Essentially the same staff as on the 1944 fourth-place club, Chicago was in first place when Borowy was acquired on July 27. And while Borowy went 11–2 the rest of the way, it should be noted that the Cubs had four other pitchers in double figures in wins—Wyse at 22–10, Passeau at 17–9, Derringer at 16–11 and Prim at 13–8. Five pitchers in double figures almost always produces a pennant contender.

One of the reasons the Cubs won the pennant was their outstanding record in doubleheaders. They played 34 and won 20 of them while losing only three. They split 10 and in one, they won the first game and the second ended in a tie, called because of darkness. So their overall record in doubleheaders was 51–16–1. Had they lost two more doubleheaders, split four more, or had any combination adding up to four more losses the Cardinals would have prevailed for a fourth straight year.

The high number of doubleheaders underscores the importance that the Cubs' spot starters played. Wyse, Passeau, Derringer and Prim carried the load until Borowy arrived on July 27. But the Cubs played 20 doubleheaders prior to July 27, some on consecutive days. They needed help for their frontliners and they got it. Chipman, Vandenberg and Erickson each won two games when called on to start as the doubleheaders piled up.

April 22 at Pittsburgh (W)
April 29 vs. Pittsburgh (L)
May 6 at St. Louis (L)
May 20 at Brooklyn (W)
May 27 vs. Brooklyn (W-T)
   second game called because of darkness
   with score tied May 30 vs New York (S)
June 3 vs. Boston (S)
June 10 vs. Cincinnati (W)
June 14 at Pittsburgh (L)
June 15 at Cincinnati (W)
June 24 at St. Louis (S)
June 29 at Brooklyn (S)
July 1 at New York (S)
July 4 at Boston (W)
July 6 at Philadelphia (W)
July 8 at Philadelphia (W)
July 12 vs. Boston (S)
July 15 vs. New York (W)

July 18 vs. Brooklyn (S)
July 22 vs Philadelphia (S)
July 29 vs. Cincinnati (W)
August 3 at Cincinnati (W)
August 5 at Cincinnati (W)
August 8 at Boston (W)
August 12 at Philadelphia (W)
August 19 at New York (W)
September 2 at St. Louis (S)
September 3 vs. Cincinnati (W)
September 5 vs. New York (W)
September 9 vs. Boston (W)
September 14 vs. Philadelphia (S)
September 16 vs. Brooklyn (W)
September 27 at Cincinnati (W)
September 29 at Pittsburgh (W)

TOTALS: 51 wins, 16 losses, 1 tie

One of the factors that contributed to the championship was Chicago's domination over several teams, particularly the Cincinnati Reds. The Cubs took 21 of the 22 games they played against each other, losing only on August 5 by a score of 4–3. The Cubs won the season series from Philadelphia 17–5. That's a 38–6 record against two teams, giving them a lot of wiggle room in case other teams gave them any problems. Only the Cardinals did. Chicago won only six games all year against St. Louis—and Borowy won three of those, another indication of the former Yankee's importance to the Cubs championship. Ott's Giants also held their own against Chicago, each team winning 11 of the 22 games.

Cubs against....

Boston	15–7	Philadelphia	17–5
Brooklyn	14–8	Pittsburgh	14–8
Cincinnati	21–1	St. Louis	6–16
New York	11–11	**TOTAL**	**98–56**

What absolutely killed the Cardinals was not the Cubs' acquisition of Borowy but their own inability to consistently beat the worst teams in the National League. The Cardinals finished three games behind the Cubs and probably would have won their fourth straight championship had they done better against the weakest teams in the league. As was noted, the Cardinals handled the Cubs easily, winning 16 and losing 6. They were 16 and 6 against Ott's Giants as well. But whereas the Cubs were 67–21 against Cincinnati, Philadelphia, Pittsburgh and Boston, the Cardinals were 50–38 against those second division clubs. Philadelphia won 46 games all year, one of the worst showings in major league baseball history. Yet nine of those wins came at the expense of the Cardinals, 20 percent of their victory total. Ironically, the Cardinals were able to stay close in the pennant race because of their mastery over the Cubs. A telling moment in the Cardinals' season came on September 27, when, just after having beaten the Cubs in two out of three games to stay in the pennant race, St. Louis lost to Pittsburgh while the Cubs were beating the Reds twice. So the Cardinals lost 1½ games in the standing in one day because of their inability to beat the Pirates, negating the game they gained in the standings with their wins over Chicago.

Cardinals against

Boston	12–10	New York	16–6
Brooklyn	13–9	Philadelphia	13–9
Chicago	16–6	Pittsburgh	12–10
Cincinnati	13–9	**Total**	**95–59**

When the Cubs began to jell in mid-June, Chicago was almost impossible to beat twice in a row. In fact, the Cubs didn't lose two consecutive games any time between June 24 and August 10 and had a 37–12 record during that time. Though Borowy gets well-deserved credit for anchoring the pitching staff in the second half of the season, the record shows that the Cubs were 48–29 in the first half of the season and had an identical record the second half.

When the Cubs won the pennant in 1935 with Grimm at the helm, a 21–game winning streak down the stretch made the difference. In 1945, it was a winning month that made the difference. Without the fabulous July, there would have been no National League pennant flying in Chicago. The Cubs' play that month is one of those phenomena in baseball that is unexplainable except to say that these kinds of things happen in baseball. A team that was five games over .500 for the first three months of the season went 26–6 in July — 26–5 if you consider that their game against Brooklyn was suspended and was completed September 15 with the Cubs losing 12–5. Consider also that this was a team that had been in first place for only two days during the season — and only once, April 29, since opening day. They lost their first game in July, then won 11 in a row. In the midst of that streak, they took over first place on July 8 and never surrendered it. They played eight doubleheaders, winning five and splitting three.

The Cubs in July:

July 1— lost to New York, 7–4
July 1— beat New York, 4–3
July 3 — beat Boston, 24–2
July 4 — beat Boston, 5–3
July 4 — beat Boston, 7–6
July 5 — beat Boston, 3–2
July 6 — beat Philadelphia, 11–3
July 6 — beat Philadelphia, 5–1
July 7 — beat Philadelphia, 3–0
July 8 — beat Philadelphia, 12–6
July 8 — beat Philadelphia, 9–2
July 12 — beat Boston, 6–1
July 12 — lost to Boston, 3–1
July 13 — beat Boston, 2–0
July 14 — beat Boston, 6–5
July 15 — beat New York, 5–3
July 15 — beat New York, 7–2

July 16 — beat New York, 4–3
July 17 — lost to New York, 2–1
July 18 — beat Brooklyn, 5–0
July 18 — lost to Brooklyn, 9–5
July 19 — beat Brooklyn, 3–1
July 20 — lost to Brooklyn, 12–5
    (game suspended due to darkness
    and completed on September 15)
July 21— beat Philadelphia, 5–3
July 22 — beat Philadelphia, 8–5
July 22 — lost to Philadelphia, 11–6
July 24 — beat Philadelphia 8–3
July 26 — beat Cincinnati, 2–1
July 27 — beat Cincinnati, 2–1
July 28 — beat Cincinnati, 8–3
July 29 — beat Cincinnati, 4–1
July 29 — beat Cincinnati, 3–2

One area in which the Cubs did not excel was in one-run games. Modern-day pennant winners are usually dominant in close games, especially with the development of fireballing relief pitchers whose job it is to come into a game in the ninth inning, sometimes only pitching to one batter and "saving" the win for another pitcher. There was no such emphasis in 1945. Starting pitchers took pride in finishing what they started and often found themselves on either side of lopsided scores. The Cubs played 45 one-run games, winning 24 and losing 21.

Grimm got the most out of an aging pitching staff and a nucleus of players with an assortment of physical problems that kept them out of military service. Many of his other players had marginal major league abilities and were on the roster primarily because better players were off at war. Thirteen men who played for the Cubs in 1945 never played another major league game after that: Pitchers Derringer, Vandenberg, Stewart, Comellas, Starr, Warneke, Henessey and Signer; catchers Gillespie and Rice; infielders Schuster and Otero; and outfielder Moore.

Furthermore, not a single member of the 1945 Cubs is in the Baseball Hall of Fame, an oddity for a World Series team. Hank Greenberg and Hal Newhouser of the 1945 Detroit Tigers, the Cubs World Series opponent, are enshrined. Of all the World Series teams in the 1940s, the 1944 St. Louis Browns are the only other team without a future Hall of Famer. Every pennant winner of every succeeding year into the 1990s has at least one Hall of Famer.

Borowy was not the only surprise of 1945. Cavarretta, always considered to be a good ballplayer, had a great year. He led the league in hitting with a .355 average, He had 94 runs batted in and 97 runs scored and would have been over the 100 mark in each of these categories had he not missed 22 games with a separated shoulder. Second baseman Johnson, who had played a full career in the minor leagues before Grimm spotted him and brought him up as a wartime replacement, hit .302, the only time in his career he hit over .300. He also led the league in sacrifice bunts.

Derringer won 16 games, the most he had won since 1940, and gave Grimm 213–plus innings in the last year of his major league career. Prim, another career minor leaguer, played only parts of six seasons in the big leagues, and in three of those he appeared in 14 or fewer games. But the silver-haired lefty, who won only 22 major league games, won 13 of them for Grimm in 1945. Vandenberg, at age 39, was a pleasant surprise in his final big league season. His 6–3 record and steady performances as spot starter and frequent reliever added depth to the pitching staff, something a pennant winner always needs.

Hack, the seemingly ever-smiling third baseman, wasn't smiling much when Jimmy Wilson was the manager. Had Grimm not talked him into coming out of retirement in 1944, he would not have gotten his 2,000th hit a year later or had the opportunity to play in his fourth World Series with the Cubs. Hack, who hit .282 while playing in 98 games in 1944, had one of his best years in 1945 and was a key to the Cubs offensive success. The lead-off hitter got 193 hits and also walked 99 times while compiling a .323 batting average. He scored 110 runs and only struck out 30 times.

Lowrey came up with the Cubs in 1942 but had only one full season in the majors, 1943, before going into the military and missing the entire 1944 season. He hit .283 and was more than just an adequate replacement for Dom Dallasandro, whom he replaced in left field when Dallasandro went into the service. Center fielder Pafko, playing his second full season, blossomed into a star. He hit .298, drove in 110 runs and probably prevented that many runs from scoring during the year with his outstanding defensive play. Pafko had a rifle arm that he said he developed milking cows as a kid. As an adult, he threw out base runners trying to take an extra base — or stopped them from trying just by fielding a ball and cocking his arm.

Becker was not a surprise to Grimm but may have been to the rest of the league. He had been a clutch hitter for Grimm in Milwaukee and the Cubs' manager thought he could do the same in the big leagues, bad feet and all. Pinch-hitting and filling in for Cavarretta, Becker hit .286 — with a slugging percentage of .421 — in 67 games. More important, he came through with several big hits when Cavarretta was out for 22 games in August with a separated shoulder. He had a single, double and triple in his first start after Cavarretta got hurt.

McCullough, who had been the Cubs regular catcher from 1940–43, missed the next two seasons because of the military. In 1945, Grimm carried four catchers on his roster. Mickey Livingston and Dewey Williams shared the majority of the catching duties and filled in well, particularly defensively and in handling pitchers.

The biggest disappointment was clearly Nicholson, who worked in a war plant until mid-April, missed all of spring training and never could get back in the groove that made him one of the National League's most formidable hitters in 1944. The only reason Nicholson wasn't the 1944 MVP was that the writers opted to go with someone who played on a pennant winner, Cardinal shortstop Marty Marion. Nicholson had MVP numbers: 33 home runs, 122 runs batted in, 116 runs scored — all good enough to lead the league. He also hit 35 doubles and had a .287 batting average. In 1945, he slumped to .243 with 28 doubles, just 13 home runs, 88 runs batted in and 82 runs scored. The drop in his numbers alone meant the Cubs had to make up for 22 fewer home runs, 34 fewer runs batted in and 44 points off his batting average. Just as unquestionably as the fact they won the pennant because of Borowy, they won it despite their most powerful hitter having a terrible year. Nicholson, who was color-blind, played several more years in the big leagues but never came close to matching his 1944 numbers. Part of his downfall might have been the return of good pitchers who had been in the service. Part of it might have been the onset of diabetes, which was not discussed much at the time he played, but the effects of which prevented him from playing in the 1950 World Series when he was a member of the Phillies.

There were other disappointments, but none of the magnitude of

Nicholson's year-long slump. Lenny Merullo was the Cubs regular short-stop and was not counted on for anything more spectacular than to be a steady influence in the infield, to keep the clubhouse loose like he always did with his constant banter, and to get a few clutch hits now and then. But Merullo, who had come a long way since the day in 1941 when he made four errors in one game, went into a slump at the end of the year that affected his overall play — so much so, that Grimm benched him for the World Series and started Roy Hughes instead.

"It broke my heart but I understood," Merullo said years later. "I hadn't been playing very well and I had been in kind of a funk. Charlie went with Roy Hughes who was a veteran, a good ballplayer, and a better hitter than I was."

Another setback that, as it turned out, probably hurt the Cubs more in the World Series than in the regular season was the shape Hi Bithorn was in when he returned from the Navy in September of 1945. Bithorn won 18 and lost 12 in 1943 and was one of the rising young stars in the National League when he went into the service. He was discharged on September 5, 1945, but was in no shape to rejoin the ballclub. In fact, Bithorn literally did not look like the same pitcher who had won 18 games just two years earlier. He had been a trim 185 pounds when he left for the service but returned 40 pounds heavier. The extra weight forced him to change his delivery, and the change in delivery took something off his fastball. He wasn't in shape to finish the season and missed the World Series as well. Two years later, he was out of the big leagues. He didn't pitch for the Cubs at all in 1945 and never regained his pre-war form.

Bithorn's rise and fall in the major leagues is a study in triumph and tragedy. In addition to being a good ballplayer growing up in Puerto Rico, he was smart and was mature at a young age. By the time he was 22, he was managing the San Juan Senators in the Puerto Rican Winter League. He was of Spanish and Dutch heritage, so his last name belied the fact that he was a Latino. That, coupled with the fact that he was lighter skinned than people of Latin extraction and had a good command of the English language, helped him advance toward the still-segregated major leagues. Then World War II came and the departure of ballplayers into the military gave him his big chance. But when he returned from the service out of shape and unable to play, it cost him his only opportunity to be in a World Series. On New Year's Day 1952, Bithorn was an innocent bystander caught in the crossfire of a police gunfight in Mexico and was shot to death. He was 35.

By contrast, the Detroit Tigers big righthander, Virgil Trucks, was discharged from the Navy at about the same time as Bithorn. He had maintained his conditioning by pitching for a good military baseball team and was ready to play big league ball when he got out. Trucks started the last regular season game for the Tigers and had a complete game victory against the Cubs in the second game of the World Series. Trucks enjoyed a long career with the Tigers, Philadelphia A's and Chicago White Sox.

Lon Warneke, one of the great Cubs pitchers on their pennant-winning teams of 1932 and 1935, winning 22 and 20 games respectively in those years, tried to help his old ballclub in 1945. He had been retired for a year but came off his Arkansas acreage to try to provide some good innings for his old skipper Grimm. But the zip was gone. Warneke was never able to get back in his old groove. He appeared in nine games, pitched 14 innings and gave up 16 hits, and had a 0–1 record with a 3.86 earned-run average.

In assessing the 1945 Cubs, the contribution of Grimm cannot be overlooked. He is not rated among baseball's greatest managers, not put in the same company as John McGraw, Connie Mack, Casey Stengel and Sparky Anderson. He was more comical than flamboyant, more prone to playing hunches than always going by the book. But the record is clear: He is one of the few managers to win a pennant in his first year, 1932, and his 1935 pennant winner won 21 games in a row. He gave way to Hartnett in 1938 but it was essentially his ballclub that won the pennant that year. And then he had the 1945 winner. Long after 1945, he remained a successful leader. He was Minor League Manager of the Year with Milwaukee in 1951 and took a struggling Braves team and built it into a contender from 1952 into the 1955 season. Grimm was never shy about talking about his successes as a manager but always gave credit to his players.

When he took over the Cubs in 1932, he inherited ballplayers who had little respect for their previous manager, Rogers Hornsby. Grimm got them on track in time to win the National League pennant that year. It took him a year longer, but he accomplished the same thing when he was hired to replace Jimmy Wilson in 1944. Again he took over an unhappy team. Hack retired rather than play another year for Wilson. Grimm managed to put the pieces back together to come up with a championship in 1945. Throughout his career, with few exceptions, everything seemed to come together under Grimm's direction. Owner Wrigley said, "Every time I call on Charlie, we win."

Noted baseball analyst Bill James gives Grimm enormous credit for the Cubs championship in 1945.

First row, from left: Bob Swift, Bob Maier, Al Benton, Arthur Mills (coach), Steve O'Neill (manager), Paul Richards, Hal Newhouser, Frank Overmire. Second row, from left: Rudy York, Roy Cullenbine, Jimmy Outlaw, Hub Walker, Hank Greenberg, Les Mueller, Skeeter Webb, Eddie Mayo. Third row, from left: Walter Wilson, Pat McLaughlin, Joe Orrell, Russell Kerns, Zeb Eaton, Ed Borom, Paul Trout. Fourth row, from left: Joe Hoover, Chuck Hostetler, Art Houtteman, Hack Miller, Dr. Forsyth.

"There is a tendency to automatically discount whatever happened during the war because the game wasn't normal," James wrote in *The Bill James Guide to Baseball Managers from 1870 to Today*.

"While this discount is appropriate for players, a manager's job certainly didn't get easier during the war. If anything, wartime performance for managers should get extra credit.... That kind of baseball is probably a truer test of the manager's skills...."

VII

The American League Pennant Race

"It was a peculiar week. We were fighting for the pennant, only we weren't fighting."

— *Senators manager Ossie Bluege*

The Detroit Tigers narrowly missed an American League championship in 1944, winning 88 games but finishing one game behind the surprising St. Louis Browns, who claimed their first championship. In 1945, the Tigers won one less game but hung on to win the pennant, setting up a rematch of the 1935 World Series when the Tigers beat the Cubs in six games.

Detroit's climb to the championship was remarkable considering the number of good ballplayers who were in the military. Right-handed pitcher Virgil Trucks won 14 games in 1942 and 16 in 1943 before going into the Navy. He missed all of the 1944 season and appeared in only one game in 1945, the last game of the season. Tommy Bridges, another starter, was nearing the end of a long career in which he had won 192 games through 1943 when he went into the service. In a three-year span from 1934 through 1936, Bridges won 66 games for the Tigers. He had a curve ball that had a break like a ball rolling off a table, according to his catcher and manager, Mickey Cochrane, and had two wins against the Cubs in the 1935 World Series. Bridges was in the Army and missed all of 1944 and most of 1945, returning in time to get into just four games. Another pitcher, Fred Hutchinson, came up with the Tigers as a rookie in 1939 and appeared in 30 games in the next two years before joining the Navy. (Hutchinson's first major league appearance was against the Yankees on May 2, 1939 — on the same day and on the same field where Lou Gehrig ended his consecutive game streak at 2,130.) Hutchinson did not return from the service until 1946 and then won 10 or more games in six consecutive seasons.

Birdie Tebbetts had been the Tigers starting catcher for four years and had been with the team for seven when he went into the Navy in 1942 and did not return until 1946. Walter "Hoot" Evers was a promising outfielder who came up briefly in 1941, then went into the Army and did not return to the Tigers until 1946. He then played 12 years in the major leagues and compiled a .278 lifetime batting average. Also in the service were third baseman Pinky Higgins, who played in 148 games in 1944 and hit .297; centerfielder Barney McCosky, who played every game in 1942 and hit .293 and then served in the military the next three years; and Jimmy Bloodworth, the starting second baseman in 1942 and 1943 before he went off to war. Dick Wakefield, an outfielder, hit .315 in 1943, .355 in a partial season in 1944 and spent 1945 in the Navy.

By far the biggest loss to the Tigers was the military service of Hank Greenberg, their tall, powerful outfielder and first baseman who hit 58 home runs in 1938 and had 132 home runs in the three-year span of 1938–1940. Greenberg played part of the 1941 season and then enlisted in the Army Air Corps. He was the first American League player to enlist and rose to the rank of captain before returning with an honorable discharge in July of 1945. Greenberg homered in his first game back, on July 1, and hit a grand-slam home run against the St. Louis Browns in the ninth inning of the last game of the season on September 30 to clinch the pennant for the Tigers.

Historians have long speculated on the potential career statistics of Bob Feller and Ted Williams, two great stars who lost several years of their careers to the military. The same can be said for Greenberg, who hit 331 home runs in his career but missed three full seasons and parts of one other due to the war. He played two more seasons after his return in 1945 and hit 44 and 25 home runs respectively. Had he been able to play a full career, it is reasonable to believe he would have had 500 or more career home runs.

The Tigers were decimated but so were most other teams. Ossie Bluege, manager of the surprising second-place Washington Senators, said, "Your whole team could change overnight." In Detroit, it was up to manager Steve O'Neill to somehow put a competitive team on the field.

O'Neill had two pitchers who could win a lot of games. Lefthander Hal Newhouser won 29 in 1944 and was the American League's most

Hal Newhouser was a moody Hall of Fame pitcher for the Tigers who led the American League in wins in 1944 and 1945. He was knocked out of the first game of the World Series but came back to win two, including the clincher.

valuable player. He coupled that with a 1945 season in which he was 25–9, leading the league in wins, winning percentage, earned-run average, starts, complete games, innings pitched and strike outs, and winning the Most Valuable Player award again—the first pitcher in major league history to achieve that honor. Newhouser was a brash, hard-nosed competitor who sometimes would glare at Detroit fielders who made errors in games he pitched and smashed up clubhouses when things didn't go his way. He was a so-so pitcher until veteran catcher Paul

Richards joined the club and became "Newhouser's catcher." Richards knew how to control Newhouser and keep his mind focused on the game. When he rose from becoming little more than a .500 pitcher to having his back-to-back MVP years, O'Neill wouldn't take credit for the transformation. He attributed it to "control, getting married, control, settling down, control, staying focused and control." A congenital heart defect kept Newhouser out of the military.

The other half of the deluxe tandem was Dizzy Trout, a big, bespectacled righthander who was 20–12 in 1943, 27–14 in 1944 and 18–15 in 1945. Trout finished second, four votes behind Newhouser in the 1944 MVP balloting, and won five games in 15 days for the Tigers as they made their stretch drive in September of 1945.

Hal Newhouser

Year	W–L	Pct.	ERA	G	IP	H	BB	SO	ShO
1944	29–9	.763	2.22	47	312.1	264	102	187	6
1945	25–9	.735	1.81	40	313.1	239	110	212	8

Paul "Dizzy" Trout

Year	W–L	Pct.	ERA	G	IP	H	BB	SO	ShO
1944	27–14	.659	2.12	49	352.1	314	83	144	7
1945	18–15	.545	3.14	41	246.1	252	79	97	4

The rotation also included Al Benton, who returned from the service in time to go 13–8 in 1945. He was a two-time All Star who got off to a 6–1 start but broke his ankle in May and never regained the same effectiveness when he returned, going 7–7 for the remainder of the season. Benton's career spanned so many decades that he is the only pitcher in baseball history to have faced both Babe Ruth and Mickey Mantle. The fourth starter was Frank "Stubby" Overmire, a lefthander who got his nickname from his build, 5 feet 7 inches and 170 pounds. Overmire pitched 10 years in the major leagues and was below .500 in six of them. He was 9–9 in 1945. But O'Neill liked him, kept him in the starting rotation and also gave him a surprise start in the third game of the World Series, ahead of Trout. He didn't win the game, losing 3–0 to Claude Passeau's one-hitter, but his appearance set up the Tiger rotation for the rest of the series.

Bridges, one of the most popular players in Tiger history, was a six-time All Star who had been to the World Series three times with the Tigers. He was discharged from the Army in early September and received a hero's welcome in his first appearance at Briggs Stadium on Labor Day in which he was the winning pitcher. Two other Detroit pitchers had claims to fame. Zeb Eaton appeared in 17 games, 14 of them in relief, and compiled a 4–2 record. Perhaps more important, Eaton hit .250 with eight hits in 32 bats, including two home runs. One of them was a grand-slam homer off Hank Borowy, who was pitching for the Yankees at the time. Two weeks later, Borowy was with the Cubs. Many have speculated that Borowy's gopher ball to Eaton was the blow that convinced Yankee general manager Larry MacPhail to get rid of him. Les Mueller, a righthander who, like Trout, wore glasses, started 18 games and had a 6–8 record. An 18-year-old lefthander who got into five games for Detroit without a win or a loss was Billy Pierce who won 211 games in his major league career, most of them with the Chicago White Sox, who got him in a trade with the Tigers in 1949. Pierce made World Series appearances with the White Sox in 1959 and the San Francisco Giants in 1962.

Dizzy Trout won five games for Detroit in September to help them clinch the pennant but did not start until the fourth game of the World Series.

With Greenberg gone, the best power hitter in the ballclub was Rudy York, a slugger who had been with the ballclub since 1934 and couldn't play anywhere but first base. When Greenberg was active, the Tigers moved him from first base to left field to accommodate York and keep both men in the lineup. York was a four-time All Star who hit 18 home runs in August of 1938, a record for homers in a month that stood for 60 years until Sammy Sosa of the Cubs clubbed 21 in July of 1998.

The Tigers had Jimmy Outlaw at third, a journeyman of average ability who had been an outfielder but was converted to a third baseman when it was necessary to move Greenberg to the outfield. Skeeter Webb played shortstop and also was O'Neill's son-in-law. This gave writers of the era an obvious and oft-used joke, saying O'Neill had both an in-law and an outlaw in his lineup. The in-law hit .199 in 407 at-bats but managed to keep his job as a starter. Eddie Mayo played second base and hit .285 in the pennant year. He was also an outstanding fielder, a team leader, and extremely popular with writers and fans. As a member of the Philadelphia A's in 1943, Mayo was injured when an errant throw went off a runner's shoulder and struck him in the eye. The A's dropped him, Uncle Sam didn't want him and the Tigers, in desperate need of players, picked him up. Mayo had the peculiar habit of ducking after every pitch. He was a left-handed batter and he had a fear of right-handed catchers beaning him when they threw the ball back to the pitcher.

Detroit's outfield was a hodge-podge. Greenberg had been the star. Roger "Doc" Cramer, whose age was estimated at anywhere from 39 to 43, played center field. But he could hit fairly well and covered ground in the outfield adequately and that's all that counted. Another outfielder was Chuck Hostetler, who was recruited for the Tigers from a semi-pro league in 1944 and hit .298 in 90 games as a 40-year-old rookie. He hit just .159 as a reserve in 1945 and his base running gaffe in the sixth game of the World Series was a turning point in the game.

The catching duties were handled by Bob Swift, who gained fame six years later for being behind the plate in 1951 when midget Eddie Gaedel batted for the Browns in a Bill Veeck publicity stunt; and Paul Richards, whose career dated back to 1928 when he played for Wilbert Robinson's Brooklyn Dodgers. He was a successful minor league manager who won two pennants while managing Atlanta and, during that time, was a mentor to Dewey Williams, a catcher on the Cubs. Richards played in the big leagues for Brooklyn, the St. Louis Browns, New York Giants and Philadelphia Athletics as well as the Tigers, who pulled him out of retirement when Birdie Tebbetts went into the service.

Detroit also had Lambert "Dutch" Meyer, who hoped to be Gehringer's successor at second base after trying his hand at the oil business for a few years. Meyer proved to be no competition for Mayo at second. His contribution to sports trivia is actually in football. Meyer was the leading receiver for quarterback Sammy Baugh at Texas Christian University and caught a pass from Baugh in TCU's 3–2 victory over Louisiana State in the 1936 Sugar Bowl game.

Trucks always claimed the best team in baseball wasn't in the majors. It was at Great Lakes Naval Air Station in Glenview, Illinois. The military team was managed by Cochrane, the old Tiger skipper, and had a record of 63–14 in 1942, 52–10 in 1943 and 48–2 in 1944. Pitchers included Trucks, Bob Feller, Schoolboy Rowe, Denny Galehouse and Johnny Rigney. Cochrane did some of the catching, as did the Cubs Clyde McCullough and the man he considered his rival, Walker Cooper of the Cardinals. The Great Lakes team had an infield of Kenny Keltner, Pinky Higgins, Billy Herman and Johnny Mize. Outfielders included McCosky, Wakefield and Gene Woodling.

Like the Cubs, Detroit did not start out the season showing any signs of being spectacular. The war seemed to have taken too big a toll on their roster. The Tigers opened the season with a 7–1 loss to the Browns at Sportsman's Park in St. Louis. Newhouser was the losing pitcher but Mueller made the big news that day by giving up a base hit to Pete Gray, the one-armed outfielder who went one-for-four and did not have a ball hit to him in the field. The Browns' win was their ninth in a row on opening day, a major league record (since tied by the New York Mets of 1975–1983).

The Tigers won six of their first 10 games and made a key transaction at the end of the month. On April 30, they traded two seldom-used reserve players, Dutch Meyer and Don Ross, to Cleveland for veteran outfielder Roy Cullenbine, a switch-hitting outfielder who had bounced around with several teams in his career. Cullenbine had come up with the Tigers in 1938 and set a major league record by scoring five runs in his first big league game. He had the habit of taking a lot of pitches, a trait that did not endear him to one of his general managers, Bill DeWitt of the Browns. DeWitt called him lazy because he never swung at pitches. But Cullenbine's patience had some advantages. He set another major league record by drawing a walk in 22 consecutive games. When he joined the Tigers outfield, he was the best of the bunch without Greenberg. Cullenbine played right field and hit .277 with 18 home runs and 93 runs batted in. He also had 23 assists in an outfield that was otherwise woefully short on defense. Cullenbine led the American League in walks with 112, one of three times in his 10-year career that he topped the 100 mark in bases on balls. After he played for the Browns in 1941, DeWitt shipped him to the Yankees where he played on their 1942 championship team. One of his teammates was Hank Borowy.

On May 9, Newhouser and Benton each pitched shutouts as the Tigers beat the Browns in a doubleheader by scores of 3–0 and 1–0. Four days later, Benton came through with a 2–0 win over the Red Sox on May 13, giving him a 5–0 record and three shutouts, easily the best start

Hank Greenberg was one of the American League's greatest sluggers when he became the first ballplayer to enlist after Pearl Harbor. When he returned home, he hit a home run in his first game back, hit the homer that decided the pennant for the Tigers on the last day of the season and pummelled Cub pitching in the World Series. (Photograph courtesy of Baseball Hall of Fame Library.)

of a season for him in his career. He almost made it six wins and four shutouts but the Senators beat him 1–0 on May 20. But Benton's season and the Tigers' pennant chances were dealt a heavy blow in his next start when a line drive off the bat of Philadelphia's Bobby Estalella shattered his ankle, sidelining him for two months. Mueller replaced him in the rotation.

By June, no American League team was showing dominance over the others, but some were starting to make their move. The Yankees, 7–4 in April, were 16–9 in May to take over the league lead. The Tigers had a 12–9 month and had moved six games over .500 at 19–13, good for second place. The defending champion Browns were 17–16 and in fourth place, a half-game behind Chicago, which had gotten off to one of its best starts in several years. The Tigers surged in June and took over first place on June 8 with a 2–1 victory over the White Sox. They won five in a row between June 6 and June 10, won 20 and lost 11 for the month, and never relinquished the top spot despite one of the most bizarre endings in American League history. One of the teams slowly rising in the standings was Clark Griffith's Washington Senators, a team that finished eighth in 1944 with a 64–90 record but climbed over .500 in June, in fourth place.

On July 1, the first-place Tigers got their superstar back. Greenberg returned to the lineup after four years in the military. UPI described the scene:

"When the big fellow walked to the plate and 47,729 Detroit fans shook the stadium with their cheers, he knew he was 'at home again' in more ways than one. This was the life Hank Greenberg dreamed about when he gave up a $55,000 a year job with the Tigers to become a $21-a-month private in Uncle Sam's army.... The first time up he didn't hit a homer, but before the game was over he rewarded the faithful by sending a whistling liner into the lower left-field stands to give him a round-trip ticket to home."

Greenberg's homer helped Detroit beat Philadelphia in the first game of a doubleheader. Detroit swept the twin bill to open up a 3½-game lead over the Yankees. On July 4, Benton made his first start since recovering from his broken ankle and was the winning pitcher as Detroit beat Boston 5–2 in the second game of a doubleheader sweep over the Red Sox. The Tigers held off the Yankees in July, but by the end of the month the surging Senators climbed into a second-place tie with New York, both teams trailing the Tigers by five games.

Washington's rise was helped in large part by four knuckleball pitchers. Dutch Leonard, 36, was in his 13th big league season but was having his best year since winning 20 games for the Senators in 1939. He would finish this year at 17–7. Leonard had been 14–14 for the eighth place Senators in 1944. Also having a big year, bigger in fact than Leonard's, was Roger Wolff, 34, who would win 20 games and lose 10 in 1945, his only winning season in a seven-year career. In 1944, he was 4–15. Mickey Haefner, 32, was a third starter. He won 16 and lost 14. He pitched eight years in the big leagues and had two winning seasons. Haefner was 12–15 for the '44 Senators. Their fourth knuckleball starter was Johnny Niggeling, 41, who started 25 games and was 7–12 in this, his next-to-last season in the big leagues. Another starter, a non-knuckler, was Marino Pieretti, a rookie who had never thrown a pitch in the big leagues. He compiled a 14–13 record and never won more than eight in five more big league seasons.

The Senators' offense was provided by first baseman Joe Kuhel, who hit 27 home runs for the White Sox in 1940 but managed only two for the Senators in 1945. But he drove in 75 runs and hit .285. Outfielder Buddy Lewis got back from the service in time to hit .333 in 69 games. Veteran outfielder George Case hit .294 and contributed speed to the starting lineup with 30 stolen bases. George Myatt also stole 30. The Senators' speed on the base paths helped them manufacture runs. They played in cavernous Griffith Stadium with its left-field wall 402 feet from home plate. Kuhel hit the only Washington home run there all year — and that was inside the park. Theirs was not a roster destined for the Hall of Fame, but it was good enough to be competitive in wartime. The Senators finished in second place and might have reached the top had it not been for some shenanigans by their eccentric owner Clark Griffith.

They were involved in yet another of major league baseball's opening day oddities. The Senators beat the Philadelphia A's 14–8 — the highest run total they would have all year.

Griffith was the loudest complainer in all of baseball when the Cubs snatched Borowy on waivers from the Yankees. Chicago would never have had the chance had Griffith or any other owner made an offer for him. As it turned out, Washington was about one Borowy short of winning the American League championship. The Senators knuckled opponents to death. By season's end, 60 of their wins would involve a knuckleballing pitcher. Without much fanfare, they began to move up in the standings. On June 1, they were in seventh place, 7½ games out of first. Six weeks later, they were in second place, 2½ games behind Detroit.

The Tigers were unspectacular but steady and Newhouser was the steadiest of all, continually mowing down American League hitters. He lost a 4–0 decision to the Red Sox and Jim Wilson on July 3 but beat the Yankees 3–2 on July 7, lost another tough one to Wilson of Boston 2–1 on July 12, then bested Haefner and the Senators 6–4 on July 18 and was the winner when Detroit crushed Philadelphia 9–1 on July 22. Newhouser beat Johnny Humphries and the White Sox 1–0 on July 27 and was the winner over the Browns, 5–4, on July 31. The most unusual game for the Tigers in July occurred on July 21 when Detroit and Philadelphia battled to a 1–1 tie in 24 innings. Mueller pitched 19⅔ innings, a feat unmatched by any other hurler in major league history for endurance in one ballgame.

The Browns languished at the bottom of the standings most of the year and on August 1 found themselves in seventh place with a 42–45 record, 10 games behind the Tigers. Similar to what the Cubs had done in the National League in July, St. Louis went on a tear in August and put themselves in contention for the American League championship. The Browns were not blessed with great hitting — Milt Byrnes was their "slugger" with eight homers and 59 RBIs — but they managed to get timely hitting and adequate pitching to win 23 games while losing only 12 to vault into third place. Nels Potter, a 19-game winner on the '44 championship team, turned in another good year, his last good year in the big leagues. By year's end, he had won 15 and lost 11. Between August 14 and August 29, the Browns won 15 of 19 games, pulling them to within four games of the Tigers. Washington was in second place, just a game and half behind with a month to play.

Griffith, recognizing that his Senators were bona fide contenders, appealed to the American League to reschedule many of Washington's games from day games to night games. He claimed it was the patriotic thing to do, so that defense workers with daytime jobs could see a ball-game at night. Shirley Povich, longtime sports editor and columnist for the *The Washington Post*, pointed out that Griffith's patriotic gesture might have been spurred by the fact that his knuckleballing pitchers were harder to hit at night.

On August 4, with the Senators chasing the Tigers at the top of the standings, Washington was involved in an unusual doubleheader with the Boston Red Sox. The Senators won the first game 4–0 as rookie Wally Holborow threw a two-hit shutout. It would be the only start of his major league career. In the second game, manager Bluege made two pitching changes that made baseball history. Trailing 6–2 in the fourth inning, Bluege pulled starter Sandy Ullrich and brought in Joe Cleary, who was making his big league debut. Cleary was tagged for three sin-gles and two walks before getting Red Sox pitcher Boo Ferriss on strikes. He then gave up another single, another walk and a double. With the score now 14–2, Bluege summoned Bert Shepard, the old pitcher who had gone into the service and lost a leg when his plane was shot down over Germany. He came back to the States and was fitted with an artificial leg. Griffith signed him pretty much as a goodwill gesture and both he and Bluege probably never envisioned him getting into a ballgame. But with Washington hopelessly behind 14–2 and Bluege not wanting to waste any of his regular pitchers with the pennant race still in the bal-ance, Shepard got the call. He struck out George Metkovich, the first man he faced, and pitched 5⅓ innings, allowing one run on three hits.

"We were fighting for the pennant," Shepard recalled in a 1995 inter-view. "Because of that, even though I hadn't done too bad in exhibition games, they weren't going to use me in regular games. Then comes the

Boston game and we're getting our socks beat off. They had loaded the bases on us with two outs and that's when I got my chance. They brought me in to pitch to Metkovich and I remember running the count to 3 and 2 and saying to myself, 'I can't walk this guy. This is my chance, my time. I can't walk him.' And you know, I struck him out."

Cleary's experience wasn't as pleasant. After Cleary surrendered four singles, three walks and a double in ⅓ of an inning, Senators manager Ossie Bluege didn't mince any words when he yanked him from the game. Onlookers described the conversation this way. Bluege said to Cleary, "Pitcher, my f&#*-ing ass." Cleary replied, "Go f&#* yourself."

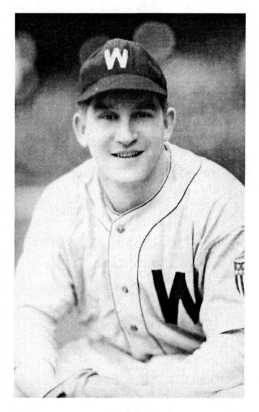

Bert Shepard lost a leg when his plane was shot down in World War II. The Washington Senators signed him as a good-will gesture and he got into one game, striking out the first batter he faced.

Neither Cleary nor Shepard ever pitched again in the majors. Cleary's earned run average for his one appearance: 189.00

There were no great teams in the American League in 1945. The war had taken care of that. The pennant race was more or less survival of the fittest, and the fit became even fitter if they were fortunate enough to have ballplayers discharged from the armed services. For most of the season, Detroit had to rely on Newhouser and Trout. In 1944, their 56 wins between them represented 64 percent of the team's 88 wins. In 1945, the two hurlers, winning 43 between them, accounted for just under half of the Tigers' 87 wins. Benton and Overmire rounded out the starting rotation. Detroit went after some pitching help for the stretch drive and got two veterans— George Caster from the Browns and Jim Tobin from the Boston Braves.

They picked up Caster on waivers on August 8. He was a relief pitcher who was prone to temper tantrums when things didn't go his way. On June 20, in a game against the White Sox, Caster blew up when Browns manager Luke Sewell came out to take him out of a game. Instead of handing the ball to his manager, Caster turned and fired it into the White Sox dugout. Chicago players reacted by charging the mound and several minutes went by before order was restored.

Tobin was a pitcher who had a no-hitter to his credit and he could also hit. He once hit three home runs in a game. The pitching staff was further strengthened when Bridges got out of the service and joined the club on August 30.

Trout was 13–13 going into September, well off his 1944 numbers. But O'Neill had confidence in him and the big righthander rose to the occasion. He won five straight between September 1 and September 15, including two shutouts, before being roughed up in his last two starts of the year. Meanwhile, Newhouser won five of six starts, losing only a 3–2 decision to the Senators on September 16. Three of his wins were shutouts.

In this zany season, Griffith, the colorful, controversial owner of the Senators— always looking for ways to make an extra buck — had used his influence to have his team's season end a week ahead of the rest of the league so that he could rent out Griffith Stadium to the Washington Redskins pro football team. The Senators ended their year in Philadelphia on September 23, losing to the A's 4–3 in 12 innings. Potter of St. Louis shut out the Tigers 3–0. At the end of the day — and the end of the Senators' season, Detroit held only a one-game lead. The pennant would be decided entirely by how the Tigers played in the final week of the season.

Washington's last game was a strange one. The Senators led the A's 3–0 in the eighth inning in the first game of a scheduled doubleheader. Philadelphia's Mayo Smith hit a routine fly to Buddy Lewis in right field. Lewis caught the ball but in flipping it back to the infield his arm hit his pant leg and he dropped the ball. Second base umpire Ed Rommel only saw the ball drop from Lewis' hand and ruled it in play. The A's rallied to score three unearned runs to tie the game. The game went into the 12th inning still tied 3–3. With Masterson pitching his fifth inning in relief without allowing a hit, light-hitting Ernie Kish came to bat for the A's with two out and nobody on. Kish lifted a routine fly ball to right fielder George Binkowski — "Bingo Binks," as he was called. Binks, who claimed to be partially deaf and often ran into his own teammates because he couldn't hear them calling for a ball, had nobody near him on this play. He had no sunglasses either. As Binkowski squinted in a desperate attempt to see the ball in the bright sunlight, it fell a few feet from him for a double. A moment later, George Kell singled in the winning run.

The Senators' improbable season was over. Detroit had four games left, two against Cleveland and two against St. Louis. They needed to split the four games to clinch the pennant. As Cramer said, "If we can't do that, we don't deserve it." Meanwhile, the Senators could only await the outcome of each of the games.

"It was a peculiar week," said Bluege. "We were fighting for the pennant, only we weren't fighting." He held a team workout Monday at Griffith Stadium, although additional seating for football had shrunk the field considerably.

The suspense grew as the Tigers were idle on Monday, September 24, and were rained out of a Tuesday game with the Indians. On Wednesday, September 26, they won the first game of a doubleheader 11–0 behind Newhouser to clinch a tie. They could win it all with a second game win. O'Neill sent out Benton, who had been knocked out in his previous 11 starts. He threw the best game since his return in July and took a one-hitter and a 2–0 lead into the sixth inning. But Cleveland scored three quick runs on a rally aided by Benton dropping a throw while covering first base. He didn't get out of the inning. Caster came on and put out the fire but it was too late. Cleveland beat Detroit 3–2, keeping the pennant race alive. Meanwhile, the Senators could only wait and listen for the results of Tigers games.

On Thursday, an off day, O'Neill got word that Trucks had been discharged from the Navy in Norman, Oklahoma. He called him and told him to take the first train to St. Louis — because he was pitching Saturday. Meanwhile, Griffith and Bluege were being as creative as possible to keep the Senators sharp. The Boston Red Sox had an off day and Griffith talked Boston management into having the Red Sox play an exhibition game against the Senators at a ballpark in Bainbridge, Massachusetts. The Red Sox were out of the pennant race, the season was nearly over, and Red Sox players were surely not anxious to play an extra game. In Griffith's talks with Red Sox ownership, it is not recorded how much money exchanged hands in order for the game to be played. But Boo Ferriss, Boston's best pitcher at 21–10, took the mound for the Red

Sox. Roger Wolff beat him 2–1 in what was better-than-the-average exhibition game.

Detroit also had a day off Friday. Trucks arrived in St. Louis and worked out with veteran catcher Richards. The Senators played the Bainbridge Commodore minor league team. Bainbridge started Ken Raffensberger, who had considerable major league experience. The Senators went with knuckleballing Leonard and won 2–0.

In St. Louis, Saturday's game against the Browns, the one Trucks was scheduled to start, was rained out. So the pennant race came down to a doubleheader against St. Louis on Sunday, September 30. The Tigers, at 87–65, had a one-game lead over the Senators. They needed one win to clinch the pennant. When the players arrived at the park, there was some question as to whether the games would even be played as St. Louis experienced its 10th straight day of rain. But too much was at stake. The owners, managers, coaches, players and fans waited for a hint of sunshine. It came about an hour after the scheduled starting time.

O'Neill, who was used to playing hunches with his patchwork ballclub all year, decided to start Trucks. It was more of a gamble than starting him on Saturday, his original plan, because if Trucks faltered on Saturday, he could always come back with Newhouser on Sunday. But the rainout Saturday changed everything. Thinking ahead, O'Neill wanted to use Newhouser in a playoff if there was one. So he went with Trucks and planned to use Trout in the second game. That would leave Newhouser fresh for a playoff game if there was one or ready to be the opening game pitcher in the World Series.

How much of a gamble was it? Though he had pitched regularly while in the Navy, Trucks hadn't pitched professionally since 1943. And now his manager put him on the mound with the American League championship at stake.

Meanwhile, Bluege sent three pitchers— Haefner, Wolff and Walt Masterson — along with catcher Rick Ferrell to Detroit so they would be fresh and rested in case there was a playoff. They listened to the radio from their rooms at the Book-Cadillac hotel as the Tigers and Browns took the field in St. Louis.

Trucks did well and made it into the sixth inning with a 2–1 lead. O'Neill didn't want to press his luck so he brought in Newhouser to finish off the Browns, and the move almost backfired. Making his fourth relief appearance of the year, Newhouser gave up a run in the seventh and another in the eighth to give St. Louis a 3–2 lead.

As the tension mounted, O'Neill still had to think ahead to tomorrow while trying to squeeze out a victory on this day. Should the Browns hold on to win, he could start Trout in the second game and have Benton or Overmire come in if Trout got in trouble. He had lost his last two starts. Then if there was a playoff on Monday, he could come back with Newhouser or Benton or Overmire, whoever had pitched the least on Sunday. There was no good scenario on Monday. The solution was to win on Sunday.

In the top of the ninth inning, Hub Walker batted for Newhouser and singled. Webb laid down a bunt along the first base line. Browns first baseman George McQueen picked up the ball, whirled and threw to second for the force out but Walker beat the throw. The Tigers had the tying and winning runs on with nobody out. Red Borom ran for Walker. Potter, the Browns' ace who had started and was still on the mound, walked Cramer intentionally — a strange move since it put the tying and winning runs in scoring position. But it also set up a force at any base with Greenberg, who was slow afoot, coming to the plate. Greenberg ended the suspense when he lined a home run into the left-field seats, clearing the bases and giving Detroit a 6–3 lead. There were handshakes all around when Greenberg crossed the plate, except for Borom, who kissed him on the cheek.

Benton, who came in to pitch the bottom of the ninth, like Newhouser was making only his fourth relief appearance of the year. He pitched a scoreless half inning to seal the championship for Detroit, which wound up with the lowest winning percentage, .575, of any American League pennant-winning team.

When the final out was recorded, fans listening to the game in the Telenews Theater in Detroit erupted with joy, so much so that theater management put on a recording of the Star Spangled Banner to calm them down. The Cubs, who had clinched the National League championship the day before, heard the news in Pittsburgh and were not unhappy. They didn't care who they played, but Briggs Stadium had more seats than Griffith Stadium, and that meant more money for the players

The acquisition of Cullenbine in April proved huge for the Tigers. He played in 154 games, led the league in walks with 113 and was second in home runs with 18. He was experienced and he brought leadership to the clubhouse and a steadying influence to the field. Also, he solidified the defense in the Tigers' outfield. York also contributed greatly, a fact that was often overlooked at the time because the big first baseman had trouble winning the hearts of Tigers fans. After his feat of hitting 18 home runs in one month (August of 1938), some fans seemed to want nothing less and booed him more than they did any other Detroit player of his era. O'Neill felt sorry for York. "I've never seen anything like it," he said. "No matter what he says or doesn't say, he had to be distressed by it." York hit 18 home runs and drove in 87 while playing in 155 games in 1945.

The contributions of Newhouser and Greenberg can't be underestimated. Newhouser led the American League in wins (25), winning percentage (.735), strikeouts (212) and earned-run average (1.81). He was the second player in major league history to win consecutive Most Valuable Player awards. Slugger Jimmie Foxx had done it in 1932 and 1933. Greenberg played only half a season so his overall numbers were not great — .311 batting average, 13 home runs and 60 runs batted in. But he was the best Tiger at getting the big hit, as evidenced by his homer in his first game back from the service on July 1 and his ninth-inning, grand-slam, pennant-winning blast against the Browns on September 30.

With this most unusual last week of this most unusual season, the Tigers now had to take on the Cubs in what was destined to be a most unusual World Series.

FINAL AMERICAN LEAGUE STANDINGS

Team	W — L	Team	W — L
Detroit	88–65	Cleveland	73–72
Washington	87–67	Chicago	71–78
St. Louis	81–70	Boston	71–83
New York	81–71	Philadelphia	52–98

It is worth noting that, just as in the case of the Cubs, where Charlie Grimm deserves credit for making the best of a bad situation, Tigers manager Steve O'Neill took what he had to work with and came out a winner. Like Grimm, O'Neill's name is not mentioned in essays and conversations naming baseball's best managers, but in 14 years as a major league manager, he never had a losing season. He took over as manager of the Cleveland Indians in 1935 and managed them through the 1937 season, finishing third, fifth, and fourth. Detroit hired him in 1943 and he stayed six years, finishing fifth in his first and last seasons there and second three times as well as the first-place finish in 1945. In 1950, he replaced an ailing Joe McCarthy with the Boston Red Sox, who were floundering with a 32–30 record. Under O'Neill, they went 62–30 the rest of the way to finish third and then finished third the following year as well. Then it was on to Philadelphia where O'Neill's Phillie ballclubs finished fourth, fourth and were in fourth place when he stepped down midway in the 1954 season. All of that adds up to 14 seasons with four different teams, with one first-place finish, three second places, three third places, four fourth-place finishes and three fifth-place finishes. Only 15 managers have a higher winning percentage than O'Neill's (.559). Of the 15, 10 are in the Hall of Fame and one is Bobby Cox of Atlanta, who is still active.

Stephen Francis O'Neill

Born July 6, 1891, in Minooka, Pennsylvania; died January 26, 1962, in Cleveland, Ohio; Managerial record: Cleveland Indians 1935–1937; Detroit Tigers 1943–1948; Boston Red Sox 1950–1951; Philadelphia Phillies 1952–1952

Year	Team	W–L	Pct.	Standing
1935	Cleve	36–23	.610	Third (a)
1936	Cleve	80–74	.519	Fifth
1937	Cleve	83–79	.539	Fourth
1943	Detroit	78–76	.506	Fifth
1944	Detroit	88–66	.571	Second
1945	Detroit	88–65	.575	First
1946	Detroit	92–62	.597	Second
1947	Detroit	85–69	.552	Second
1948	Detroit	78–76	.506	Fifth
1950	Bos (A)	62–30	.674	Third (b)
1951	Bos	87–67	.565	Third
1952	Phil (N)	59–32	.648	Fourth (c)
1953	Phil	83–71	.539	Third
1954	Phil	40–37	.519	Third (d)
14 years		1039–819	.559	

(a) Took over Cleveland team in fifth place; finished third
(b) Took over Boston team in fourth place; finished third
(c) Took over Philadelphia team in sixth place; finished fourth
(d) Left Philadelphia team in third place; it finished fourth

WORLD SERIES

Year	Team	W–L
1945	Detroit	4–3

VIII

The World Series

"We shoulda took 'em; we shoulda took 'em."
— *Hank Borowy*

In the fall of 1945, Firestone stores in Detroit offered motor tune-up specials for $4 and brake maintenance for $1.19. The new 1946 Pontiacs were on display in the General Motors building lobby. Pringle's Furniture Company was advertising its "Post-War Furniture Show." Hugh Connelly & Son Jewelers was offering solid gold mountings for $16.50. World War I flying ace Eddie Rickenbacker, now president of Eastern Airlines, was to address the Detroit Economic Club. And of course there were the Tigers, champions of the American League, who were to take on the Chicago Cubs in the World Series.

Frederick Lieb, the great baseball writer and historian, captured the mood of the nation and set the scene for the World Series in a magnificent piece he wrote for *The Sporting News* published in the October 4, 1945 edition. (The article refers to the series "scheduled to open October 3" because, like many publications, *The Sporting News* was actually printed and distributed a few days before its official publication date.)

"Happy days are here again with the nation adjusting itself to peacetime living and the first World's Series since 1941 to be played in near-normal conditions, scheduled to open at Briggs Stadium October 3, with those two old blue-ribbon rivals, the Tigers of Detroit and the Cubs of Chicago, again snarling, gnashing and clawing at each other in the same cage.

"Three World's Series rolled by while the nation was engaged in the greatest of all wars, two Cardinal-Yankee affairs and the all-St. Louis battle of 1944. While interest held up amazingly well and receipts and attendance for single games were established in 1942 and 1943 at Yankee Stadium, no one forgot, even for a moment, the bigger show on alien fields thousands of miles away.

"While Uncle Sam accepted his war World's Series as a diversion for workers at home and fighting nephews and nieces overseas, he is again ready to munch peanuts in his bleacher seat and give the 1945 Series his full and undivided attention. A happy thought is that men still overseas will listen to the Series returns from victory barracks in Berlin and Tokyo rather than from foxholes and jungle swamps...."

While Lieb patriotically set the scene, the Cubs and Tigers were still working their way through wartime adjustments. For one thing, the home-road World Series travel schedule had been altered from the traditional two-three-two home-and-away schedule to three-four to lessen train travel, save fuel and free up trains to transport returning servicemen home. The series, which started in the home park of the American and National league champions in alternate years, was to start in Detroit this year. While typically the home team for the first two games had the potential for playing four home games— the first and second games and the sixth and seventh — this year the "home field" advantage would swing to the other side with four consecutive games, the last four, to be played at Wrigley Field in Chicago if the series went that long.

Stripped of the romanticism of being the first post-war World Series, it was, like the season that led to it, a series featuring many athletes whose best days were behind them, men who had been pulled from retirement to fill holes in rosters and men who bore some type of illness, weakness or deformity that kept them at home.

A comment attributed to Chicago sports writer Warren Brown provided perspective far different than the red-white-and-blue mosaic painted by Lieb in *The Sporting News*. Speaking of the Cubs and Tigers, Brown said, "I've seen them both play. I don't think either team can win."

It was to be a wacky series in many ways and the Cubs got an inkling of the crazy days ahead when they arrived in Detroit for the first three games. Hotels had been overbooked so that there was no room to accommodate all of the Cubs players and personnel and their wives. Nine players and their spouses were dispatched to a steamship docked in the Detroit River where arrangements had been made for them to stay in cabins that were hardly the equivalent of spacious, comfortable hotel rooms. Bill Nicholson and Len Merullo and their wives refused to stay on the boat and instead, went to the Book-Cadillac Hotel where the other players and wives were staying, demanded the same accommodations that the other players and spouses were receiving, and vowed to take up residence in the lobby until they received it. Rooms were found for them.

The Sporting News gave a pre-series breakdown of both ballclubs, position by position.

First base: Advantage, Chicago. Phil Cavarretta had a batting average 90 points higher than Detroit's Rudy York.

Second base: Advantage, Detroit. Eddie Mayo was considered the Tigers' "pepperpot" and was considered a team leader, giving him a slight edge over Chicago's Don Johnson, who hit .302 and had his best year in the major leagues.

Shortstop: A draw. Skeeter Webb, manager Steve O'Neill's son-in-law, hit .199. Chicago's Len Merullo had been erratic both at the plate and in the field. His replacement, Roy Hughes, had played most of his career at second base.

Third base: Advantage, Chicago: Stan Hack was still considered one of baseball's stars and got his 2,000th big league hit in August. Detroit's third baseman, Jimmy Outlaw, was adequate but was no comparison to Hack.

Left field: Advantage, Detroit: Chicago had speedster Peanuts Lowrey. Detroit had future Hall of Famer Hank Greenberg, regaining his old, powerful form since returning from the service in July.

Center field: Advantage, Chicago: Andy Pafko was 24, a good hitter and a great fielder with one of baseball's best arms. Detroit's Roger Cramer was 39, and while still a solid ballplayer, he could no longer match the skills that Pafko possessed.

Right field: Advantage, Detroit: Nobody would have predicted this at the start of the year, because Chicago's Bill Nicholson was coming off a 1944 season in which he led the league in home runs and RBIs. But he suffered through a season-long slump in 1945 in which he hit only 13 home runs while Detroit's Roy Cullenbine was, if not great, steady most of the year.

Catcher: Advantage, Detroit: The Tigers had a veteran, Paul Richards, who was Hal Newhouser's regular catcher and was considered one of the smartest players in the game in terms of baseball savvy. The backup was Bob Swift. The Cubs had the unusual situation of having five catchers — Mickey Livingston, Dewey Williams, Len Rice, Paul Gillespie and, just home from the service, Clyde McCullough. Richards' presence was enough to give the edge to the Tigers.

Pitching: Advantage, Chicago: The Cubs had a starting rotation of

Hank Borowy and Hank Wyse — both 20 game winners — veteran Claude Passeau and lefty Ray Prim, who had his best year in the majors. They also had Paul Derringer, an aging veteran with World Series experience. Paul Erickson, the hero of the pennant-clinching game, Hy Vandenberg and Bob Chipman were mainstays of a deep bullpen. Detroit had Newhouser and Paul "Dizzy" Trout, who had not been consistent; Virgil Trucks, who was young and had been in the service most of the year; Al Benton, who had been hurt for two months during the season; Tommy Bridges, an aging hero of the past; and Stubby Overmire, a veteran lefty.

As the Cubs prepared to take the field at Briggs Stadium in Detroit, their owner, Phil Wrigley, was back in Chicago trying work out problems caused by scalpers of game tickets being sold for the upcoming games in Chicago. Wrigley spoke to the fans through an advertisement he placed in the *Chicago Tribune.*

Under the headline "We're Burned Up, Too," Wrigley wrote:

"The Cubs went to a lot of trouble and extra expense to engage outside office space and a large force of bank tellers and clerks to try and do an extra good job of distributing evenly and fairly the comparatively limited supply of World Series tickets, the sale of which, because the proceeds of which go into a special account of the Commissioner of Baseball, have to balance out to the penny; to say nothing of settling up with Uncle Sam for the exact tax on the printed price on each ticket.

"However, once the tickets are in the hands of the public, there is nothing to prevent individuals from selling their seats at a neat profit through scalpers.

"Unfortunately, there are always a few people who prefer a quick profit to anything else. We all know this to be true, but as we said to start with — we still do not like it."

—CHICAGO NATIONAL LEAGUE BALLCLUB

Oddsmakers made the Cubs 7–5 favorites to win the World Series and had them 2½ to 1 to win the first game. Grimm had originally thought of starting either Passeau or Wyse in the opener, hoping to give Borowy an extra day or two of rest. But with the weather forecast for Detroit being wet and cold, Grimm decided to give the extra rest to Passeau, whose tired arm often ached more than usual in that kind of weather. So Borowy got the nod for the opener as Grimm chose to lead with his ace. Borowy, who had a 21–7 combined record with the Yankees and Chicago — 10–5 with New York, 11–2 with the Cubs — had experience pitching against Detroit. He was 11–3 lifetime against Detroit. In 1945, before coming over to Chicago, Borowy was 2–0 in three starts against the Tigers while a member of the Yankees, including a 7–3 victory on May 11 when the losing pitcher was Newhouser. On July 8, Borowy was the winner and Trout the loser in an 8–6 Yankee victory. A week later, Borowy didn't get the decision in a 5–4 Yankee win over the Tigers—the game in which he gave up the home run to Detroit relief pitcher Zeb Eaton that Borowy thought might have led to general manager MacPhail unloading him.

The pitching rotations were such that if the series went seven games, Newhouser and Borowy might clash three times, although the travel schedule, with just one day off between games six and seven, meant that O'Neill and Grimm would have to juggle their regular rotations or that pitchers like Borowy and Newhouser would have to pitch without their usual rest.

The Cubs had a scare before the series started. Second baseman Johnson injured his neck in a freak play in Cincinnati on September 27. In the seventh inning of the first game of a crucial doubleheader, with the National League pennant still at stake, Johnson leaped to try to catch a line drive and collided with second base umpire Babe Pinelli, who was not hurt. He went to a Cincinnati hospital where he was diagnosed as having a sprained neck, but he was able to play in the World Series.

As the series opened, an indication of the age of the respective teams could be found in a look at their respective bullpens. For the Cubs, there was Warneke, who was a non-factor in the Cubs pennant run in 1945 but had won two games in the 1935 World Series against the Tigers— the only two games the Cubs won — including a 3–0 opening game shutout. In the Detroit bullpen, Bridges sat and awaited the call to come in. Bridges won two games for the Tigers in that same 1935 World Series. Both had been outstanding pitchers in their day but were now relegated to roles of "experienced veterans" and "guys who have been there" because their days of making a difference were behind them.

GAME ONE, OCTOBER 3, BRIGGS STADIUM, DETROIT

As predicted, Detroit was cold and damp as the series started on Wednesday, October 3, featuring the classic match-up of Borowy and Newhouser. But the classic match-up didn't last long. In the first inning, Hack led off the game and grounded weakly to Jimmy Outlaw at third, who threw him out easily. Johnson also hit a dribbler but it made it into center field for a single. When Johnson stole second, his spikes clipped second baseman Mayo on his fingers. The game was held up while trainers administered to Mayo, who stayed in the game. After Lowrey flied out to Cramer in center field, Cavarretta hit a slow roller to Mayo at second and beat it out for a base hit, Johnson taking third on the play. When Richards, the Tigers' catcher, let a Newhouser pitch get by him for a passed ball, Johnson scored. So Newhouser was behind 1–0, having given up a ground ball single up the middle and an infield hit and having been victimized by a stolen base and a passed ball. The Tigers intentionally walked Pafko to get to Nicholson, who had just come off one of the worst years of his career. Nicholson tripled off the right-field wall, scoring Cavarretta and Pafko. Then Livingston, the Cubs' catcher, delivered a base hit, scoring Nicholson. The inning ended when Richards threw out Livingston trying to steal. The Cubs had four runs on four hits before the Tigers even came to bat.

Detroit might have had a chance to get most or all of it back in the bottom of the first, but a double play killed the rally and saved Borowy from having a similar nightmare to Newhouser's in the top half of the inning. Staked to a 4–0 lead, Borowy gave up a lead-off single to Webb and a single also to Mayo. Cramer then hit a ground ball to shortstop Hughes, who turned it into a 6–4–3 twin killing as Webb went to third. Borowy got back into trouble by walking Greenberg and Cullenbine to load the bases and put the tying run at the plate with Rudy York. But York fouled out to Cavarretta to end the inning.

Neither team scored in the second. In the third inning, the Cubs hit Newhouser hard. Johnson doubled. Lowrey laid down a sacrifice bunt, moving Johnson over to third. Then Cavarretta singled, scoring Johnson, and Pafko doubled, scoring Cavarretta. Nicholson popped out but Livingston, one of the surprise hitters in the series, delivered his second straight single, scoring Pafko and sending Newhouser to the showers down 7–0. As Prince Hal made his way to the clubhouse, he took a baseball bat and angrily smashed light bulbs along the way. Benton came in to pitch for the Tigers and the inning ended when, for the second straight time, Richards threw out Livingston trying to steal.

Benton and Jim Tobin held the Cubs in check for the next three innings. Cavarretta homered in the seventh — it would be the Cubs only home run of the series — and Chicago picked up another run in the same inning when Pafko singled, went to second and third on a stolen base and passed ball, and scored on Nicholson's single.

Borowy, shakey at the start but helped by two double plays, threw a six-hit shutout as the Cubs won 9–0.

In the locker room after the game, O'Neill said, "We'll be better tomorrow — I hope. Chicago deserved to win. I don't think there was any question about that. And you can't blame any one man or play when the score is 9–0. They hit the ball with men on, and we didn't. That was most of the difference.

"I do think they got some breaks, however. That passed ball with two out in the first inning that started them to four runs—that hurt. Then they had a few cheap hits sprinkled in."

O'Neill got his first look at Pafko, the Cubs young outfielder, and was impressed by what he saw. "Pafko made the greatest play of the game when he picked up Greenberg's drive in the fifth and caught Mayo at third with that great throw to Hack. Why, that ball was 30 feet to his left. He had to run to his left, grab it, turn and throw. That was the big play."

Greenberg, the Detroit slugger who was walked and hit with a pitch, seemed amused by the clamoring of all the media in the Tigers' clubhouse. "If we have this many experts in here when we lose, what will it be when we win?" he asked.

Newhouser told reporters, "I had plenty of stuff and my control was all right, too. If only I could have gotten past that first inning, things would have been different."

Over on the Cubs' side, Borowy, pitching in his third World Series, seemed relieved that he had gotten through the game unscathed. "For five innings, I just couldn't seem to get my arm loose. I never did stay warm and my arm never really was loose," he said.

Box Score

Chicago	AB	R	H	Detroit	AB	R	H
Hack 3b	5	0	1	Webb ss	4	0	1
Johnson 2b	5	2	2	McHale (d)	1	0	0
Lowrey lf	4	0	0	Mayo 2b	4	0	2
Cavarretta 1b	4	3	3	Cramer cf	3	0	0
Pafko cf	4	3	3	Greenberg lf	2	0	1
Nicholson rf	4	1	2	Cullenbine rf	3	0	0
Livingston c	4	0	2	York 1b	3	0	1
Hughes ss	3	0	0	Outlaw 3b	3	0	1
Borowy p	3	0	0	Richards c	2	0	0
Totals	36	9	13	Hostetler (b)	1	0	0
				Newhouser p	1	0	0
				Benton p	1	0	0
				Eaton (a)	1	0	0
				Tobin p	1	0	0
				Mueller p	0	0	0
				Borom (c)	1	0	0
				Totals	31	0	6

```
Chicago    4 0 3 0 0 0 2 0 0 — 9  13  0
Detroit    0 0 0 0 0 0 0 0 0 — 0   6  0
```

(a) struck out for Benton in fourth; (b) grounded out for Richards in ninth; (c) grounded out for Mueller in ninth; (d) flied out for Webb in ninth.

Doubles— Johnson, Pafko. Triple — Nicholson. Home run — Cavarretta. Sacrifices— Lowrey, Borowy. Runs batted in — Nicholson 3; Livingston, Pafko, Cavarretta 2. Stolen bases— Johnson, Pafko. Double plays— Hughes, Johnson and Cavarretta; Johnson, Hughes and Cavarretta.

	IP	H	R	BB	SO
Borowy	9	6	0	5	4 (winner)
Newhouser	2.2	8	7	1	3 (loser)
Tobin	3	4	2	1	1
Mueller	2	0	0	1	1
Benton	1.1	1	0	0	1

Hit by pitcher— by Borowy (Greenberg). Passed balls— Richards 2. Left on base — Detroit 10; Chicago 5. Umpires— Bill Summers (AL), Lou Jorda (NL), Art Passerella (AL), Jocko Conlan (NL). Time — 2:30. Attendance — 54,637.

GAME 2, OCTOBER 4, BRIGGS STADIUM, DETROIT

The second game matched Hank Wyse, the Cubs 22-game winner, against Virgil Trucks for the Tigers, who had only been out of the Navy for about a week. Trucks had pitched in one game and pitched only 5⅓ innings since being out of the service. O'Neill could have gone with Dizzy Trout, his 18-game winner, but Trout had been inconsistent in late September and Trucks, if nothing else, was a fresh arm. If Detroit could win the second game, the series would be even and O'Neill still had Trout ready to go. If Detroit fell behind two games to none, O'Neill could come back with Trout and then Newhouser to try to even the series.

Unfortunately for Detroit, the second game started much as the first game had, with a scratch hit. Hack led off the game with a ground ball to deep short that Webb fielded cleanly but could not make the throw in time. Johnson, who led the National League in sacrifice bunts during the regular season, laid down another good one, putting Hack in scoring position. Then Lowrey singled to left. Greenberg fielded the ball and threw out Hack trying to score. Cavarretta grounded out to York to end the inning.

The game remained scoreless until the fourth inning when one of the many daffy fielding plays in the series occurred. Cavarretta hit a lazy fly ball into right center field. Cramer and Cullenbine both gave chase and both watched as the ball dropped between them. Cavarretta got a double out of it and scored on a Nicholson single to right, giving the Cubs a 1–0 lead.

Virgil Trucks came out of the military in time to start the last game of the season for the Tigers and then started two games in the World Series. (Photograph courtesy of Baseball Hall of Fame Library).

In the bottom of the fifth inning, Wyse retired the first two bat-ters— Richards on a deep fly that Lowrey caught in left field and Trucks on a ground ball to Johnson at second. After that, Webb singled to left and Mayo walked. Cramer singled to left, scoring Webb and moving Mayo around to third. Wyse, pitching carefully to Greenberg, had the count at one-and-one when he threw him a curve ball. Chicago sportswriter Warren Brown wrote that Greenberg got a curve but he hit it straight — into the left field stands, giving the Tigers a 4–1 lead that turned out to be the final score.

The Greenberg homer was a momentum builder. John Drebinger, writing in *The New York Times,* said, "It was a clout that provided the first occasion for genuine rejoicing by the folks in this American League bailiwick, and it was a full-throated roar that welled up from the arena as the 34-year-old veteran jogged around the bases behind two of his colleagues."

For Wyse, it was a crushing blow. The

Hank Wyse threw one bad pitch in the second game of the World Series, Hank Greenberg hit it for a three-run homer and Wyse was relegated to the bullpen for the rest of the series.

Cubs seemed on their way to winning their second straight series game. The Tigers had been held scoreless for the first 13 innings and, as it turned out, did not score after the Greenberg blast. In fact, the Tigers had scored in only one inning in the first two games and yet were tied with the Cubs, one game apiece. Prior to the game, Wyse told sports writers, "I think I know how to pitch to Hank. I watched every pitch Borowy threw yesterday and he knows these boys better than anyone."

The Greenberg homer changed the dynamics of the World Series — and of the Cubs pitching plans. Whether Wyse lost confidence in himself or Grimm lost confidence in him, the fact is he didn't start another game and pitched only 1⅔ innings in two relief appearances.

Box Score

Chicago	AB	R	H	Detroit	AB	R	H
Hack 3b	3	0	3	Webb ss	4	1	2
Johnson 2b	3	0	0	Mayo 2b	3	1	0
Lowrey lf	4	0	2	Cramer cf	4	1	3
Cavarretta 1b	4	1	1	Greenberg lf	3	1	1
Pafko cf	4	0	0	Cullenbine rf	2	0	0
Nicholson rf	3	0	1	York 1b	4	0	0
Gillespie c	4	0	0	Outlaw 3b	4	0	1
Hughes ss	3	0	0	Richards c	4	0	0
Wyse p	3	0	0	Trucks p	3	0	0
Secory (a)	1	0	0	Totals	31	4	7
Erickson p	0	0	0				
Becker (b)	1	0	0				
Totals	32	1	7				

```
Chicago      0 0 0 1 0 0 0 0 0 — 1 7 0
Detroit      0 0 0 0 4 0 0 0 0 — 4 7 0
```

(a) fled out for Wyse in seventh; (b) struck out for Erickson in ninth.

Doubles — Cavarretta, Hack. Home run — Greenberg. Sacrifice — Johnson. Runs batted in — Nicholson, Cramer, Greenberg 3.

	IP	H	R	BB	SO
Wyse	6	5	4	3	1 (loser)
Erickson	2	2	0	1	1
Trucks	9	7	1	3	4 (winner)

Left on base — Chicago 8; Detroit 7. Time — 1:48. Attendance — 53,636

Game 3, October 5, Briggs Stadium, Detroit

Having tied the series at one game each, O'Neill again decided to save Trout for another day and instead started 26-year-old lefthander Frank "Stubby" Overmire in game three, a man whose nickname came from his stature. Overmire was 5 feet, 7 inches tall and weighed 170 pounds. He was in his third year in the major leagues and was pretty much of a .500 pitcher, going 7–6 in 1943, 11–11 in 1944 and 9–9 in 1945. He started 22 games for the Tigers in their pennant year and had nine complete games.

The Cubs went according to Grimm's original plan, tossing veteran righthander Passeau, Chicago's most experienced pitcher who won 17 games during the regular season. The game was scoreless for the first three innings. The Cubs' only hit came in the first inning, a single to left by Lowrey. The Tigers also had one hit, a base hit to left field by York in the bottom of the second.

In the Cubs fourth inning, Lowrey led off with his second hit of the game, a double off the left-field wall. Manager Grimm, anticipating that the game would remain tight, played for one run and had Cavarretta, his top hitter, sacrifice Lowrey over to third. Overmire, pitching carefully to Pafko, walked him, and then Nicholson singled to left, the ball just skipping by the outstretched glove of Webb at shortstop, and Lowrey scored the first run of the game. After Livingston flied out to Cramer in center field, Hughes singled passed Mayo, scoring Pafko. Overmire then struck out Passeau to end the inning.

The Cubs kept their 2–0 lead until the seventh, when Livingston doubled to right off Benton, who had come in to relieve Overmire. Hughes sacrificed Livingston to third after which Passeau helped his own cause by hitting a fly ball to Cramer, driving in the third Cub run of the game. By game's end, Passeau had mowed down every Detroit batter except for York's second inning single and a harmless walk to Bill Swift in the sixth, who was wiped out in a double play. Passeau had come within one batter of throwing a perfect game. It was the greatest game ever pitched in the World Series, topping Ed Reulbach's one-hitter for the Cubs in the 1906 series against the White Sox. Reulbach won the game 7–1 and walked six batters. Eleven years after Passeau's one-hitter, Don Larsen of the New York Yankees threw a 2–0 perfect game against the Brooklyn Dodgers at Yankee Stadium. Larsen's gem has left Passeau's effort in the shadows of the record books today, but it was the best ever at the time.

And York, who knew Passeau from their days as roommates in the minor leagues, apologized the next day for ruining his old friend's brush with history. "I never would have swung if I knew it would have messed up your game," he told Passeau.

The Cub righthander was just glad to have won the game. Years later, in an interview with the author, he reflected on it.

"I was just going out there to do my best, that's all," he said. "It was just another day. After the game starts, it's just another ballgame. That's the way you have to look at it. I threw a one-hitter and I won. It doesn't always work that way. I threw four one-hitters in my career and only won but one of them. I was just one of those fellows who couldn't get many runs. If something strange could happen, it always did."

Passeau's impressive performance gave the Cubs a 2–1 lead in the series as the clubs headed to Chicago for the next four games. All the Cubs had to do was split four home games to win their first title since 1908. Based on what he had seen the past two days, Grimm decided to move Passeau ahead of Wyse in the pitching rotation.

Box Score

Chicago	AB	R	H	Detroit	AB	R	H
Hack 3b	5	0	2	Webb ss	3	0	0
Johnson 2b	5	0	0	McHale (d)	1	0	0
Lowrey lf	4	1	2	Mayo 2b	3	0	0
Cavarretta 1b	2	0	1	Cramer cf	3	0	0
Pafko cf	2	1	0	Greenberg lf	3	0	0
Nicholson rf	4	0	1	Cullenbine rf	3	0	0
Livingston c	4	1	1	York 1b	3	0	1
Hughes ss	3	0	1	Outlaw 3b	3	0	0
Passeau p	4	0	0	Swift c	1	0	0
Totals	33	3	8	Borom (a)	1	0	0
				Richards c	1	0	0
				Overmire p	1	0	0
				Walker (b)	1	0	0
				Benton p	1	0	0
				Hostetler (c)	1	0	0
				Totals	28	0	1

```
Chicago     0 0 0 2 0 0 1 0 0 — 3 8 0
Detroit     0 0 0 0 4 0 0 0 0 — 0 1 2
```

(a) ran for Swift in sixth; (b) grounded into double play for Overmire in sixth; (c) grounded out for Benton in ninth; (d) fouled out for Webb in ninth.

Errors—Webb, Mayo. Doubles—Lowrey, Livingston, Hack. Sacrifices—Cavarretta, Hughes, Pafko. Runs batted in—Nicholson, Hughes, Passeau. Double play—Johnson and Cavarretta.

	IP	H	R	BB	SO
Passeau	9	1	0	1	1 (winner)
Overmire	6	4	2	2	2 (loser)
Benton	3	4	1	0	3

Left on base—Chicago 8; Detroit 1. Time—1:55. Attendance—55,500.

Game 4, October 6, Wrigley Field, Chicago

The World Series shifted to Wrigley Field in Chicago with the Cubs in great shape after taking two out of three in the visitors' ballpark. Their task was not difficult to figure out. They needed two wins in their home ballpark and they would have four tries at it if they needed them.

Try as he did, owner Phil Wrigley could not stop scalpers from plying their trade on Addison, Sheffield, and Clark Street and Waveland Avenue outside Wrigley Field. Some fans paid $150 for $7.20 box seat tickets. Inside the ballpark, William Sianis, owner of the Billy Goat Tavern, was on his way to two of those $7.20 seats he purchased for himself and his goat, just as he had done from time to time during the regular season. But Wrigley didn't want the goat in the ballpark during the World

A large crowd gathers outside the ballpark before a World Series game with the Tigers. The familiar Wrigley Field sign identifies the Cubs in what was to become an unfamiliar way for the next half-century and more: "National League champions."

Series and had security evict Sianis and the goat. Wrigley's reasoning: "The goat smells," he said.

In retaliation, Sianis declared he was putting a curse over the Cubs—one that is still referred to nearly 60 years later as the Cubs strive to get back into a World Series for the first time since 1945 — or since the Sianis "curse" kicked in. When the World Series ended, a still irate Sianis sent a three-word telegram to Wrigley: "Now who smells?"

On the field, Grimm, like O'Neill, wanted to try to provide as much rest as he could for his top guns Borowy, Passeau and Wyse so southpaw Ray Prim got the call in game four. O'Neill went with Trout, his 18-game winner, who had not yet appeared in the series.

Both pitchers threw shutout ball for three innings. In fact, Prim, the gray-haired lefty who was nicknamed "Pop" because of his hair color, set down the first 10 Tigers batters, creating a buzz in the pressbox because of Passeau's feat just the day before. But in the fourth inning, after Webb grounded out to Hack at third, Mayo walked, Cramer singled to right, breaking up the no hitter, and then Greenberg singled to left, breaking up the shutout. Cullenbine followed with a double down the left-field line, Greenberg stopping at third. Derringer, the veteran who had won World Series games with Cincinnati five years before and who had been the Cubs opening day pitcher this year, came in to relieve Prim. He walked York intentionally to load the bases. Outlaw hit a ground ball to Johnson, who flipped to Hughes for the force out at second, but the throw to first was too late for the double play. Greenberg scored. Richards then singled, driving home the fourth run of the inning.

In the sixth inning, the Cubs scored their only run of the game, but it was marked by yet another play of dubious distinction. Johnson led off the sixth with a triple. When Lowrey hit a ground ball to third baseman Outlaw, who was playing back and conceding the run, Johnson at first started toward home, then whirled around inexplicably and headed back toward third. First baseman York took Outlaw's throw to retire Lowrey and then fired back to third to try to get the retreating Johnson. When York's throw sailed over Outlaw's head, Johnson trotted home with the Cubs first and only run.

At game's end the Tigers and Trout had beaten the Cubs 4–1 to tie the series at two games apiece. Prim had pitched decently for the Cubs but the fourth inning, his second time through the Detroit lineup, had been his undoing. The Tigers had now scored in only two innings of the first four games—being shut out in 33 of 35 innings—and yet had managed to win two games.

"Hang in there," Grimm told sports writers after the game. "It's Hank Borowy and more base hits tomorrow."

Grimm acknowledged that Trout was tough and said he kept the Cubs off balance by how long he took to deliver the ball.

"Dizzy Trout was plenty fast and he had control when he needed it. However, he wasn't as fast as Virgil Trucks was Thursday. A couple of base hits in the right spot would have meant a different story. But of course he never allowed us to get them. In fact, occasionally, we wondered if old Diz was going to allow us the chance to swing at the ball. He took all day out there, wiping his glasses, mopping his forehead and playing with the resin bag. He wouldn't be counted out of the picture even when time was called once.

"First, the catcher, Paul Richards, called 'time.' Then the umpire, Jocko Conlan, called 'time,' too. He had us on the hook and he was thoroughly enjoying it. But don't forget, I had some pretty good pitching out there today, too."

Prim took the loss in stride. "They were hittin' 'em where they ain't today," he said. "But then, that's what they're hoping to do every time they take a swing up there. And if they succeed, it's just your hard luck."

The Tigers credited their manager with helping Trout get back into form after having a tough second half of the regular season and losing 15 games overall. Richards, his catcher, said, "Ol Diz is back at center stage, back where he belongs. O'Neill really handled the big fellow perfectly. It may have been accidental, but the psychology he used on Trout was perfect.

"Diz likes to be up in that limelight, like anyone else. He loves it. Well, O'Neill keeps him out of action for two weeks, out of the series for three games. He was really ready today, physically and mentally. Diz had to win today to get back in the limelight where he belongs— and he did."

Box Score

Detroit	AB	R	H	Chicago	AB	R	H
Webb ss	5	0	0	Hack 3b	4	0	0
Mayo 2b	3	1	0	Johnson 2b	4	1	2
Cramer cf	4	1	2	Lowrey lf	4	0	1
Greenberg lf	3	1	1	Cavarretta 1b	4	0	0
Cullenbine rf	3	1	1	Pafko cf	4	0	0
York 1b	3	0	0	Nicholson rf	4	0	0
Outlaw 3b	4	0	1	Livingston c	3	0	1
Richards c	4	0	1	Hughes ss	1	0	0
Trout	4	0	1	Becker (b)	1	0	1
Totals	33	4	7	Merullo (c) ss	1	0	0
				Prim p	0	0	0
				Derringer p	0	0	0
				Secory (a)	1	0	0
				Vandenberg p	1	0	0
				Gillespie (d)	1	0	0
				Erickson p	1	0	0
				Totals	31	1	5

```
Detroit    0 0 0 4 0 0 0 0 0 — 4 7 0
Chicago    0 0 0 0 0 1 0 0 0 — 1 5 0
```

(a) struck out for Derringer in fifth; (b) singled for Hughes in seventh; (c) ran for Becker in seventh; (d) grounded out for Vandenberg in seventh.

Errors— York, Nicholson. Double — Cullenbine. Triple — Johnson. Sacrifice – Prim Runs batted in — Greenberg, Cullenbine, Outlaw, Richards.

	IP	H	R	BB	SO
Trout	9	4	1	1	6 (winner)
Prim	3.1	3	4	1	1 (loser)
Derringer	1.2	2	0	2	1
Vandenberg	2	0	0	0	0
Erickson	2	2	0	1	2

Passed ball — Livingston. Left on base — Detroit 6; Chicago 5. Time — 2:00. Attendance — 42,923.

GAME 5, OCTOBER 7, WRIGLEY FIELD, CHICAGO

O'Neill, having gotten good performances out of Overmire and Trout and having won two games with his team scoring in only two innings, now exuded confidence for the rest of the series.

"We should beat Borowy," he said prior to game five. "Sure he shut us out Wednesday, but it could have been a wholly different story if we had made one hit where it counted. He was really in trouble. Newhouser and Trucks are two of the best pitchers in baseball and should be able to end the series Monday. There's no doubt in my mind about it. We have the edge from here on."

Game five was a rematch between the opening game aces, Borowy and Newhouser, but the outcome was much different. This time, it was Newhouser who was on his game and Borowy who struggled. The only thing that kept the Cubs in the ballgame was the Tigers' inept fielding. The game was filled with mental and physical errors and foreshadowed what was ahead for both teams.

The Tigers threatened to score in the first inning when Mayo singled to right and Greenberg reached when Hack misplayed his ground ball. But Borowy struck out Cullenbine to end the inning, stranding the two base runners.

In the third inning, Pafko's outstanding fielding continued to amaze O'Neill and the Tigers but Detroit managed to score the first run of the game. After Newhouser struck out to start the inning, Webb walked. Mayo got his second straight hit, a single to right, moving Webb over to third. Cramer hit a fly ball to deep center that Pafko raced back for and caught near the vines. Webb scored easily from third. Greenberg became the third straight batter to hit the ball hard, lining the ball into right center field, but Pafko again made a great catch to end the inning. In the bottom of the third, the Cubs got the run back in a hurry. After Livingston bounced out, Borowy helped his own cause with a double to left. Hack drove him in with a run-tying single that Cramer fumbled in center field, ending any chance for a play at the plate. Hack was picked off first to end the inning.

The score remained tied until the sixth inning when Detroit broke the game open with yet another four-run inning, which seemed to be the Tigers' staple. Cramer opened the inning with a single to center and went to second when the ball went under Pafko's glove and through his legs. Greenberg doubled to left, scoring Cramer, as the Tigers continued to hammer Borowy. Cullenbine beat out an infield hit, advancing

Greenberg to third. When York singled, scoring Greenberg, that sent Borowy to the showers. The veteran Hy Vandenberg, making his second series appearance, came in to pitch. Outlaw laid down a sacrifice bunt, advancing the base runners to second and third. With first base open, Richards was walked to set up what the Cubs hoped would be an inning-ending double play with the pitcher Newhouser coming up. But Vandenberg walked Newhouser, forcing in the third run of the inning and keeping the bases loaded for the top of the Tigers' lineup. Webb hit a ground ball to Johnson, who flipped the ball to Merullo for one out, but the throw to first was too late to get Webb. York scored on the play. Chipman then relieved Vandenberg and walked Mayo. Johnson fielded Cramer's ground ball and threw him out to end the inning.

The fielding shenanigans continued in the seventh inning. Derringer came in to pitch for the Cubs. Greenberg blooped a double into short left field. Cullenbine bunted, trying to advance Greenberg to third. Derringer fielded the ball, but instead of going to first for the sure out, he tried to get Greenberg at third but threw too late. Cramer's sacrifice fly gave Detroit a 6–1 lead. The Cubs edged closer in the bottom of the seventh, scoring two runs on a single by Lowrey, a walk to Cavarretta, and a force out by Pafko that left runners on first and third. Nicholson hit a double-play ground ball to Outlaw at third, but his throw to second was late. Lowrey scored and the other two runners were safe. Livingston then doubled, scoring Pafko, but Newhouser got out of the inning by fanning Dewey Williams, batting for Merullo.

This less-than-artistic performance by both teams continued in the ninth inning when Paul Erickson, the hero of the Cubs pennant-clincher at Pittsburgh but a man known for his unpredictability, plunked lead-off hitter Cramer with a pitch. Greenberg then hit his third double of the game, moving Cramer to third. Cullenbine followed with another double, driving in two runs. York also hit the ball hard but lined to Hack at third for the first out. Outlaw and Richards both grounded out to end the inning. Newhouser entered the bottom of the ninth with an 8–3 lead but his teammates gave the Cubs another run. Cavarretta led off with a routine fly to right center field. Cramer and Cullenbine both loped over and watched as the ball fell between them. Nicholson's base hit scored Cavarretta with the final run of the game. Cramer explained the misplay in the outfield this way: "I could have caught the ball but Cullenbine kept shouting, 'All right, all right.' When I heard this, I stopped." Cramer said Cullenbine told him later that "all right, all right" meant "all right, you catch it."

"It was a weird contest at best," wrote John Drebinger in *The New York Times*, who attributed some of the erratic fielding to the notorious Wrigley Field wind.

"We won even though we looked bad," O'Neill said succinctly.

Warren Brown of the *Chicago Sun*, the man who said before the series began that he had seen both teams play and didn't think either team could win, told his readers after game five, "Newhouser won a doubleheader today. He beat both the Cubs and his own team."

The loss wiped out a home-field advantage for Chicago. Having won two out of three at Detroit, the Cubs needed only to split the remaining four games in their home ballpark. Now they faced elimination if they didn't win the next two games.

Box Score

Detroit	*AB*	*R*	*H*	*Chicago*	*AB*	*R*	*H*
Webb ss	4	1	1	Hack 3b	3	0	1
Mayo 2b	4	0	2	Johnson 2b	3	0	0
Cramer cf	4	2	1	Lowrey lf	4	1	1
Greenberg lf	5	3	3	Cavarretta 1b	3	1	1
Cullenbine rf	4	1	2	Pafko cf	4	1	0
York 1b	5	1	1	Nicholson rf	4	0	1
Outlaw 3b	4	0	0	Livingston c	4	0	1
Richards c	4	0	1	Merullo ss	2	0	0
Newhouser p	3	0	0	Williams (b)	1	0	0
Totals	37	8	11	Schuster ss	1	0	0
				Borowy p	1	1	1
				Sauer (a)	1	0	0
				Vandenberg p	0	0	0
				Chipman p	0	0	0
				Derringer p	0	0	0
				Secory (c)	1	0	1
				Erickson p	0	0	0
				Totals	32	4	7

Detroit   0 0 1 0 0 4 1 0 2 — 8 11 0
Chicago   0 0 1 0 0 1 2 0 1 — 4 7 2

(a) struck out for Chipman in sixth; (b) struck out for Merullo in seventh; (c) singled for Derringer in eighth.

Errors—Hack, Pafko. Double—Borowy, Greenberg 3, Cullenbine, Livingston, Cavarretta. Sacrifices—Outlaw, Cullenbine, Johnson. Runs batted in—Cramer, Hack, Greenberg, York, Newhouser, Webb, Outlaw, Nicholson 2, Livingston, Cullenbine 2. Double plays—Mayo, York, Webb and Mayo; Johnson, Merullo and Cavarretta.

	IP	*H*	*R*	*BB*	*SO*
Newhouser	9	7	4	2	9 (winner)
Borowy	5	8	5	1	4 (loser)

	IP	H	R	BB	SO
Vandenberg	.2	0	0	2	0
Chipman	.1	0	0	1	0
Derringer	2	1	1	0	0
Erickson	1	2	2	0	0

Hit by pitch — by Erickson (Cramer). Left on base- Detroit 9; Chicago 4. Time — 2:18. Attendance — 42,463.

GAME 6, OCTOBER 8, WRIGLEY FIELD, CHICAGO

The sixth game of the 1945 World Series is the one that became the defining game of the series — the one that fans, writers and historians would look back on as the one that was the best example of how the quality of baseball had slipped during the war years. The series had already been marked by fielders throwing to the wrong base, pitchers walking batters with the bases loaded, inept base running and fly balls dropping between outfielders who should have made easy catches. None of that would compare with some of the bizarre happenings in the sixth game, including one that decided the game.

The starting pitchers were Trucks, who hadn't worked since his win in game two, and Passeau, the veteran who threw the one-hitter in game three. Passeau's masterful performance pushed him ahead in the rotation over Wyse, the 22-game winner who gave up the three-run homer to Greenberg in game two and had not pitched since that game. This would leave Wyse ready for game seven, if there was one, where he would surely face Newhouser.

Neither team scored in the first inning. In the Tigers second, with one out, Cullenbine walked, York doubled and Outlaw was intentionally walked to fill the bases and set up a double play. Then Passeau walked Richards to force in a run — the third time in the series that a batter had walked with the bases loaded, and it wouldn't be the last. In the bottom of the second inning, an error actually led to a double play. Pafko singled. After Nicholson fouled out, Livingston hit an easy ground ball to Mayo, who flipped the ball to shortstop Webb for the force out. But Webb, trying for the double play, threw the ball over York's head. Livingston headed for second but was thrown out by catcher Richards, who was backing up first base. The second error of the game occurred in the Tigers fourth inning when Johnson bobbled Cullenbine's ground ball, but the Cubs got out of the inning without any runs scoring.

In the Cubs fifth, erratic fielding took center stage again. Livingston, one of the hottest hitters in the series, led off with a single. Hughes laid down a sacrifice bunt that Trucks misplayed and York fell down trying

to field. Passeau also bunted toward Trucks, who threw to third too late
to force Livingston. The bases were loaded with nobody out — and two
of the runners had reached base on balls that were hit about 45 feet.
Hack then singled to center driving in the tying run and when Hughes
also tried to score, he made it when Cramer's throw to the plate skipped
by Richards for an error on the catcher, giving the Cubs a 2–1 lead.
Passeau and Hack moved up to third and second and stayed there as
Johnson grounded out to Mayo. Lowrey walked, loading the bases again,
and Cavarretta drove in two runs with a single to center. George Caster
relieved Trucks, who had not been hit hard but was losing 4–1 and not
getting any breaks. Caster got Pafko to pop out and Nicholson struck
out, ending an inning that could have been much worse.

In the top of the sixth inning, a play occurred that Cubs players say
was the turning point in the World Series. Passeau was sailing along with
a 4–1 lead. Cullenbine led off with a single to center and stole second
base. York fanned. Then Outlaw ripped a ball up the middle that Passeau
tried to stop with his bare hand — his pitching hand. The force of the
drive bent his middle finger back and tore his fingernail but he managed
to throw out Outlaw for the second out. Bob Maier, batting for Richards,
hit another ball up the middle. This one Passeau knocked down with
his glove but could not make a play. It didn't matter because John
McHale, batting for Caster, took a called third strike. In the bottom of
the sixth, with Tommy Bridges making his first World Series appearance since 1935, the Cubs made it 5–1 on back-to-back doubles by Livingston and Hughes.

As the Tigers batted in the seventh, it was obvious that Passeau's
injury from the previous inning was bothering him. But the Cubs defense
wasn't much help. Pinch hitter 42-year-old Chuck Hostetler reached
base when Hack mishandled his ground ball. Hostetler took second when
Mayo grounded out to Cavarretta. Cramer lined a single to left that
should have scored Hostetler. But as he rounded third base and headed
for the plate he fell down on the base path and struggled to scramble to
his feet. He was tagged out by Hughes before he was able to get his aging
body off the ground. While all of this was happening, Cramer took second. Passeau, pitching carefully to Greenberg, walked him. Then Cullenbine singled to center, scoring Cramer.

Grimm summoned Wyse from the bullpen to preserve the 5–2 lead
and a win for the injured Passeau. But York greeted Wyse with a single
to drive in Greenberg before Outlaw grounded out to end the inning.

The Cubs padded their lead to 7–3 in the bottom of the seventh.

After Lowrey reached on an infield hit, the aging Bridges walked Cavarretta, Nicholson and Livingston, forcing in a run. Benton came in with a mission to throw strikes. He threw one to Hughes, who lined a base hit off Benton's leg, driving in Cavarretta.

Chicago took the field at the start of the eighth inning with a 7–3 lead in a game it had to win — with its 22-game winner on the mound. But Swift walked to start the eighth and moved around to third when pinch hitter Hub Walker doubled to right. Hack then misplayed Joe Hoover's grounder for his second error of the game as Swift scored. When Mayo singled to center, Walker scored, cutting the Cubs' lead to 7–5. Chicago got a break when Mayo tried to stretch his hit into a double and was thrown out by Pafko— the second time the Cubs' center fielder had nailed Mayo on the base paths. Lefty Ray Prim relieved Wyse and was greeted by a scorching line drive on which Peanuts Lowrey made a great catch. But Hoover scored to make it 7–6. Then Greenberg homered to tie the game. Prim got Cullenbine to ground out to end the inning.

The ninth inning featured two starting pitchers in the ballgame, Trout for Detroit, who had also pitched in the eighth, and Borowy, who had already pitched a complete game in game one and had worked five innings the previous day. After all the antics and actions of the first eight innings, the ballgame settled down. Trout and Borowy held their opponents scoreless through 11 innings. Borowy then set the Tigers down in the 12th. In the bottom of the 12th, Dewey Williams, who had replaced catcher Livingston, grounded out. Then pinch hitter Frank Secory pinch hit for Lenny Merullo, who had injured his wrist in the top of the 12th when he was spiked by Hoover trying to steal. Secory singled to center and was replaced by pinch runner Schuster. After Borowy, batting for himself, struck out, Hack hit a ground ball single to left field. As Greenberg approached the ball, it skipped over his shoulder and Schuster scampered home with the winning run.

This game, which had been filled with so many mishaps, ended with one in the press box. Official scorers gave Greenberg an error on the play that ended the game. But hours later, upon learning the ball had hit a sprinkler head in the outfield grass causing it to suddenly bounce over Greenberg's shoulder, the scorers erased the error and gave Hack a double.

"At the finish, there wasn't much, except the price of the ticket, that reminded the customers they had been looking at a World Series battle," wrote Irving Vaughan in the next morning's *Chicago Tribune*.

It was a game that left many scars. There was Passeau's finger and

Merullo's wrist. There was the reputation of the two teams. New York writer Frank Graham called the game "the worst game ever played in the World Series. It is the fat men against the tall men at the annual office picnic."

Edward Burns in the *Chicago Tribune* was equally blunt. "Tragedy and farce. Bad plays and good ones. Thousands and thousands of dollars in the balance. And to cap off the wildness of baseball's wildest day, the three official scorers made the great Hank Greenberg the goat in their on-the-spot ruling, then, five hours later, reversed themselves...."

And then there was Hostetler, whose base-running blunder would haunt him like Fred Merkle's had from a generation past and like Bill Buckner's fielding error would in a generation hence. Trucks summed it up. "It was a very sad occasion for him," he said.

His embarrassment stayed with him the rest of his life. Shortly

before his death in 1971, Hostetler told historian Fred Smith, "I'll never forget it. I played only two years in the majors with the Tigers but this is what anyone ever talked about."

Passeau's injury changed the dynamics of the series. He was winning 5–1 when he hurt his hand. While it is impossible to guess the outcome of the game had he not been injured, he had already thrown a one-hit shutout in game three and was cruising along with a 5–1 lead in the sixth inning of game six. The Cubs were in good position to win the game, enjoy the only day off of the series, and then come back with Wyse or Borowy or Prim in game seven.

But Passeau lost his

Stan Hack got the winning hit in the 12th inning of the sixth game of the World Series, one of the zaniest and most exciting World Series games ever played.

rhythm in the seventh inning as the Tigers started to chip away at him. "He couldn't follow through," Grimm said after the game. So the Cubs' skipper went to the bullpen, summoning first his ace righthander Wyse and then lefty Prim, neither of whom could stop the bleeding. When he brought in Borowy in the ninth inning, he had used his entire starting staff just to salvage the sixth game, and Borowy wound up going four innings. Grimm's dilemma, including his lack of confidence in any other pitcher, was demonstrated by how he chose not to pinch hit for Borowy in the top of the 12th.

For some, it brought back memories of the 1935 World Series, also featuring the Cubs, managed by Grimm, and the Tigers. Once again, the Cubs were down three games to two as Chicago battled to stay alive at Briggs Stadium in Detroit. In the ninth inning, Stan Hack hit a lead-off triple off Tommy Bridges. A hit, a fly ball, a ground ball to deep short, a slow roller in the infield — any of these would have produced the big run. But Billy Jurges struck out. The next batter was the Cubs' starting pitcher Larry French, who had gone all the way and allowed two runs on ten hits. Grimm chose not to pinch hit for him and French hit an easy ground ball to Bridges, who held Hack at third and threw the base runner out at first. Augie Galan then flied out, stranding Hack at third base. Much like the situation 10 years later, Grimm was trying to stretch a pitching staff because of the injury of a hurler, Lon Warneke. He took a lot of criticism for not pinch hitting for French but said years later, "If I had it to do all over again, I'd play it the same way."

The one big difference in 1945 is that the Cubs had won the game. Grimm now had to decide who would start game seven against the well-rested Newhouser for the Tigers.

BOX SCORE

Detroit	AB	R	H	Chicago	AB	R	H
Webb ss	3	0	0	Hack 3b	5	1	4
Mayo 2b	6	0	1	Johnson 2b	4	0	0
Cramer cf	6	1	2	Lowrey lf	5	1	1
Greenberg lf	5	2	1	Cavarretta 1b	5	1	2
Cullenbine rf	5	1	2	Pafko cf	6	0	2
York 1b	6	0	2	Nicholson rf	5	0	0
Outlaw 3b	5	0	1	Livingston c	3	2	2
Richards c	0	0	0	Gillespie (e)	1	0	0
Maier (a)	1	0	1	Hughes ss	4	1	3
Swift c	2	1	1	Becker (f)	0	0	0
Trucks p	1	0	0	Secory (h)	1	0	1
Caster p	1	0	0	Block (g)	0	0	0

Detroit	AB	R	H	Chicago	AB	R	H
McHale (b)	1	0	0	Merullo ss	0	0	0
Bridges p	0	0	0	Schuster (i)	0	1	0
Benton p	0	0	0	Passeau p	3	1	0
Walker (d)	1	1	1	Wyse p	1	0	0
Trout p	2	0	0	Prim p	0	0	0
Hostetler (c)	1	0	0	Borowy p	2	0	0
Hoover ss	3	1	1	Totals	46	8	15
Totals	48	7	13				

Detroit   0 1 0 0 0 0 2 4 0 0 0 0 — 7 13 1
Chicago   0 0 0 0 4 1 2 0 0 0 0 1 — 8 15 3

(a) singled for Richards in sixth; (b) struck out for Caster in sixth; (c) reached on error for Webb in seventh; (d) doubled for Benton in eighth; (e) grounded out for Livingston in ninth; (f) walked for Hughes in ninth; (g) hit into force play for Becker in ninth; (h) singled for Merullo in 12th; (i) pinch ran for Secory in 12th.

Errors—Richards, Hack 2, Johnson. Doubles—York, Livingston, Hughes, Walker, Pafko, Hack. Home run—Greenberg. Sacrifices—Johnson 2. Runs batted in—Richards, Hack 3, Cavarretta 2, Hughes 2, York, Livingston, Cullenbine, Hoover, Greenberg, Mayo, Cramer. Stolen base—Cullenbine. Double plays—Mayo, Webb, 2 Richards and Merullo; Johnson and Cavarretta; Mayo, Hoover and York; Hack, Pafko. Double—Borowy, Greenberg 3, Cullenbine, Livingston, Cavarretta.

	IP	H	R	BB	SO
Passeau	6.2	5	3	6	2
Wyse	.2	3	3	1	0
Prim	.2	1	1	0	0
Borowy	4	4	0	0	0 (winner)
Trucks	4.1	7	4	2	3
Caster	.2	0	0	0	1
Bridges	1.2	3	3	3	1
Benton	.1	1	0	0	1
Trout	4.2	4	1	2	3 (loser)

Left on base—Detroit 12, Chicago 12. Time—3:28. Attendance—41,708.

GAME 7, OCTOBER 10, WRIGLEY FIELD, CHICAGO

What happened in game seven really begins with what happened after game six in the Chicago Cubs locker room.

The parade of Cubs pitchers in game six, including all four starters, provided some drama in the midst of the victory celebration. The big question for Grimm was: Who would be the starting pitcher in game seven?

Shortstop Lenny Merullo, who was spiked on the wrist in the top half of the 12th inning of the sixth game, was getting stitched up in the clubhouse when his triumphant team mates came in after the game. He said at first he heard Grimm talking about how the veteran Derringer would start game seven. A United Press International reporter heard

Grimm and immediately sent a dispatch that Derringer would be the starter.

But then Grimm changed his mind.

Merullo remembers it this way. "I was lying on the trainer's table when the game ended and of course we won so everyone came in screamin' and yellin.' The clubhouse was a madhouse. And while I'm layin' there on the table, I see Grimmy go up to Hy Vandenberg and tell him 'You're my guy'— meaning he was going to start the seventh game of the World Series.

"Vandenberg was a good pitcher who had been around a long time and we used him mostly in middle relief. Anyway, a few minutes later, Borowy comes in after talking with the writers and he goes up to Grimm and says, 'Skip, I'm all right. I'll get a good night's sleep tonight.' And Grimm says, 'All right, you're my guy.' It wasn't but a minute or two after he had said the same thing to Vandenberg. That's exactly how it happened."

Borowy remembers it a little differently: "Charlie was going around the clubhouse saying, 'Who's ready? Who's ready?' Well, I was dead tired of course, but you know, sometimes something inside you takes over. Sometimes in sports, the adrenalin kicks in and you just get a hard-on. That's part of being competitive, of being a professional athlete. And so I told him I was ready."

Borowy, who had pitched five innings in game five and four innings in game six, got the nod to start game seven. The only rest he would get was the off day — the only off day of the series— between games six and seven.

Second baseman Johnson said, "If Passeau hadn't gotten hurt, he probably would have won that game by himself. Now we go into the seventh game and we got nobody fresh. I remember Borowy begged Charlie to start him — and he did."

Williams, the reserve catcher, said, "I tried to get 'em not to start Borowy. I talked my head off. I talked to Grimm. I talked to Cavarretta. I talked to Merullo. Vandenberg should have started that game. But for some reason, Grimm had it in for Vandenberg and so Borowy started."

One thing was clear. Grimm had lost confidence in Wyse, the man who, before the season started, Grimm had predicted would win 20 games— and he won 22. Wyse had been the ace of the staff, the go-to man until Borowy arrived on July 27. Wyse made one bad pitch in game two, the one Greenberg hit out of the ballpark with two men on, and in game six, coming in for a rare relief appearance, he couldn't hold the lead. Vandenberg had not pitched at all in game six and had worked ⅔ of an inning in game five and two innings in game four without allowing a hit or a run. Derringer had worked in two games and had pitched 3⅔ innings and had not pitched since game five. But Grimm decided that Borowy, who had started game five and worked five-plus innings and had pitched the last four innings of game six, was "my guy" for game seven. Borowy had been brilliant in game six and had the game one shutout to his credit. His general manager at the Yankees, Larry MacPhail, had criticized Borowy for not being a second-half pitcher. But for the Cubs, he was 11–2 in the second half including two key wins against the Cardinals, whom Chicago beat only six times all year. He had pitched in the 1942 and 1943 World Series for New York and was 2–1 in his three appearances in this World Series. Borowy had earned his stripes. When everything was on the line, as it was in game seven, he was the man Grimm wanted to have the ball. Another classic match-up was in the making—Borowy against Newhouser.

There was excitement at Wrigley Field long before the game started. October 9 was an off-day for the ballclubs, the only off-day in the series. Owner Philip Wrigley made arrangements to sell 36,000 tickets for the seventh game starting at 8 a.m. that morning. Fans began gathering at midnight near the 28 ticket windows surrounding the Addison Street entrance to the ballpark. Temperatures were in the low 40s as die-hards lit fires in garbage cans and stood around them to keep warm. Others brought wooden crates they used as chairs. Some stood wrapped in blankets and looked like Indians, according to one newspaper account. In the upstairs offices, Wrigley, dressed in suit and tie, supervised ticket manager George Doyle and his staff as they got the rolls of tickets ready and talked about their own "game plan" for game seven.

As a means of crowd control, Andy Frain, president of the company that provided ushers for Cubs games, provided some men to help with crowd control and had to call for more help, summoning men who had returned home after working the boxing matches at Marigold Arena and at Chicago Coliseum, where an ice skating exhibition had taken place.

The ticket windows opened as scheduled at 8 a.m., and the crowd, which was about 200 at midnight and had grown larger and larger throughout the night, was estimated at more than 20,000 when the sales began. At game time, 41,590 were settling in for the final game.

Webb led off for the Tigers and Borowy missed the strike zone with his first two pitches. The count went to 3–2 before Webb lined a single to right. As Borowy threw his first pitch to Mayo, Webb took off for second. Mayo singled to right, executing the hit-and-run perfectly, and Webb scampered around to third. Cramer took a pitch for ball one and then singled to left, scoring Webb. It was the beginning of a nightmare afternoon for Grimm and the Cubs. Borowy's tired arm was offering little more than batting practice for the Tigers and Grimm had to get him out of there. He had been hoping to get several innings from Borowy. He had gotten nine pitches. Now, he not only had to replace him, but he needed a long reliever. Ironically, whoever came into the game with nobody out in the first inning would be someone Grimm had been reluctant to start. He chose Derringer, who had been inconsistent during the season and in the series but who was a warhorse with big-game experience as a member of the pennant-winning Reds in 1940.

With Cramer and Mayo on first and second, Derringer faced the powerful Greenberg. And Greenberg surprised the Cubs, the crowd and the writers by laying down a sacrifice bunt. Cullenbine was walked intentionally to load the bases and set up what Chicago hoped would be an inning-ending double play. York popped out for the second out. Derringer was one out away from getting out of the inning and keeping the Cubs just one run down. But he walked Outlaw to force in a run and Richards followed with a double into the left-field corner, clearing the bases and giving Detroit and Newhouser a 5–0 lead.

The Cubs got a run in the bottom of the first, helped by a Newhouser error. With one out, Johnson doubled. Lowrey attempted to sacrifice, and when Newhouser fumbled the ball, he was safe at first while Johnson held at second. Cavarretta drove Johnson home with a single to right.

In the second inning, the Tigers scored again. With two out and nobody on, Cramer singled to right and Greenberg and Cullenbine both walked. Derringer had exactly the same situation as in the first inning, when he got York to pop out with the bases loaded. This time, he walked York, forcing in a run. So Derringer, who went 15 years without walking in a run, did it twice in the seventh game of the World Series. It marked the fifth time in the past three games in which a runner had come home on a bases-loaded walk.

The Cubs got a run in the fourth on a Pafko triple — a ball that Cramer circled under in center field but somehow didn't make the play. Sports writer Warren Brown, recalling it in his book *The Chicago Cubs*, said, "Cramer forgot to catch it." That drove in Cavarretta who had singled. Chicago added another run in the eighth when Nicholson drove in his eighth run of the series with a single that scored Lowrey. The Tigers, meanwhile, had scored a run in the seventh on yet another double by Richards and tacked on two more in the eighth off Passeau, who, still feeling the effects of the finger injury, came in with the score 7–2 after Grimm had already used Borowy, Derringer, Vandenberg and Erickson. By choosing to bring in the injured Passeau to mop up, he left not only Chipman and Prim in the bullpen but also Wyse. Passeau gave up two runs and did not return for the ninth. It was then that Grimm summoned Wyse, who retired the Tigers in order. The Cubs went down harmlessly in the bottom of the ninth, with Newhouser recording his 10th strikeout. The Tigers were the world champions.

After the game, Borowy sounded much like Newhouser had after Newhouser's battering in game one. "With a little luck, I might have made it," he said.

Interviewed by the author a half-century later, Borowy said, "The zip just wasn't there. You gotta have a winner and you gotta have a loser — that's baseball. But we shoulda took 'em. We shoulda took 'em."

"Borowy didn't have a lot when he warmed up and I knew it," said Grimm, echoing what warm-up catcher Dewey Williams had said. "I knew it but I wanted to give it a try," said Grimm.

Reflecting on the series many years later, Passeau looked back to the sixth game, the one in which he departed with the injured finger and in which the Cubs blew a four-run lead before winning it in 12 innings. "We should have won it long before that," he said in an interview with the author.

"Borowy pitched the seventh game because we didn't have anybody else."

Wyse, also interviewed by the author shortly before his death in 2000, disagreed with Borowy. "I should have pitched that seventh game. I thought so then and I still do.

"Grimm was hung up on Borowy. He had done a good job for us when he came over from the Yankees and Grimm went with him. I had expected to pitch that game. Grimm didn't say anything to me about it. He just said Borowy was pitching. That was it. It was a mistake. It was Grimm's fault."

Johnson, also interviewed shortly before his death in 2000, said, "I don't have a problem with Borowy starting. The whole staff was tired, and we wouldn't have been in the series if it hadn't been for him. It was a lot to ask of Borowy. He wasn't that big a guy. There wasn't much heft to him and he just didn't have anything left."

Had he won, Borowy would have been the first pitcher since Stan Coveleskie to win three games in the World Series. Coveleskie did it with the 1920 Cleveland Indians. His catcher was Steve O'Neill.

Box Score

Detroit	AB	R	H	*Chicago*	AB	R	H
Webb ss	4	2	1	Hack 3b	5	0	0
Mayo 2b	5	2	2	Johnson 2b	5	1	1
Cramer cf	5	2	3	Lowrey lf	4	1	2
Greenberg lf	2	0	0	Cavarretta 1b	4	1	3
Cullenbine rf	2	2	0	Pafko cf	4	0	1
York 1b	4	0	0	Nicholson rf	4	0	1
Outlaw 3b	4	1	1	Livingston c	4	0	1
Richards c	4	0	2	Hughes ss	3	0	1
Swift c	1	0	0	Borowy p	0	0	0
Newhouser p	4	0	0	Derringer p	0	0	0
Mierkowicz	0	0	0	Vandenberg p	1	0	0
Totals	39	9	9	Sauer (a)	1	0	0
				Erickson p	0	0	0
				Secory (b)	1	0	0
				Passeau p	0	0	0
				Wyse p	0	0	0
				McCullough (c)	1	0	0
				Totals	37	3	10

```
Detroit     5 1 0 0 0 0 1 2 0 — 9 9 1
Chicago     1 0 0 1 0 0 0 1 0 — 3 10 0
```

(a) struck out for Vandenberg in fifth; (b) struck out for Erickson in seventh; (c) struck out for Wyse in ninth.

Error—Newhouser. Doubles—Richards 2, Mayo, Nicholson, Johnson. Triple—Pafko. Sacrifice—Greenberg. Runs batted in—Cramer, Outlaw, Richards 4, Cavarretta, York, Pafko, Mayo, Greenberg, Nicholson. Stolen bases—Outlaw, Cramer. Double play—Webb, Mayo and York.

	IP	H	R	BB	SO
Newhouser	9	10	3	1	10 (winner)
Borowy	0	3	3	0	0 (loser)
Derringer	1.2	2	3	5	0
Vandenberg	3.1	1	0	1	3
Erickson	2	2	1	1	2
Passeau	1	1	2	1	0
Wyse	1	0	0	0	0

Wild pitch—Newhouser. Left on base—Detroit 8, Chicago 8. Time—2:32. Attendance—41,500

158

The Cubs Win the Pennant!

COMPOSITE BOX SCORE

Detroit	G	AB	R	H	D	T	HR	RBI	AVE.
Maier ph	1	1	0	1	0	0	0	0	1.000
Walker ph	2	2	1	1	1	0	0	0	.500
Cramer cf	7	29	7	11	0	0	0	4	.379
Hoover ss	1	3	1	1	0	0	0	1	.333
Greenberg lf	7	23	7	7	3	0	2	7	.304
Mayo 2b	7	28	4	7	1	0	0	2	.250
Swift c	3	4	1	1	0	0	0	0	.250
Cullenbine rf	7	22	5	5	2	0	0	4	.227
Richards c	7	19	0	4	2	0	0	6	.211
Webb ss	7	27	4	5	0	0	0	1	.185
York 1b	7	28	1	5	1	0	0	3	.179
Outlaw 3b	7	28	1	5	0	0	0	3	.179
Trout p	2	6	0	1	0	0	0	0	.167
Mierkowicz lf	1	0	0	0	0	0	0	0	.000
Newhouser p	3	8	0	0	0	0	0	0	.000
Benton p	3	0	0	0	0	0	0	0	.000
Tobin p	1	1	0	0	0	0	0	0	.000
Mueller p	1	0	0	0	0	0	0	0	.000
Trucks p	2	4	0	0	0	0	0	0	.000
Overmire p	1	0	0	0	0	0	0	0	.000
Caster p	1	0	0	0	0	0	0	0	.000
Bridges p	1	0	0	0	0	0	0	0	.000
McHale ph	3	3	0	0	0	0	0	0	.000
Borom ph-pr	2	1	0	0	0	0	0	0	.000
Eaton ph	1	1	0	0	0	0	0	0	.000
Hostetler ph	3	0	0	0	0	0	0	0	.000
Totals	7	242	32	54	10	0	2	32	.223

Chicago	G	AB	R	H	D	T	HR	RBI	AVE.
Becker ph	3	2	0	1	0	0	0	0	.500
Cavarretta 1b	7	26	7	11	2	0	1	5	.423
Secory ph	5	5	0	2	0	0	0	0	.400
Hack 3b	7	30	1	11	3	0	0	4	.367
Livingston c	6	22	3	8	3	0	0	4	.364
Lowrey lf	7	29	4	9	1	0	0	0	.310
Hughes ss	6	17	1	5	1	0	0	3	.294
Pafko cf	7	28	5	6	2	1	0	2	.214
Nicholson rf	7	28	1	6	1	1	0	8	.214
Johnson 2b	7	29	4	5	2	1	0	0	.172
Borowy p	4	6	1	1	1	0	0	0	.167
Gillespie c-ph	3	6	0	0	0	0	0	0	.000
Merullo pr-ss	3	2	0	0	0	0	0	0	.000
Schuster ss-pr	2	1	1	0	0	0	0	0	.000
Williams ph-c	2	2	0	0	0	0	0	0	.000
Wyse p	3	3	0	0	0	0	0	0	.000
Erickson p	4	0	0	0	0	0	0	0	.000
Passeau p	3	7	1	0	0	0	0	1	.000

Chicago	G	AB	R	H	D	T	HR	RBI	AVE.
Prim p	2	0	0	0	0	0	0	0	.000
Vandenberg p	3	1	0	0	0	0	0	0	.000
Chipman p	1	0	0	0	0	0	0	0	.000
Derringer p	2	0	0	0	0	0	0	0	.000
Block pr	1	0	0	0	0	0	0	0	.000
McCullough ph	1	1	0	0	0	0	0	0	.000
Sauer ph	2	2	0	0	0	0	0	0	.000
Totals	7	247	29	65	16	3	1	27	.263

Detroit	G	IP	H	R	ER	BB	SO	W-L	ERA
Mueller	1	2	0	0	0	1	1	0–0	0.00
Caster	1	.2	0	0	0	0	1	0–0	0.00
Trout	2	13.2	9	2	1	3	9	1–1	0.66
Benton	3	4.2	6	1	1	0	5	0–0	1.93
Overmire	1	6	4	2	2	2	2	0–1	3.00
Trucks	2	13.3	14	5	5	5	7	1–0	3.38
Tobin	1	3	4	2	2	1	0	0–0	6.00
Newhouser	3	20.2	25	14	14	4	22	2–1	6.10
Bridges	1	1.1	3	3	3	3	1	0–0	16.20
Totals	7	65.2	65	29	28	19	48	4–3	3.84

Chicago	G	AB	R	H	D	T	HR	RBI	AVE.
Vandenberg	3	6	1	0	0	3	3	0–0	0.00
Chipman	1	.1	0	0	0	1	0	0–0	0.00
Passeau	3	16.2	7	5	5	8	3	1–0	2.70
Erickson	4	7	8	3	3	3	5	0–0	3.86
Borowy	4	18	21	8	8	6	8	2–2	4.00
Derringer	3	5.1	5	4	4	7	1	0–0	6.75
Wyse	3	7.2	8	7	6	4	1	0–1	7.04
Prim	2	4	4	5	4	1	1	0–1	9.00
Totals	7	65	54	32	30	33	22	3–4	4.15

IX

Afterthoughts

"Grimm had nothing but weary gentlemen at his command."
— *Irving Vaughan in the Chicago Tribune*

Several years after the 1945 World Series, Paul Derringer ran into his old general manager, Jim Gallagher, at a social gathering. Recalling his wild spell in the seventh game, he said, "You know, it's funny. I can't ever remember any other time when I walked someone with the bases loaded."

"What's funny about that?" said Gallagher.

Gallagher's terse question, like Borowy's "we shoulda took 'em" lament, are testimony to the sense of frustration the Cubs felt in letting the World Series championship slip away by losing three out of four games at Wrigley Field after winning two out of three to start the series in Detroit.

The "would haves" and "could haves" and "should haves" are the legacy of the series for the Cubs.

They allowed the Tigers to score in only one inning of the first three games and in only two innings of the first four games—and yet Detroit somehow won two of those games. The Cubs knocked out Newhouser in the third inning of the first game and, in his three starts, pummeled him for 14 runs on 25 hits, leaving him with an earned-run average of 6.10 for the series. Yet, Newhouser won two of those games.

In addition, Detroit played so sloppily that twice they tested the throwing arm of Pafko, resulting in base runners being thrown out twice, snuffing out rallies; twice Cramer and Cullenbine, playing center and right fields, hovered around routine fly balls and both times let them drop between them, keeping Cubs' rallies alive; and they experienced the biggest base running gaffe of the series when Hostetler stumbled between third and home and was humiliatingly tagged out as he staggered to get off the ground.

It was a series that in some respects seemed as one-sided as the 1960 World Series 15 years later between Pittsburgh and New York in which the Yankees held the Pirates to just 15 runs in the first six games, won two of those games 12–0 and 16–3, outscored the Pirates 55 to 25 for the series, and yet lost to the Pirates in seven games.

Grimm took a chance in pitching Borowy in three straight games, starting games five and seven and pitching four innings in relief in game six. "Good pitching beat good try," he said after the Cubs lost the seventh game. The irony for the Cubs was that the problem they thought they solved during the long, regular season — lack of pitching depth — wound up killing them in the short series. The manner in which the two managers manipulated their pitching rotations also proved to be important.

Wyse gave up a three-run homer to Greenberg in the second game. It was enough to beat the Cubs 4–1 and enough that Grimm apparently lost confidence in his 22-game winner. After going with a rotation of Borowy, Wyse, Passeau and Prim in the first four games, and then going with Borowy again in game five, Grimm passed over Wyse and went with Passeau in game six, a game the Cubs had to win to stay alive. Passeau had tossed a one-hitter in game three. When he got hurt and had to leave game six, Wyse was summoned in an unusual role — relief — but it seemed like a great move on Grimm's part at the time. Any manager would love to have the luxury of being able to bring in a 22-game winner in relief to wrap up a victory. But Wyse, idle for three days and more accustomed to the starter's role of pacing himself for the long haul, got knocked around in a hurry by a Tigers team glad to see Passeau out of there. He gave up three runs on three hits in ⅔ of an inning. And suddenly, Grimm's pitching advantage disintegrated. Faced with elimination if the Cubs didn't win, he yanked Wyse and brought in Prim, another starter, to put out the fire. But Prim gave up a run, the tying run, on a Greenberg homer in ⅓ of an inning. So Grimm turned to Borowy to pitch the ninth inning — and then the 10th, 11th and 12th innings as the Cubs hung on to win in a contest writer Charles Einstein called "the worst World Series game ever played."

In the space of a few innings in that pivotal game, Chicago's pitching was in shambles. Passeau had been sailing along before Outlaw's line drive clipped his pitching hand. Had he been able to complete the game or at least turn it over to Chipman, Vandenberg or Erickson in the eighth or ninth innings, the Cubs could have come back in game seven with Borowy on two days rest (the same as Newhouser) or Prim or Wyse, with three and four days rest, respectively. Instead, Grimm used all four of his starters in game six. The disastrous results: One got hurt, two were ineffective, and the other, Borowy, pitched four innings after having started game five.

Yet Grimm went with his ace, Borowy, in game seven, following the old Dizzy Dean adage of "you gotta dance with who brung ya." But everything Borowy threw, the Tigers hit and he was gone after only nine pitches.

Meanwhile, throughout the series, O'Neill had to make several decisions with his pitching staff and some of them were, if not risky, surprising. Trout, his number two pitcher, was battling a cold and had not been effective in his last two starts of the regular season. Still, it would have been tempting to start him in game two after Newhouser lost the first game. Instead, O'Neill went with Trucks, who had been out of the Navy for a week and had pitched only six innings on the last day of the season. Trucks was the victor when Greenberg homered off Wyse. With the series even at one game apiece, O'Neill could have gone with Trout. Instead, he started Stubby Overmire, a .500 career pitcher who was 9–9 during the regular season with the Tigers. Overmire pitched well but lost a 3–0 decision in the game in which Passeau threw the one-hitter. So O'Neill found himself down two games to one but had a full arsenal of pitchers rested and raring to go. Trout, making his series debut, threw a five-hitter to beat Prim 4–1 in game four. Newhouser came back to beat Borowy in game five, setting up the marathon sixth game.

None of this maneuvering on either side would have mattered much had it not been for the extraordinary timely hitting of Greenberg. He destroyed Wyse and the Cubs with one swing in game two. He singled to drive in a run in game four and scored what turned out to be the winning run. He doubled and drove in a run in game five. In game six, it was Greenberg's home run that tied the game in the eighth and forced Grimm to bring in Borowy in relief in the ninth. Greenberg topped off his series by fooling everybody in the seventh game when he laid down a perfect sacrifice bunt in the five-run first inning.

Irving Vaughan, writing in the *Chicago Tribune*, wrote afterwards that rather than pinning blame on Grimm for his handling of the pitching staff or on Borowy for not coming through in the seventh game, the answer to the Cubs' plight might simply be that despite their glorious if improbable season, they might have been overrated going into the series.

"Grimm's team didn't possess anyone even close to the equal of Hal Newhouser," wrote Vaughan. "The Cubs were not only without a New-houser, who, after winning 25 games in the regular season, won two of the series battles after being knocked out of the opener, but they weren't timely in the power department, to which Hank Greenberg gave some attention in behalf of the new champions. Hank won the second game almost single-handedly with one of his two homers.

"And even getting past Newhouser, the Cubs, as the series developed, still were shy in the pitching department, the latter doing so poorly as a whole that there is reason to wonder just how they managed to win the pennant. It was because of the all-around weakness of the staff that when the Cubs finally reached the seventh and deciding game, Grimm had nothing but weary gentlemen at his command."

Grimm always said the Cubs would have won the series had Passeau not gotten hurt in the sixth game. He was assuming that Passeau would have won it and that Borowy would have been fresher for game seven. O'Neill didn't have as deep a starting staff as Grimm — and it would have been worse had Trucks not been released from the Navy a week before the season ended.

Another factor that gave the edge to the Tigers was the condition of two pitchers who got out of the service in time to join their teams at the end of the season. Trucks started the season finale and won a game in the World Series. Bithorn, the big Cubs righthander who had won 18 games in 1942, came home 40 pounds heavier and was not in shape to play. Had he been ready, he would have added an important dimension for the Cubs, just as Trucks had for the Tigers.

The 1945 World Series, while not memorable for its artistry, nonetheless left its mark on baseball history at that time for several reasons. The seven-game attendance of 333,457 was a World Series record, besting the old mark of 328,051 set in the 1926 World Series between the St. Louis Cardinals and New York Yankees. Players' shares were also records for their day — $6,123 for each of the winning Tigers, $4,277 for the losing Cubs.

Other World Series records, most of them long-since broken, included:

Most players used in a game by both teams— 38 in the sixth game.

Longest game (in terms of time)— 3 hours and 28 minutes, in the sixth game.

Most times hitting over .400 in a World Series— 2, Phil Cavarretta of the Cubs (tied with four other players.)

Most chances by an outfielder — 27, by Andy Pafko of the Cubs.

Most putouts by a third baseman — 12 by Stan Hack of the Cubs.

Most earned runs off a pitcher who won two or more games — 14, off the Tigers Hal Newhouser.

Most runs scored by a losing team — 29 by the Cubs.

Most bases on balls received by one club — 33 by the Cubs.

Most strikeouts by one club — 48 by the Cubs.

It is often said that championship teams occur when several players have "career years" in the same year. With the exception of Pafko, Lowrey, Cavarretta or Chipman, no Cubs player ever reached the same level of play that he achieved in 1945. Indeed, 14 players who appeared in at least one game for the 1945 Cubs never played in the major leagues again and several others were out of major league baseball within a few years.

Grimm remained with the Cubs until 1949. The ballclub had been on a downhill slide since the championship year and had finished eighth in 1948, just three years after being on top. On June 12, 1949, Grimm resigned, with the hope that a new manager would inject some new life into the ballclub, just as he had done in 1932, replacing Rogers Hornsby and winning a pennant, and in 1938 when Gabby Hartnett replaced him and won a pennant. This time the new manager was Frankie Frisch, but he didn't have much to work with and the Cubs finished eighth again.

Grimm later explained the ballclub's shortcomings. "What happened to the Cubs? The year 1945 had been the last war year," he said. "One of the reasons we won is that we had a veteran club which had not been hit as deeply as others in the league for military service. This was great for 1945. But some of these players were past their peak and this temporary advantage was lost in the post-war seasons when other teams came up with war-freed athletes."

Grimm took a front office job with the Cubs in 1949 but was back in uniform within a year, once again managing the Milwaukee Brewers. In 1952, he was hired during the season to replace Tommy Holmes as manager of the floundering Boston Braves. When the Braves moved to Milwaukee in 1953, Grimm was a great fit as manager because he had been such a fan favorite in his days while twice being a minor league manager there. He stayed with the Braves through part of the 1956 season. He was to return to the Cubs one more time, in 1960, when Wrigley hired him to replace Bob Scheffing. "Every time we hire Charlie, we win," said Wrigley. Not this time. The Cubs got off to a slow start, 6–11, and by early May, both Wrigley and Grimm knew it was time to make a change. But instead of firing his favorite manager, Wrigley engineered a unique trade: Grimm went to the WGN radio broadcasting booth while Hall of Famer Lou Boudreau, who had been a Cubs radio broadcaster, went down to the field to become the Cubs manager. Grimm stayed in the broadcast booth a few more years, then retired to his home in Scottsdale, Arizona, where he died on November 15, 1983, at the age of 85. Fittingly, his ashes were spread over Wrigley Field.

The baseball journeys of many of the Cubs stars were not pleasant after 1945. Borowy continued to have problems with blisters on the fingers of his pitching hand and also developed shoulder problems. He pitched three more years for the Cubs but didn't come close to the success he'd had in 1945 or his previous three years with the Yankees. Borowy proved that the Yankees' MacPhail was wrong in questioning his effectiveness late in a season — the reason he said he put him on waivers and the Cubs picked him up. But Borowy may have been one of the athletes who was a wartime wonder, having his best years when the best ballplayers were overseas. He was 12–10 in 1946, 8–12 in 1947 and 5–10 in 1948. Borowy was traded to the Philadelphia Phillies where he was 12–12 in 1949. He spent the 1950 season with three teams, the Phillies, the Pittsburgh Pirates and the Detroit Tigers. His major league career ended after a 2–4 season with the Tigers in 1951. After Borowy won 21 games and lost 7 with the Yankees and Cubs in 1945, his record was 41–50 with four teams in the remaining years of his career.

Was Borowy shipped to the Cubs because MacPhail wanted to get rid of him or because he owed Gallagher a favor for the Billy Herman deal four years earlier? When MacPhail and Gallagher died, the answer to that question died with them.

Wyse, 22–10 in 1945, slipped to 14–12 in 1946 and hurt his arm during practice before a 1947 game. He said his arm was put in a cast, he was sent home, and he never pitched again for the Cubs. He had a 2–4 record when his season ended. He pitched for Shreveport in 1948 and for the Cubs Triple A Los Angeles club in 1949. He won nine games for Connie Mack's 1950 Philadelphia A's team and was 1–2 with the A's and the Washington Senators before retiring in 1951. After his stellar 1945 season with the Cubs, Wyse produced a 30–37 record over the next six years. He died October 22, 2000, at the age of 83, in Salina, Oklahoma. To his dying day, Wyse thought he should have been the starter in the seventh game of the World Series.

Passeau, who won nine consecutive games and finished with a 17–9 record during the 1945 season and then tossed a one-hitter in the third game of the World Series, pitched two more seasons. Like Borowy and Wyse, he didn't come close to matching his 1945 statistics, going 9–8 in 1946 and 2–6 in 1947.

Derringer was released after the 1945 season. At age 40, he signed with Triple A Indianapolis and won 9 and lost 11 in 1946, after which he retired. Derringer compiled a record of 223–212 over 15 major league seasons.

Erickson, the hero of the Cubs' pennant-clinching victory over the Pirates, had one more decent year with the Cubs and then faded into retirement. In 1946, he pitched 174 innings, his career high for one season, and won a career-high nine games and lost seven. He was involved in some confusion at the start of the season through no fault of his own. The Cubs put him on waivers in April of 1946. The Pirates claimed him, thinking they were purchasing Hal Erickson, a pitcher in the Cincinnati Reds organization. Then the Pirates changed their mind, so Hal Erickson stayed with the Reds and Paul Erickson stayed with the Cubs. Hal Erickson was shipped to Columbia, the Reds farm club in the Sally League, along with Ted Kluszewski, who would later be a big league star. Hal Erickson didn't make it to the majors until 1953 and only lasted one year. Meanwhile Paul Erickson had his most productive year with the Cubs. But he slipped to 7–12 in 1947 and appeared in nine games with the Cubs, Philadelphia Phillies and New York Giants before retiring at the age of 33.

Prim, the lefthander who won some clutch games as the Cubs made their climb to the top in July, won only two more games in his major league career. He was 2–3 with the Cubs in 1946, after which, at the age of 39, he was sent to the club's Triple A farm team in Los Angeles. After toiling to a 2–3 record for that ballclub, Prim retired.

Chipman, the soft-throwing lefthander, enjoyed seven more seasons in the major leagues after the Cubs championship year. In fact, 34 of his 51 lifetime wins came between 1946 and 1952. He played with the Cubs through the 1949 season and spent his last three years with the Boston Braves.

Vandenberg, the 39-year-old warhorse who was 7–3 with three complete games, one shutout and one save in the 1945 season and who made three relief appearances in the World Series without allowing a run, never pitched again in the major leagues. He stayed in professional baseball several more years and, at age 42, was a member of the Oakland Oaks team that won the Pacific Coast League championship for the first time in 21 years. The Oaks were managed by Casey Stengel, who was soon to become the new manager of the New York Yankees.

Cavarretta played with the Cubs through the 1953 season, several of which were productive years, but none came close to matching his MVP totals of 1945. In the middle of the 1951 season, owner Phil Wrigley fired manager Frankie Frisch and called on Cavarretta to be a playing-manager. In 1952, under his direction, the Cubs finished at .500, 77–77. It was the last time they would achieve a .500 record until 1963 when they were 82–80 under Bob Kennedy.

In 1953, the Cubs faltered again, finishing 65–89 and in seventh place. In spring training 1954, Wrigley asked Cavarretta about the team's chances and, in characteristic style, Cavarretta was blunt in his assessment that the Cubs were not a very good team. Wrigley fired Cavarretta, making him the first skipper ever to be fired in spring training. Cubs favorite Hack replaced him and the Cubs finished seventh again, winning one less game than they had under Cavarretta the previous year. Cavarretta finished his playing career with the Chicago White Sox, retiring after the 1955 season. His last game with the Cubs was in 1953 — and he had appeared in exactly 1,953 games with them, dating back to 1934.

Johnson is an example of a player who had a "career year" in 1945 when he hit .302. A favorite player of Grimm's, Johnson played three more years with the Cubs, never hitting better than .259. He then became a free agent. At age 38, he signed with Sacramento in the Pacific Coast League for the 1949 season but retired before the season was over.

Merullo, who was the Cubs regular shortstop in 1945, played in only 65 games in 1946 and hit .151. He hit .241 in 1947, one point higher than his lifetime batting average, but never played in another major league game after that. In spring training 1948, he incurred a sciatica injury affecting a nerve in his leg that limited his mobility on the field and made it painful for him to stand or sit for long periods of time. Merullo said it was at about that time that Roy Smalley, a shortstop in the Cubs minor league system, was ready for major league duty. He came up and Merullo bowed out. Merullo remained in the organization as a Cubs scout until 1973 when the major leagues started a scouting bureau that employed him for the next 25 years. Among the players he helped sign are Ron Santo, the Cubs star third baseman, and Moe Drabowsky, who started his career as a Cubs starting pitcher and later gained fame as a Baltimore Oriole relief pitcher.

Hack, the smiling, popular third baseman who came out of retirement in 1944 at the urging of manager Grimm and then helped lead the Cubs to the pennant in 1945, played parts of two more seasons. He retired with 2,193 hits and a .301 lifetime batting average. In 1954, after owner

Wrigley fired Cavarretta in spring training, he called on Hack to take over as manager. Under Hack, the Cubs won 64, lost 90 and finished seventh. They improved a little, to 72–81 and a sixth place finish in 1955. But in 1956, they finished last, winning only 60 games. Hack was fired and replaced by yet another old Cubs ballplayer, Bob Scheffing. Hack resurfaced in 1958 as a coach for the St. Louis Cardinals and was interim manager for the last 10 games of the season.

Pafko played five more seasons with the Cubs and was an All Star three of those years. He played primarily in the outfield but also was a backup third baseman. In 1951, he was traded to Brooklyn. That trade allowed Pafko to play in one of the most famous games in baseball history. On October 3, 1951, he was in left field for the Dodgers and watched Bobby Thomson's home run sail over his head and into the seats at the Polo Grounds, giving the National League pennant to the New York Giants. He played in the World Series for the Dodgers in 1952 and 1953 and with the Milwaukee Braves in 1957 and 1958. He is one of the few players to have played in four World Series with three different teams. In 1959, he played in another famous game. On May 12, he was in the Braves' lineup when Harvey Haddix threw 12 perfect innings against Milwaukee before losing the game on Henry Aaron's game-winning hit in the 13th inning. He retired with a career average of .285 and had 213 home runs.

Lowrey played 10 more years in the major leagues, with Cincinnati, St. Louis and Philadelphia. Though Lowrey was a consistently good player for the Cubs and hit .289 with 89 RBI in their pennant year, he was involved in one of the club's best trades ever in 1949. Lowrey and Harry Walker were sent to the Cincinnati Reds in exchange for outfielders Hank Sauer and Frankie Baumholtz, both of whom became among the Cubs' best players in the early 1950s. Lowrey had an off-year with Cincinnati and was traded to the Cardinals the following year. He hit .303 for the Cardinals in 1951 and led the National League in pinch hits in 1952 and 1953, with 13 and 22 respectively. He ended his career with Philadelphia in 1955 and retired with a lifetime batting average of .273. Lowrey later was a coach with the Cubs.

Nicholson played with the Cubs for three more seasons but, partially because of vision problems, never achieved the success he experienced during the war years. Nonetheless, when he was traded to the Philadelphia Phillies after the 1948 season, Cubs fans were outraged. He finished his career as a part-time player and pinch hitter for the Philadelphia Phillies and was a member of the famed "Whiz Kids" pennant winner of 1950 but did not play in the World Series. On Labor Day 1950, the Phillies disclosed that Nicholson was suffering from diabetes and would miss the remainder of the season. Nicholson finished his career with 235 home runs—eight of them as a pinch hitter.

Livingston, the man who was catching for the Cubs because he couldn't wear an Army helmet, hit .364 (8 for 22) in the World Series after appearing in 71 games for the Cubs in 1945. He never caught that many games in parts of five more seasons with the Cubs, Giants, Braves and Dodgers, ending his career with Brooklyn in 1951 with a lifetime batting average of .238.

Becker, the man with the notoriously bad feet, had foot surgery after the 1945 season, but in 1946 he and the Cubs parted company. Becker was not happy with his role as a reserve player and went home on May 13. Two weeks later, his contract was sold to Nashville but he didn't stay in the minor leagues long. The Cleveland Indians brought him up and Becker responded in his first game on July 16 with a single and a pair of doubles as the Indians beat Boston 6–3. Becker was involved in a famous defensive strategy in that game. Cleveland manager Lou Boudreau introduced what came to be known as the "Ted Williams shift" in which three of the four Indian infielders were positioned on the right side. Jimmy Wasdell was the regular Indian first baseman, but Becker was the first baseman in the first game in which Boudreau used it against Williams and Becker is identified as the first baseman in some of the published diagrams of the shift.

He played in 50 games for Cleveland and hit .299 but did not figure in the Indians' plans for 1947. He was released after appearing in only two games and returned to his beloved Milwaukee Brewers, where he had been a popular star when Charlie Grimm managed them before both Grimm and Becker moved up to the Cubs. With Milwaukee, Becker achieved one more season in the limelight, winning the American Association batting title with a .363 average, and then played for the Seattle Raniers in the Pacific Coast League in 1949. But he never played major league baseball again and retired as a player at the age of 31.

Bithorn, who the Cubs hoped would be a great starter for them, was relegated to the bullpen where he was 6–5 with the Cubs in 1946. He then went to the White Sox in 1947 where he was 1–0 in limited action, his last year in the major leagues. Bithorn pitched in the minor leagues and in the Mexican League for a few years. On January 1, 1952, he was shot and killed by police in Mexico in a bar altercation in which he is believed to have been a bystander. He was 35 years old. A baseball stadium in San Juan, Puerto Rico is named in his honor. He was the first Puerto Rican to play in the major leagues.

Hanyzewski, whose win ended the Cubs 13-game losing streak in 1944, never lived up to his potential or to manager Grimm's expectations of him. He appeared in only two games in 1945 with no decisions and was done in the major leagues after the 1946 season, compiling a five-year career record of 12–13.

Williams, who shared catching duties and appeared in 59 games for the Cubs in 1945, played in seven games with the Cubs in 1946 and 1947 combined and was out of the major leagues after appearing in 48 games with the Cincinnati Reds in 1948. When he retired from baseball, he returned home to Williston, North Dakota, where he coached American Legion baseball for many years. One of his players was Phil Jackson, who later played pro basketball with the New York Knicks and became one of the most successful coaches of all time with the Chicago Bulls and Los Angeles Lakers. Williams's advice to the young athlete Jackson: "Stick with basketball."

Gillespie, the reserve catcher with the crew cut, never appeared in a major league game after the 1945 World Series.

Rice, like Gillespie, saw limited action for the Cubs in 1945. He was released at the end of the season and never played in the major leagues after that.

Secory, the reserve outfielder, had 62 major league at-bats before the 1945 season and 43 at-bats after the 1945 season. His major league playing career was over after 1946. He spent one year in the minors before calling it quits. Secory got up five times as a pinch hitter in the 1945 World Series and got two singles, including one that led to the winning run in the 12th inning of the sixth game. Secory had the unusual situation of, despite limited playing time, having a slugging percentage of over .500 in both 1944 and 1946. In 1944, five of 18 hits were for extra bases— one double and four home runs. In 1946, he had only 10 hits but had three doubles and three home runs. In 1952, Secory became a National League umpire, a position he held through 1970.

Hughes, who won the starting shortstop job over Merullo in the World Series, never played another game for the Cubs. The Philadelphia Phillies picked him up on waivers in January of 1946. He hit .236 and retired at season's end.

Schuster played his last major league game with the 1945 Cubs. In 1946, at the age of 33, he was playing in the Pacific Coast League where he remained for the next seven years and where one of his teammates was Heinz Becker with the Seattle Raniers.

Block who, along with Stan Musial, was considered to be one of the National League's top rookie prospects in 1942, lost three years to the Coast Guard and never got the attention he thought he deserved to make it in the major leagues. When he returned to the Cubs at the end of the 1945 season, he got into the World Series as a pinch hitter. He played in six games in 1946 and was done as a major league player in 1947 at the age of 28. Block spent most of 1946 with Nashville and was with the Cubs for a short time in 1947, making his last major league appearance. He quit baseball, started an insurance company and became a millionaire.

Warneke, the Cubs pitching hero from a past era who came out of retirement and tried to help the club in 1945, never pitched in the major leagues again. He became a Pacific Coast League umpire in 1946 and moved up to the National League where he was a highly-respected ump from 1949 through 1955.

McCullough, the first man ever to play in a World Series who did not play during the regular season, was with the Cubs through the 1948 season, then played four years with the Pittsburgh Pirates, then returned to the Cubs through 1956 when he retired. He was platooned most of his career and never achieved his dream of being considered in the same class of catchers as Walker Cooper.

X

Major League Career Statistics of 1945 Cubs

Here is a look at the lifetime major league records of manager Charlie Grimm and the 37 men who appeared in at least one game for the 1945 Chicago Cubs championship team.

Charles John Grimm

Born August 28, 1898, in St. Louis, Missouri; died November 15, 1983, in Scottsdale, Arizona. 5'11", 173 lbs.; B-left, T-left.

PLAYING CAREER

Year	Team	G	AB	R	H	D	T	HR	RBI	AVE.
1916	Phil (A)	12	22	0	2	0	0	0	0	.091
1918	StL (N)	50	141	11	31	7	0	0	12	.220
1919	Pitt	12	44	6	14	1	3	0	6	.318
1920	Pitt	148	533	38	121	13	7	2	54	.227
1921	Pitt	151	562	62	154	21	17	7	71	.274
1922	Pitt	154	593	64	173	28	13	0	76	.292
1923	Pitt	152	563	78	194	29	13	7	99	.345
1924	Pitt	151	542	53	156	25	12	2	63	.288
1925	Chi (N)	141	519	73	159	29	5	10	76	.306
1926	Chi	147	524	58	145	30	6	8	82	.277
1927	Chi	147	543	68	169	29	6	2	74	.311
1928	Chi	147	547	67	161	25	5	5	62	.294
1929	Chi	120	463	66	138	28	3	10	91	.298
1930	Chi	114	429	58	124	27	2	6	66	.289
1931	Chi	146	531	65	176	33	11	4	66	.331
1932	Chi	149	570	66	175	42	2	7	80	.307
1933	Chi	107	384	38	99	15	2	3	37	.247
1934	Chi	75	267	24	79	8	1	5	47	.296

Year	Team	G	AB	R	H	D	T	HR	RBI	AVE.
1935	Chi	2	8	0	0	0	0	0	0	.000
1936	Chi	39	132	13	33	4	0	1	16	.250
20 years		2164	7917	908	2299	394	108	79	1078	.290

WORLD SERIES

Year	Team	G	AB	R	H	D	T	HR	RBI	AVE.
1929	Chi (N)	5	18	2	7	0	0	1	4	.389
1932	Chi	4	15	2	5	2	0	0	1	.333
2 years		9	33	4	12	2	0	1	5	.364

MANAGERIAL CAREER

Year	Team	W — L	Pct.	Standing
1932	Chi (N)	37–20	.649	First
1933	Chi	86–68	.558	Third
1934	Chi	86–65	.570	Third
1935	Chi	100–54	.649	First
1936	Chi	87–67	.565	Third
1937	Chi	93–61	.604	Second
1938	Chi	45–36	.556	Third
1944	Chi	74–69	.517	Fourth
1945	Chi	98–56	.636	First
1946	Chi	82–71	.536	Third
1947	Chi	69–85	.448	Sixth
1948	Chi	64–90	.416	Eighth
1949	Chi	19–31	.380	Eighth
1952	Bos (N)	51–67	.432	Seventh
1953	Mil	92–62	.567	Second
1954	Mil	89–65	.578	Third
1955	Mil	85–69	.552	Second
1956	Mil	24–22	.522	Fifth
1960	Chi (N)	6–11	.353	Eighth
19 years		1287–1069	.546	

WORLD SERIES

Year	Team	W—L	Pct.
1932	Chi (N)	0–4	.000
1935	Chi	2–4	.333
1945	Chi	3–4	.429
3 years		5–12	.294

Heinz Reinhard Becker

Born August 26, 1915, in Berlin, Germany; died November 11, 1991, in Dallas, Texas; 6'2", 190 lbs.; B-both, T-right.

PLAYING CAREER

Year	Team	G	AB	R	H	D	T	HR	RBI	AVE.
1943	Chi (N)	24	69	5	10	0	0	0	2	.145
1945	Chi	67	133	25	38	8	2	2	27	.286
1946	Chi-Cleve	59	154	15	46	10	1	0	18	.299
1947	Cleve	2	2	0	0	0	0	0	0	.000
4 years		152	358	45	94	18	3	2	47	.263

WORLD SERIES

Year	Team	G	AB	R	H	D	T	HR	RBI	AVE.
1945	Chi (N)	3	2	0	1	0	0	0	0	.500

Seymour Block

Born May 4, 1919, in Brooklyn, New York; 6', 180 lbs.; B-right, T-right.

PLAYING CAREER

Year	Team	G	AB	R	H	D	T	HR	RBI	AVE.
1942	Chi (N)	9	33	6	12	1	1	0	4	.364
1945	Chi	2	7	1	1	0	0	0	1	.143
1946	Chi	6	13	2	3	0	0	0	0	.231
3 years		17	53	9	16	1	1	0	5	.302

WORLD SERIES

Year	Team	G	AB	R	H	D	T	HR	RBI	AVE.
1945	Chi (N)	1	1	0	0	0	0	0	0	.000

Henry Ludwig Borowy

Born May 12, 1916, in Bloomfield, New Jersey; 6', 175 lbs, B-right, T-right.

PLAYING CAREER

Year	Team	W-L	Pct.	ERA	G	IP	H	BB	SO
1942	NY (A)	15–4	.789	2.52	25	178.1	157	66	85

Year	Team	W–L	Pct.	ERA	G	IP	H	BB	SO
1943	NY	14–9	.609	2.82	29	217.1	195	72	113
1944	NY	17–12	.586	2.64	35	252.2	224	88	107
1945	NY-Chi (N)	21–7	.750	2.65	33	254.2	212	105	82
1946	Chi	12–10	.545	3.76	32	201	220	61	95
1947	Chi	8–12	.400	4.38	40	183	190	63	75
1948	Chi	5–10	.333	4.89	39	127	156	49	50
1949	Phil (N)	12–12	.500	4.19	28	193.1	188	63	43
1950	Phil-Pitt-Det	2–4	.333	4.83	27	63.1	60	29	24
1951	Det	2–2	.500	6.95	26	45.1	58	27	16
10 years		108–82	.568	3.50	314	1716	1660	623	690

WORLD SERIES

Year	Team	W–L	Pct.	ERA	G	IP	H	BB	SO
1942	NY (A)	0–0	.000	18.00	1	3	6	3	1
1943	NY	1–0	1.000	2.25	1	8	6	3	4
1945	Chi	2–2	.500	4.00	4	18	21	6	8
3 years		3–2	.600	4.97	6	29	33	12	13

Philip Joseph Cavarretta

Born July 19, 1916, in Chicago, Illinois; 5'11", 175 lbs.; B-left, T-left.

PLAYING CAREER

Year	Team	G	AB	R	H	D	T	HR	RBI	AVE.
1934	Chi (N)	7	21	5	8	0	1	1	6	.381
1935	Chi	146	589	85	162	28	12	8	82	.275
1936	Chi	124	458	55	125	18	1	9	56	.273
1937	Chi	106	329	43	94	18	7	5	56	.286
1938	Chi	92	268	29	64	11	4	1	28	.239
1939	Chi	22	55	4	15	3	1	0	0	.273
1940	Chi	65	193	34	54	11	4	2	22	.280
1941	Chi	107	346	46	99	18	4	6	40	.286
1942	Chi	136	482	59	130	28	4	3	54	.270
1943	Chi	143	530	93	154	27	9	8	73	.291
1944	Chi	152	614	106	197	35	15	5	82	.321
1945	Chi	132	498	94	177	34	10	6	97	.355
1946	Chi	139	510	89	150	28	10	8	78	.294
1947	Chi	127	459	56	144	22	5	2	63	.314
1948	Chi	111	334	41	93	16	5	3	40	.278
1949	Chi	105	360	46	106	22	4	8	49	.294
1950	Chi	82	256	49	70	11	1	10	31	.273
1951	Chi	89	206	27	64	7	1	6	28	.311
1952	Chi	41	63	7	15	1	1	1	8	.238
1953	Chi	27	21	3	6	3	0	0	3	.286

Year	Team	G	AB	R	H	D	T	HR	RBI	AVE.
1954	Chi (A)	71	158	21	50	6	0	3	24	.316
1955	Chi	6	4	1	0	0	0	0	0	.000
22 years		2030	6754	990	1977	347	99	95	920	.293

WORLD SERIES

Year	Team	G	AB	R	H	D	T	HR	RBI	AVE.
1935	Chi (N)	6	24	1	3	0	0	0	0	.125
1938	Chi	4	13	1	6	1	0	0	0	.462
1945	Chi	7	26	7	11	2	0	1	5	.423
3 years		17	63	9	20	3	0	1	5	.317

Robert Howard Chipman

Born October 11, 1918, in Brooklyn, NY; died November 8, 1973, in Huntington, NY; 6'2", 190 lbs; B-left, T-left.

PLAYING CAREER

Year	Team	W-L	Pct.	ERA	G	IP	H	BB	SO
1941	Brklyn	1–0	1.000	0.00	1	5	3	1	3
1942	Brklyn	0–0	.000	0.00	2	1.1	1	2	1
1943	Brklyn	0–0	.000	0.00	1	1.2	2	2	0
1944	Brklyn-Chi	12–10	.545	3.65	37	165.1	185	64	61
1945	Chi	4–5	.444	3.50	25	72	63	34	29
1946	Chi	6–5	.545	3.13	34	109.1	103	54	42
1947	Chi	7–6	.438	3.68	32	134.2	135	66	51
1948	Chi	2–1	.667	3.58	34	60.1	73	24	16
1949	Chi	7–8	.467	3.97	38	113.1	110	63	46
1950	Bos (N)	7–7	.500	4.43	27	124	127	37	40
1951	Bos	4–3	.571	4.85	33	52	59	19	17
1952	Bos	1–1	.500	2.81	29	41.2	28	20	16
12 years		51–46	.526	3.72	293	880.2	889	386	322

WORLD SERIES

Year	Team	W–L	Pct.	ERA	G	IP	H	BB	SO
1945	Chi (N)	0–0	.000	0.00	1	.1	0	1	0

Lloyd Eugene Christopher

Born December 31, 1919, in Richmond, California; died September 5, 1991, in Richmond, California; 6'2", 190 lbs.; B-right, T-right.

PLAYING CAREER

Year	Team	G	AB	R	H	D	T	HR	RBI	AVE.
1945	Bos-Chi	9	14	4	4	0	0	0	4	.286
1947	Chi (A)	7	23	1	5	0	1	0	0	.217
2 years		16	37	5	9	0	1	0	4	.243

Jorge Comellas

Born December 7, 1916, in Havana, Cuba; 6', 185 lbs.; B-right, T-right.

PLAYING CAREER

Year	Team	W–L	Pct.	ERA	G	IP	H	BB	SO
1945	Chi (N)	0–2	.000	4.50	7	12	11	6	6

Paul Derringer

Born October 17, 1906, in Springfield, Kentucky; died November 17, 1987, in Sarasota, Florida; 6'3", 205 lbs; B-right, T-right

PLAYING CAREER

Year	Team	W–L	Pct.	ERA	G	IP	H	BB	SO
1931	StL (N)	18–8	.692	3.36	35	211.2	225	65	134
1932	StL	11–14	.440	4.05	39	233.1	296	67	78
1933	StL–Cin	7–27	.206	3.30	36	248	264	60	89
1934	Cin	15–21	.417	3.59	47	261	297	59	122
1935	Cin	22–13	.629	3.51	45	276.2	295	49	120
1936	Cin	19–19	.500	4.02	51	282.1	331	42	121
1937	Cin	10–14	.417	4.04	43	222.2	240	55	94
1938	Cin	21–14	.600	2.93	41	307	315	49	132
1939	Cin	25–7	.781	2.93	38	301	321	35	128
1940	Cin	20–12	.625	3.06	37	296.2	280	48	115
1941	Cin	12–14	.462	3.31	29	228.1	233	54	76
1942	Cin	10–11	.476	3.06	29	208.2	203	49	68
1943	Chi	10–14	.417	3.57	32	174	184	39	75

Year	Team	W–L	Pct.	ERA	G	IP	H	BB	SO
1944	Chi	7–13	.350	4.15	42	180	205	39	69
1945	Chi	16–11	.593	3.45	35	213.2	223	51	86
15 years		223–212	.513	4.46	579	3645	3912	761	1507

WORLD SERIES

Year	Team	W–L	Pct.	ERA	G	IP	H	BB	SO
1931	StL (N)	0–2	.000	4.26	3	12.2	14	7	14
1939	Cin	0–1	.000	2.35	2	15.1	9	3	9
1940	Cin	2–1	.667	2.75	3	19.1	17	10	6
1945	Chi (N)	0–0	.000	6.75	3	5.1	5	7	1
4 years		2–4	.333	3.42	11	52.2	45	27	30

Paul Walford Erickson

Born December 14, 1915, in Zion, Illinois; died April 5, 2002, in Fond du Lae, Wisconsin; 6'2", 200 lbs.; B-right, T-right.

PLAYING CAREER

Year	Team	W–L	Pct.	ERA	G	IP	H	BB	SO
1941	Chi (N)	5–7	.417	3.70	32	141	126	64	85
1942	Chi	1–6	.143	5.43	18	63	70	41	26
1943	Chi	1–3	.250	6.12	15	42.2	47	22	24
1944	Chi	5–9	.357	3.55	33	124.1	113	67	82
1945	Chi	7–4	.636	3.32	28	108.1	94	48	53
1946	Chi	9–7	.563	2.43	32	137	119	65	70
1947	Chi	7–12	.368	4.34	40	174	179	93	82
1948	Chi-Phil-NY	2–0	1.000	5.25	9	24	26	25	10
8 years		37–48	.435	3.86	207	814.1	774	425	432

WORLD SERIES

Year	Team	W–L	Pct.	ERA	G	IP	H	BB	SO
1945	Chi (N)	0–0	.000	3.86	4	7	8	3	5

Paul Allen Gillespie

Born September 18, 1920, in Sugar Valley, Georgia; died August 11, 1970, in Anniston, Alabama; 6'2", 180 lbs.; B-left, T-right.

PLAYING CAREER

Year	Team	G	AB	R	H	D	T	HR	RBI	AVE.
1942	Chi (N)	5	16	3	4	0	0	2	4	.250

Year	Team	G	AB	R	H	D	T	HR	RBI	AVE.
1944	Chi	9	26	2	7	1	0	1	2	.269
1945	Chi	75	163	12	47	6	0	3	25	.288
3 years		89	205	17	58	7	0	6	31	.283

WORLD SERIES

Year	Team	G	AB	R	H	D	T	HR	RBI	AVE.
1945	Chi (N)	3	6	0	0	0	0	0	0	.000

Stanley Camfield Hack

Born December 6, 1909, in Sacramento, California; died December 16, 1979, in Dixon, Illinois; 6', 170 lbs.; B-left, T-right.

PLAYING CAREER

Year	Team	G	AB	R	H	D	T	HR	RBI	AVE.
1932	Chi (N)	72	178	32	42	5	6	2	19	.236
1933	Chi	20	60	10	21	3	1	1	2	.350
1934	Chi	111	402	54	116	16	6	1	21	.289
1935	Chi	124	427	75	133	23	9	4	64	.311
1936	Chi	149	561	102	167	27	4	6	78	.298
1937	Chi	154	582	106	173	27	6	2	63	.297
1938	Chi	152	609	109	195	34	11	4	67	.320
1939	Chi	156	641	112	191	28	6	8	56	.298
1940	Chi	149	603	101	191	38	6	8	40	.317
1941	Chi	151	586	111	186	33	5	7	45	.317
1942	Chi	140	553	91	166	36	3	6	39	.300
1943	Chi	144	533	78	154	24	4	3	35	.289
1944	Chi	98	383	65	108	16	1	3	32	.282
1945	Chi	150	597	110	193	29	7	2	43	.323
1946	Chi	92	323	55	92	13	4	0	26	.285
1947	Chi	76	240	28	65	11	2	0	12	.271
17 years		1938	7278	1239	2193	363	81	57	642	.301

WORLD SERIES

Year	Team	G	AB	R	H	D	T	HR	RBI	AVE.
1932	Chi (N)	1	0	0	0	0	0	0	0	.000
1935	Chi	6	22	2	5	1	1	0	0	.227
1938	Chi	4	17	3	8	1	0	0	1	.471
1945	Chi	7	30	1	11	3	0	0	4	.367
4 years		18	69	6	24	5	1	0	5	.348

Edward Michael Hanyzewski

Born September 18, 1920, in Union Mills, Indiana; died October 8, 1991, in Fargo, North Dakota; 6'1", 200 lbs.; B-right, T-right.

PLAYING CAREER

Year	Team	W–L	Pct.	ERA	G	IP	H	BB	SO
1942	Chi (N)	1–1	.500	3.79	6	19	17	8	6
1943	Chi	8–7	.533	2.56	33	130	120	45	55
1944	Chi	2–5	.286	4.47	14	58.1	61	20	19
1945	Chi	0–0	.000	5.79	2	4.2	7	1	0
1946	Chi	1–0	1.000	4.50	3	6	8	5	1
5 years		12–13	.480	3.30	58	218	213	79	81

George Hennessey

Born October 28, 1907, in Slatington, Pennsylvania; died January 15, 1988, in Princeton, New Jersey; 5'10", 168 lbs.; B-right, T-right.

PLAYING CAREER

Year	Team	W–L	Pct.	ERA	G	IP	H	BB	SO
1937	StL (A)	0–1	.000	10.29	5	7	15	6	4
1942	Phil (N)	1–1	.500	2.65	5	17	11	10	2
1945	Chi (N)	0–0	.000	7.36	2	3.2	7	1	2
3 years		1–2	.333	5.20	12	27.2	33	17	8

Roy John Hughes

Born January 11, 1911, in Cincinnati, Ohio; died March 5, 1995, in Asheville, North Carolina; 5'10", 167 lbs.; B-right, T-right

PLAYING CAREER

Year	Team	G	AB	R	H	D	T	HR	RBI	AVE.
1935	Cleve	82	266	40	78	15	3	0	14	.293
1936	Cleve	152	638	112	188	35	9	0	63	.295
1937	Cleve	104	346	57	96	12	6	1	40	.277
1938	Cleve	58	96	16	27	3	0	2	13	.281
1939	StL (A)Phil(N)	82	260	28	56	5	1	1	17	.215
1944	Chi (N)	126	478	86	137	16	6	1	28	.287
1945	Chi	69	222	34	58	8	1	0	8	.261

Year	Team	G	AB	R	H	D	T	HR	RBI	AVE.
1946	Phil (N)	89	276	23	65	11	1	0	22	.236
8 years		762	2582	396	705	105	27	5	205	.273

WORLD SERIES

Year	Team	G	AB	R	H	D	T	HR	RBI	AVE.
1945	Chi (N)	6	17	1	5	1	0	0	3	.294

Donald Spore Johnson

Born December 7, 1911, in Chicago, Illinois; died April 6, 2000, in Laguna Beach, California; 6', 170 lbs.; B-right, T-right.

PLAYING CAREER

Year	Team	G	AB	R	H	D	T	HR	RBI	AVE.
1943	Chi (N)	10	42	5	8	2	0	0	1	.190
1944	Chi	154	608	50	169	37	1	2	71	.278
1945	Chi	138	557	94	168	23	2	2	58	.302
1946	Chi	83	314	37	76	10	1	1	19	.242
1947	Chi	120	402	33	104	17	2	3	26	.259
1948	Chi	6	12	0	3	0	0	0	0	.250
6 years		511	1935	219	528	89	6	8	175	.273

WORLD SERIES

Year	Team	G	AB	R	H	D	T	HR	RBI	AVE.
1945	Chi (N)	7	29	4	5	2	1	0	0	.172

Thompson Orville Livingston

Born November 15, 1914, in Newberry, South Carolina; died April 3, 1983, in Newberry, South Carolina; 6'1", 185 lbs.; B-right, T-right.

PLAYING CAREER

Year	Team	G	AB	R	H	D	T	HR	RBI	AVE.
1938	Wash	2	4	0	3	2	0	0	1	.750
1941	Phil (N)	95	207	16	42	6	1	0	18	.203
1942	Phil	89	239	20	49	6	1	2	22	.205
1943	Phil-Chi	120	376	36	95	14	3	7	34	.253
1945	Chi	71	224	19	57	4	2	2	23	.254
1946	Chi	66	176	14	45	14	0	2	20	.256

Year	Team	G	AB	R	H	D	T	HR	RBI	AVE.
1947	Chi-NY (N)	24	39	2	8	2	0	0	3	.205
1948	NY	45	99	9	21	4	1	2	12	.212
1949	NY-Bos (N)	47	121	12	32	4	1	4	18	.264
1951	Brklyn	2	5	0	2	0	0	0	2	.400
10 years		561	1490	128	354	56	9	19	153	.238

WORLD SERIES

Year	Team	G	AB	R	H	D	T	HR	RBI	AVE.
1945	Chi (N)	6	22	3	8	3	0	0	4	.364

Harry Lee Lowrey

Born August 27, 1918, in Culver City, California; died July 2, 1986,
in Inglewood, California; 5'8", 170 lbs.; B-right, T-right

PLAYING CAREER

Year	Team	G	AB	R	H	D	T	HR	RBI	AVE.
1942	Chi (N)	27	58	4	11	0	0	1	4	.190
1943	Chi	130	480	59	140	25	12	1	63	.292
1945	Chi	143	523	72	148	22	7	7	89	.283
1946	Chi	144	540	75	139	25	5	4	54	.257
1947	Chi	115	448	56	126	17	5	5	37	.281
1948	Chi	129	435	47	128	12	3	2	54	.294
1949	Chi-Cin	127	420	66	115	21	2	4	35	.274
1950	Cin-StL	108	320	44	75	14	0	2	15	.234
1951	StL(N)	114	370	52	112	19	5	5	40	.303
1952	StL	132	374	48	107	18	2	1	48	.286
1953	StL	104	182	26	49	9	2	5	27	.269
1954	StL	74	61	6	7	1	2	0	5	.115
1955	Phil (N)	54	106	9	20	4	0	0	8	.189
13 years		1401	4317	564	1177	186	45	37	479	.273

WORLD SERIES

Year	Team	G	AB	R	H	D	T	HR	RBI	AVE.
1945	Chi (N)	7	29	4	9	1	0	0	0	.310

Clyde Edward McCullough

Born March 4, 1917, in Nashville, Tennessee; died September 18, 1982, in San Francisco, California; 5'11", 180 lbs.; B-right, T-right.

PLAYING CAREER

Year	Team	G	AB	R	H	D	T	HR	RBI	AVE.
1940	Chi (N)	9	26	4	4	1	0	0	1	.154
1941	Chi	125	418	41	95	9	2	9	53	.227
1942	Chi	109	337	39	95	22	1	5	31	.282
1943	Chi	87	266	20	63	5	2	2	23	.237
1946	Chi	95	307	38	88	18	5	4	34	.287
1947	Chi	86	234	25	59	12	4	3	30	.252
1948	Chi	69	172	10	36	4	2	1	7	.209
1949	Pitt	91	241	30	57	9	3	4	21	.237
1950	Pitt	103	279	28	71	16	4	6	34	.254
1951	Pitt	92	259	26	77	9	2	8	39	.297
1952	Pitt	66	172	10	40	5	1	1	15	.233
1953	Chi (N)	77	229	21	59	3	2	6	23	.258
1954	Chi	31	81	9	21	7	0	3	17	.259
1955	Chi	44	81	7	16	0	0	0	10	.198
1956	Chi	14	19	0	4	1	0	0	1	.211
15 years		1098	3121	308	785	121	28	52	339	.252

WORLD SERIES

Year	Team	G	AB	R	H	D	T	HR	RBI	AVE.
1945	Chi (N)	1	1	0	0	0	0	0	0	.000

Leonard Richard Merullo

Born May 5, 1917, in Boston Massachusetts; 5'11", 166 lbs,; B-right, T-right

PLAYING CAREER

Year	Team	G	AB	R	H	D	T	HR	RBI	AVE.
1941	Chi (N)	7	17	3	6	1	0	0	1	.353
1942	Chi	143	515	53	132	23	3	2	37	.256
1943	Chi	129	453	37	115	18	3	1	25	.254
1944	Chi	66	193	20	41	8	1	1	16	.212
1945	Chi	121	394	40	94	18	0	2	37	.239
1946	Chi	65	126	14	19	8	0	0	7	.151
1947	Chi	108	373	24	90	16	1	0	29	.241
7 years		639	2071	191	497	92	8	6	152	.240

WORLD SERIES

Year	Team	G	AB	R	H	D	T	HR	RBI	AVE.
1945	Chi (N)	3	2	0	0	0	0	0	0	.000

John Francis Moore

*Born March 23, 1902, in Waterville, Connecticut; died April 4,
1991, in Bradenton, Florida; 5'10", 175 lbs.; B-left, T-right*

PLAYING CAREER

Year	Team	G	AB	R	H	D	T	HR	RBI	AVE.
1928	Chi (N)	4	4	0	0	0	0	0	0	.000
1929	Chi	37	63	13	18	1	0	2	8	.286
1931	Chi	39	104	19	25	3	1	2	16	.240
1932	Chi	119	443	59	135	24	5	13	64	.305
1933	Cin	135	514	60	135	19	5	1	44	.263
1934	Cin-Phil	132	500	73	165	35	7	11	98	.330
1935	Phil (N)	153	600	84	194	33	3	19	93	.323
1936	Phil	124	472	85	155	24	3	16	68	.328
1937	Phil	96	307	46	98	16	2	9	59	.319
1945	Chi	7	6	0	1	0	0	0	2	.167
10 years		846	3013	439	926	258	53	79	452	.307

WORLD SERIES

Year	Team	G	AB	R	H	D	T	HR	RBI	AVE.
1932	Chi (N)	2	7	1	0	0	0	0	0	.000

William Beck Nicholson

*Born December 11, 1914, in Chestertown, Maryland; died March
8, 1996, in Chestertown, Maryland; 6', 205 lbs.; B-left, T-right.*

PLAYING CAREER

Year	Team	G	AB	R	H	D	T	HR	RBI	AVE.
1936	Phil (A)	11	12	2	0	0	0	0	0	.000
1939	Chi (N)	58	220	37	65	12	5	5	38	.295
1940	Chi	135	491	78	146	27	7	25	98	.297
1941	Chi	147	532	74	135	26	1	26	98	.254
1942	Chi	152	588	83	173	22	11	21	78	.294
1943	Chi	154	608	95	188	30	9	29	128	.309
1944	Chi	156	582	116	167	35	8	33	122	.287
1945	Chi	151	559	82	136	28	4	13	88	.243

Year	Team	G	AB	R	H	D	T	HR	RBI	AVE.
1946	Chi	105	296	39	65	13	2	8	41	.220
1947	Chi	148	487	69	119	28	1	26	75	.244
1948	Chi	143	494	68	129	24	5	19	67	.261
1949	Phil (N)	98	299	42	70	8	3	11	40	.234
1950	Phil	41	58	3	13	2	1	3	10	.224
1951	Phil	85	170	23	41	9	2	8	30	.241
1952	Phil	55	88	17	24	3	0	6	19	.273
1953	Phil	38	62	12	13	5	1	2	16	.210
16 years		1677	5546	837	1484	272	60	235	948	.268

WORLD SERIES

Year	Team	G	AB	R	H	D	T	HR	RBI	AVE.
1945	Chi (N)	7	28	1	6	1	1	0	8	.214

John Thaddeus Ostrowski

Born October 17, 1917, in Chicago, Illinois; died November 13, 1992, in Chicago, Illinois; 5'10", 170 lbs.; B-right, T-right.

PLAYING CAREER

Year	Team	G	AB	R	H	D	T	HR	RBI	AVE.
1943	Chi N)	10	29	2	6	0	1	0	3	.207
1944	Chi	8	13	2	2	1	0	0	2	.154
1945	Chi	7	10	4	3	2	0	0	1	.300
1946	Chi	64	160	20	34	4	2	3	12	.213
1948	Bos (A)	1	1	0	0	0	0	0	0	.000
1949	Chi (A)	49	158	19	42	9	4	3	31	.266
1950	Chi-Wash	77	190	26	44	4	2	6	25	.232
7 years		216	561	73	131	20	9	14	74	.234

Regino Joseph Gomez Otero

Born September 7, 1915, in Havana, Cuba; died October 21, 1988, in Hialeah, Florida; 5'11", 160 lbs.; B-left, T-right.

PLAYING CAREER

Year	Team	G	AB	R	H	D	T	HR	RBI	AVE.
1945	Chi (N)	14	23	1	9	0	0	0	5	.391

Andrew Pafko

Born February 25, 1921, in Boyceville, Wisconsin; 6', 190 lbs.; B-right, T-right.

PLAYING CAREER

Year	Team	G	AB	R	H	D	T	HR	RBI	AVE.
1943	Chi (N)	13	58	7	22	3	0	0	10	.379
1944	Chi	128	469	47	126	16	2	6	62	.269
1945	Chi	144	534	64	159	24	12	12	110	.298
1946	Chi	65	234	18	66	6	4	3	39	.282
1947	Chi	129	513	68	155	25	7	13	66	.302
1948	Chi	142	548	82	171	30	2	26	101	.312
1949	Chi	144	519	79	146	29	2	18	69	.281
1950	Chi	146	514	95	156	24	8	36	92	.304
1951	Chi-Brklyn	133	455	68	116	16	3	30	93	.255
1952	Brklyn	150	551	76	158	17	5	19	85	.287
1953	Mil	140	516	70	153	23	4	17	72	.297
1954	Mil	138	510	61	146	22	4	14	69	.286
1955	Mil	86	252	29	67	3	5	5	34	.266
1956	Mil	45	93	15	24	5	0	2	9	.258
1957	Mil	83	220	31	61	6	1	8	27	.277
1958	Mil	95	164	17	39	7	1	3	23	.238
1959	Mil	71	142	17	31	8	2	1	15	.218
17 years		1852	6292	844	1796	264	62	213	976	.285

WORLD SERIES

Year	Team	G	AB	R	H	D	T	HR	RBI	AVE.
1945	Chi (N)	7	28	5	6	2	1	0	2	.214
1952	Brklyn	7	21	0	4	0	0	0	2	.190
1957	Mil	6	14	1	3	0	0	0	0	.214
1958	Mil	4	9	0	3	1	0	0	1	.333
4 years		24	72	6	16	3	1	0	5	.222

Claude William Passeau

Born April 9, 1909, in Waynesboro, Mississippi; 6'3", 190 lbs, B-right, T-right

PLAYING CAREER

Year	Team	W–L	Pct.	ERA	G	IP	H	BB	SO
1935	Pitt	0–1	.000	12.00	1	3	7	2	1
1936	Phil (N)	11–15	.423	3.48	49	217.1	247	55	85

Year	Team	W–L	Pct.	ERA	G	IP	H	BB	SO
1937	Phil	14–18	.438	4.34	50	292.1	348	79	135
1938	Phil	11–18	.379	4.52	44	239	281	93	100
1939	Phil-Chi	15–13	.536	3.28	42	274.1	269	73	137
1940	Chi (N)	20–13	.606	2.50	46	280.2	259	59	124
1941	Chi	14–14	.500	3.35	34	231	262	52	80
1942	Chi	19–14	.576	2.68	35	278.1	284	74	89
1943	Chi	15–12	.556	2.91	35	257	245	66	93
1944	Chi	15–9	.625	2.89	34	227	234	50	89
1945	Chi	17–9	.654	2.46	34	227	205	59	98
1946	Chi	9–8	.529	3.13	21	129.1	118	42	47
1947	Chi	2–6	.250	6.25	19	63.1	97	24	26
13 years		162–150	.519	3.32	444	2719.2	2856	728	1104

WORLD SERIES

Year	Team	W–L	Pct.	ERA	G	IP	H	BB	SO
1945	Chi (N)	1–0	1.000	2.70	3	16.2	7	8	3

Raymond Lee Prim

Born December 30, 1906, in Salitpa, Alabama; died April 29, 1995, in Monte Rio, California; 6', 178 lbs; B-right, T-left

PLAYING CAREER

Year	Team	W–L	Pct.	ERA	G	IP	H	BB	SO
1933	Wash	0–1	.000	3.14	2	14.1	13	2	6
1934	Wash	0–2	.000	6.75	8	14.2	19	8	3
1935	Phil (N)	3–4	.429	5.77	29	73.1	110	15	27
1943	Chi (N)	4–3	.571	2.55	29	60	67	14	27
1945	Chi	13–8	.619	2.40	34	165.1	142	23	88
1946	Chi	2–3	.400	5.79	14	23.1	28	10	10
6 years		22–21	.512	3.56	116	351	379	72	161

WORLD SERIES

Year	Team	W–L	Pct.	ERA	G	IP	H	BB	SO
1945	Chi (N)	0–1	.000	9.00	2	4	4	1	1

Leonard Oliver Rice

Born September 2, 1918, in Lead, South Dakota; died June 13, 1992, in Sonora, California; 5'11", 165 lbs.; B-right. T-right.

PLAYING CAREER

Year	Team	G	AB	R	H	D	T	HR	RBI	AVE.
1944	Cin	10	4	1	0	0	0	0	0	.000
1945	Chi (N)	32	99	10	23	3	0	0	7	.232
2 years		2	103	11	23	3	0	0	7	.223

Edward Sauer

Born January 3, 1920, in Pittsburgh, Pennsylvania; died July 1, 1988, in Thousand Oaks, California; 6'1", 188 lbs.; B-right, T-right.

PLAYING CAREER

Year	Team	G	AB	R	H	D	T	HR	RBI	AVE.
1942	Chi (N)	14	55	3	15	3	0	0	9	.273
1944	Chi	23	50	3	11	4	0	0	5	.220
1945	Chi	49	93	8	24	4	1	2	11	.258
1949	StL-Bos	103	259	31	67	14	1	3	32	.259
4 years		189	457	45	117	25	2	5	57	.256

WORLD SERIES

Year	Team	G	AB	R	H	D	T	HR	RBI	AVE.
1945	Chi (N)	2	2	0	0	0	0	0	0	.000

William Charles Schuster

Born August 4, 1914, in Buffalo, New York; died June 28, 1987, in El Monte, California; 5'9", 164 lbs.; B-right, T-right.

PLAYING CAREER

Year	Team	G	AB	R	H	D	T	HR	RBI	AVE.
1937	Pitt	3	6	2	3	0	0	0	1	.500
1939	Bos (N)	2	3	0	0	0	0	0	0	.000
1943	Chi (N)	13	51	3	15	2	1	0	0	.294
1944	Chi	60	154	14	34	7	1	1	14	.221

Year	Team	G	AB	R	H	D	T	HR	RBI	AVE.
1945	Chi	45	47	8	9	2	1	0	2	.191
5 years		123	261	27	61	11	3	1	17	.234

WORLD SERIES

Year	Team	G	AB	R	H	D	T	HR	RBI	AVE.
1945	Chi (N)	2	1	0	0	0	0	0	0	.000

Frank Edward Secory

Born August 24, 1912, in Mason City, Iowa; died April 7, 1995, in Port Huron, Michigan; 6'1", 200 lbs.; B-right, T-right.

PLAYING CAREER

Year	Team	G	AB	R	H	D	T	HR	RBI	AVE.
1940	Det.	1	1	0	0	0	0	0	0	.000
1942	Cin	2	5	1	0	0	0	0	0	.000
1944	Chi (N)	22	56	10	18	1	0	4	17	.321
1945	Chi	35	57	4	9	1	0	0	6	.158
1946	Chi	33	43	6	10	3	0	3	12	.233
5 years		93	162	21	37	5	0	7	36	.228

WORLD SERIES

Year	Team	G	AB	R	H	D	T	HR	RBI	AVE.
1945	Chi (N)	5	5	0	2	0	0	0	0	.400

Walter Donald Signer

Born October 12, 1910, in New York, New York; died July 23, 1974, in Greenwich, Connecticut; 6', 165 lbs.; B-right, T-right.

PLAYING CAREER

Year	Team	W–L	Pct.	ERA	IP	H	BB	SO
1943	Chi (N)	2–1	.667	2.88	25	24	4	5
1945	Chi	0–0	.000	3.38	8	11	5	0
2 years		2–1	.667	3.00	33	35	9	5

Raymond Francis Starr

Born April 23, 1906, in Nowata, Oklahoma; died February 9, 1963, in Baylis, Illinois; 6'1", 178 lbs.; B-right, T-right.

PLAYING CAREER

Year	Team	W–L	Pct.	ERA	G	IP	H	BB	SO
1932	StL (N)	1–1	.500	2.70	3	20	19	10	6
1933	NY-Bos	0–2	.000	4.35	15	41.1	51	19	17
1941	Cin	3–2	.600	2.65	7	34	28	6	11
1942	Cin	15–13	.536	2.67	37	276.2	228	106	83
1943	Cin	11–10	.524	3.64	36	217.1	201	91	42
1944	Pitt	6–5	.545	5.02	27	89.2	116	36	25
1945	Pitt-Chi	1–2	.333	8.10	13	20	27	11	5
7 years		37–35	.514	3.53	138	699	670	279	189

William Macklin Stewart

Born September 23, 1914, in Stevenson Alabama; died March 21, 1960, in Macon, Georgia; 6', 167 lbs.; B-right, T-right.

PLAYING CAREER

Year	Team	W–L	Pct.	ERA	G	IP	H	BB	SO
1944	Chi (N)	0–0	.000	1.46	8	12.1	11	4	3
1945	Chi	0–1	.000	4.76	16	28.1	37	14	9
2 years		0–1	.000	3.76	24	40.2	48	18	12

Harold Harris Vandenberg

Born March 17, 1906, in Abilene, Kansas; died July 31, 1994, in Bloomington, Minnesota; 6'2", 195 lbs.; B-right, T-right.

PLAYING CAREER

Year	Team	W–L	Pct.	ERA	G	IP	H	BB	SO
1935	Bos (A)	0–0	.000	20.25	3	5.1	15	4	2
1937	NY (N)	0–1	.000	7.88	1	1	10	6	2
1938	NY	0–1	.000	7.50	6	18	28	12	7
1939	NY	0–0	.000	5.68	2	6.1	10	6	3
1940	NY	1–1	.500	3.90	13	32.1	27	16	17
1944	Chi (N)	7–4	.636	3.63	35	126.1	123	51	54
1945	Chi	6–3	.667	3.49	30	95.1	91	33	35
7 years		14–10	.583	4.32	90	291.2	304	128	120

WORLD SERIES

Year	Team	W–L	Pct.	ERA	G	IP	H	BB	SO
1945	Chi (N)	0–0	.000	0.00	3	6	1	3	3

Lonnie Warneke

Born March 28, 1909, in Mount Ida, Arkansas; died June 23, 1976, in Hot Springs, Arkansas; 6'2", 185 lbs.; B-right, T-right.

PLAYING CAREER

Year	Team	W–L	Pct.	ERA	G	IP	H	BB	SO
1930	Chi (N)	0–0	.000	33.75	1	1.1	2	5	0
1931	Chi	2–4	.333	3.22	20	64.1	67	37	27
1932	Chi	22–6	.786	2.37	35	277	247	64	106
1933	Chi	18–13	.581	2.00	36	287.1	262	75	133
1934	Chi	22–10	.688	3.21	43	297.1	273	66	143
1935	Chi	20–13	.606	3.06	42	261.2	257	50	120
1936	Chi	16–13	.552	3.44	40	240.2	246	76	113
1937	StL (N)	18–11	.621	4.53	36	238.2	280	69	87
1938	StL	13–8	.619	3.97	31	197	199	64	89
1939	StL	13–7	.650	3.78	34	162	160	49	59
1940	StL	16–10	.615	3.14	33	232	235	47	85
1941	StL	17–9	.654	3.15	37	246	227	82	83
1942	StL-Chi	11–11	.500	2.73	27	181	173	36	59
1943	Chi	4–5	.444	3.16	21	88.1	82	18	30
1945	Chi	1–1	.500	3.86	9	14	16	1	6
15 years		193–121	.615	3.18	445	2782.2	2726	739	1140

WORLD SERIES

Year	Team	W–L	Pct.	ERA	G	IP	H	BB	SO
1932	Chi (N)	0–1	.000	5.91	2	10.2	15	5	8
1935	Chi	2–0	1.000	0.54	3	16.2	9	4	5
2 years		2–1	.667	2.63	5	27.1	24	9	13

Dewey Edgar Williams

Born February 5, 1916, in Durham, North Carolina; 6', 160 lbs.; B-right, T-right.

PLAYING CAREER

Year	Team	G	AB	R	H	D	T	HR	RBI	AVE.
1944	Chi (N)	79	262	23	63	7	2	0	27	.240

Year	Team	G	AB	R	H	D	T	HR	RBI	AVE.
1945	Chi	59	100	16	28	2	2	2	5	.280
1946	Chi	4	5	0	1	0	0	0	0	.200
1947	Chi	3	2	0	0	0	0	0	0	.000
1948	Cin	48	95	9	16	2	0	1	5	.268
5 years		193	464	48	108	11	4	3	37	.233

WORLD SERIES

Year	Team	G	AB	R	H	D	T	HR	RBI	AVE.
1945	Chi (N)	2	2	0	0	0	0	0	0	.000

Henry Washington Wyse

Born March 1, 1918, in Lunsford, Arkansas; died October 22, 2000, in Salina, Oklahoma; 5'11", 185 lbs, B-right, T-right

PLAYING CAREER

Year	Team	W–L	Pct.	ERA	G	IP	H	BB	SO
1942	Chi (N)	2–1	.667	1.93	4	28	33	6	8
1943	Chi	9–7	.563	2.94	38	156	160	34	45
1944	Chi	16–15	.516	3.15	41	257.1	277	57	86
1945	Chi	22–10	.688	2.68	38	278.1	272	55	77
1946	Chi	14–12	.538	2.68	40	201.1	206	52	52
1947	Chi	6–9	.400	4.31	37	142	158	64	53
1950	Phil (A)	9–14	.391	5.85	41	170.2	192	87	33
1951	Phil-Wash	1–2	.333	8.63	12	24	41	18	8
8 years		79–70	.530	3.52	251	1257.2	1339	373	362

WORLD SERIES

Year	Team	W–L	Pct	ERA	G	IP	H	BB	SO
1945	Chi (N)	0–1	.000	7.04	3	7.2	8	4	1

Bibliography

Ahrens, Art, and Gold, Eddie. *Day by Day in Chicago Cubs History*. West Point, N.Y.: Leisure Press, 1982.

Allen, Lee. *The Cincinnati Reds*. New York: G.P. Putnam's Sons, 1948.

"Batting and Pitching Give Series Edge to Cubs." *The Sporting News*, Oct. 4, 1945.

Block, Seymour "Cy." *So You Want to Be a Major Leaguer*. Self-published.

Brown, Warren. *The Chicago Cubs*. New York: G.P. Putnam's Sons, 1946.

"Chicago Share Worth $4277; Vote 33.5 Cuts." *Chicago Tribune*, Oct. 11, 1945.

"Cubs Hope to Forget Woes on Hunting Trip." *Chicago Tribune*, Oct. 12, 1945.

"Cubs Win 8-7; Tie Series in 12 Inning Game." *Chicago Tribune*, Oct. 9, 1945.

Durant, John. *The Story of Baseball*. New York: Hastings House, 1973.

Fulk, David, and Riley, Dan. *The Cubs Reader*. Boston: Houghton Mifflin, 1991.

Gettelson, Leonard. *Official World Series Records*. St. Louis: The Sporting News, 1976.

"Girls of Summer," *Michigan History*, September/October 1997.

Goldstein, Richard. *Spartan Seasons: How Baseball Survived the Second World War*. New York: Macmillan, 1980.

Grimm, Charlie, and Prell, Edward. *Jolly Cholly's Story: Baseball, I Love You*. Chicago: Henry Regnery, 1968.

"Grimm Heads for Peace and Quiet of Farm." *Chicago Tribune*, Oct. 12, 1945.

"Grimm's Cubs of '45 Measure Up to Pre-War Standards." *Chicago Cub News*, April 17, 1945.

Helyar, John. *Lords of the Realm: The Real History of Baseball*, New York: Villard Books, 1994.

Holtzman, Jerome. *The Jerome Holtzman Baseball Reader*. Chicago: Triumph Books, 2003.

"I Remember That Guy..." *Vine Line Alumni Notebook*, January 1998; April 1998; August 1998.

"In the Wake of the News." *Chicago Tribune*, Oct. 11, 1945.

James, Bill. *The Bill James Guide to Baseball Managers: From 1870 to Today*. New York: Scribner, 1997.

Lieb, Frederick G. *The St. Louis Cardinals*. New York: G.P. Putnam's Sons, 1947.

_____ and Baumgartner, Stan. *The Philadelphia Phillies*. New York: G.P. Putnam's Sons, 1953.

Marazzi, Rich, and Fiorito, Len. *Aaron to Zuverink*. New York: Avon Books, 1982.

Myers, Doug. *Essential Cubs*. Chicago: Contemporary Books, 1999.

"Newhouser Today, Trucks Tomorrow." *Chicago Sun*, Oct. 7, 1945.

Neyer, Rob. "A Last Great Season: The Senators in 1945." ESPN.com, 2003.

"1945 Series Featured the Hostetler Flop." *The Detroit News*, Sept. 20, 1999.

"Open Letter to Chicago Cub Fans." *Chicago Tribune*, Aug. 3, 1971.

"Passeau Hurls Today; Cubs Trail, 3-2." *Chicago Tribune*, Oct. 8, 1945.

Phillips, John. *The 4-F World Series of 1945*. Perry, Ga.: Capital Publishing, 1997.

Schoor, Gene. *The Pee Wee Reese Story*. New York: Julian Messner, 1956.

"7th Game Ticket Fans Besiege Cubs Park." *Chicago Tribune*, Oct. 9, 1945.

Skipper, John C. *Take Me Out to the Cubs Game*. Jefferson, N.C.: McFarland, 2000.

Smith, Ira L. *Baseball's Famous First Basemen*. New York: A.S. Barnes, 1956.

Smith, Kurt. *Voices of the Game*. South Bend, Ind.: Diamond Communications, 1987.

"Stan Hack, 70, Played Third Base for the Cubs." *The New York Times*, Dec. 16, 1979.

"Talk About Scared: Try Being Drafted." *St. Petersburg Times*, Sept. 18, 2001.

Talley, Rick. *The Cubs of '69: Recollections of the Team That Should Have Been*. Chicago: Contemporary Books, 1989.

"Tigers Earn $6,123 Each; Rout Cubs 9-3." *Chicago Tribune*, Oct. 11, 1945.

"Tigers Prevail." *The New York Times*, Oct. 4, 1945.

"Tigers Rout Prim, Cubs 4-1." *Chicago Sun*, Oct. 7, 1945.

"Tigers Will Be Better Thursday — O'Neill." *Detroit Times*, Oct. 3, 1945.

"Tommy Bridges, Detroit Pitcher." *The New York Times*, April 20, 1968.

"12 Years Uphill Made Star of Don Johnson of Cubs." *The Sporting News*, Dec. 7, 1944.

Walton, Ed. *The Rookies*. New York: Stein and Day, 1982.

Warfield, Don. *The Roaring Redhead: Larry MacPhail: Baseball's Great Innovator*. South Bend, Ind.: Diamond Communications, 1987.

Index